ORTHODOX CHRISTIAN LAITY

ORTHODOX CHRISTIAN LAITY, INC.
30 NORTH LaSALLE STREET, SUITE 4020
CHICAGO, ILLINOIS 60602-2507

Orthodox Christian Laity, Inc.
30 North LaSalle Street, Suite 4020
Chicago, Illinois 60602-2507

ISBN 0-937032-95-6

The Icon of the Holy Trinity is based on the Old Testament Event of the visit of the Lord God to Abraham at the plains of Mambre. The Lord appeared in the form of Three Men, who sat under an oak tree and were treated with great hospitality and respect by Abraham and Sarah (Genesis 18). Iconographer St. Andrea Rublev (1405-1425) shows three angels in a kind of sweeping circle gathered at the tree with Abraham's house and mountain visible. A eucharistic chalice stands on the white table-altar.

In Orthodox Christian iconography the representation of The Holy Spirit and Holy Trinity have been difficult to manifest. We present an accepted and loved icon.

Prayer Honoring the Holy Spirit

Heavenly King and Comforter, Spirit of Truth, present everywhere, who fillest creation, the Treasure of all blessings and Giver of life, come and dwell within us. Purify us from every blemish and save our souls, O gracious God.

We **DEDICATE** this book to the Spirit of Truth present in all of us baptized, chrismated, Orthodox Christians and we pray that, through prayer, discipline, faith and study, we learn to listen and trust the Holy Spirit in us and to act responsibly, as is our duty, for the Good of Christ's Church.

PREFACE

The Board of Directors of Orthodox Christian Laity (OCL) presents the **Project for Orthodox Renewal**, (seven studies of key issues facing Orthodox Christians in America) written for the good of the Church. This publication enables OCL to fulfill its educational mission of providing the "royal priesthood" of believers, clergy, hierarchy, and other interested Christians with information that fosters meaningful discussion on renewal of the Orthodox Church in the United States.

The summaries and recommendations of the Board have been placed by the editors in the beginning of the book to stimulate the reader to become engrossed in the **Project for Orthodox Renewal**.

The development of OCL discussion papers was suggested by Stephen J. Sfekas, Esquire, in a letter written to the Board in July, 1990. The seven topics approved by the membership at the Third Annual Meeting in Chicago, October, 1990, were:

Faith, Language and Culture
Spiritual Renewal
Orthodox Women and Our Church
Mission and Outreach
Selection of Hierarchy
Administration and Accountability
Orthodox Unity

Stephen J. Sfekas was appointed to the Board of Directors and became Task Force project chairman. Topics were assigned and six of them were completed and presented at the Fourth OCL Annual Meeting in Baltimore, October 1991. Twelve hundred draft copies were distributed to members, annual meeting participants, clergy, hierarchy, theologians and lay leaders of the Orthodox Church at that time.

At the Fifth Annual Meeting in St. Louis, October 1992, the Board voted to publish the revised papers in a formal book format. Board member, George Matsoukas, an educator, was appointed co-editor and fund raiser for the project.

The papers represent the independent scholarship of the authors, their committees and individual members who offered suggestions and comments. They are not necessarily official OCL viewpoints. The seven papers are interrelated in the fact that all the authors share a love of and concern for the Orthodox Church and its mission of bringing those created in the image of God closer to Him. The discussion papers exist to raise relevant questions and generate thoughtful debate within the Body of Christ so that Christian ends can be achieved. The **RECOMMENDATIONS**, on the other hand, are official OCL Board approved suggestions to be considered and incorporated into Church policy in order to further the renewal of our Church.

The OCL board believes this entire project, process, and product bears a powerful witness to our Orthodox Christian faith established in the United States by our immigrant ancestors. It is a testament to their progressive thinking and concern for the religious future of our people. The project reinforces their example of active lay participation in the continuous development of the Orthodox Church. Prayerfully, this **"Project for Orthodox Renewal"** can be utilized to strengthen the Orthodox Church in the United States as we begin the third millennium of our Orthodox Christian witness to the Resurrection of Christ.

George Matsoukas
Co-Editor

iv

ACKNOWLEDGEMENTS

The Editors thank the Orthodox Christian Laity Board members 1990-93 who encouraged and supported the development and completion of the "Project for Orthodox Renewal." Their vision to undertake such a monumental project with such limited resources is testimony to their love of the Orthodox Church.

The dedicated and hard-working authors and task force members, who helped in the preparation of the seven topic areas, are commended for their patience and scholarship. The members of the OCL and others who offered written and oral comments, and participants of the Fourth Annual Meeting (Baltimore, 1991) who also served as critical listeners of the information presented in workshop sessions, are acknowledged for their contribution to the successful completion of the project.

The editors are thankful for the technical, critical and editorial assistance offered by Board members Van Livadas, Minerva Stergianopoulos and Soteri Tsoutsouras and member Alice Kopan. Editorial and stylistic suggestions were also provided by Steven Brahlek, Communications Professor, Palm Beach Community College. Special appreciation is extended to the law firm of Weinberg and Green, Baltimore, Maryland for their support. The cover icon was suggested by Fr. Stephen Juli, Washington, D.C. We are thankful for his prayers imploring the successful completion of this project.

There was an initial publication of 1,200 copies of the Commission Papers for Workshop distribution, October 1991, made possible by the support of OCL Board member George Coupounas.

The final format you are reading is the result of the generous contribution and matching grant offered by OCL member Helen Datel, Washington, D.C. Her generous contribution was matched by individual OCL Board members and others to whom we are grateful.

Finally, the editors acknowledge Marian S. Valerio who served as secretary and word processor during the three-year period it took to complete the manuscript. In addition to her technical skills as typist, formatter and editor, she was confidant, conflict resolver and a Christian inspiration. Her patience and good cheer held this project together.

We also thank you, the reader. We pray that the insights offered herein create constructive dialogue and contribute to creating renewal within the Orthodox Church in America.

George Matsoukas
Stephen J. Sfekas
July 1, 1993

AUTHORS ACKNOWLEDGED

We wish to acknowledge the extraordinary efforts of everyone who took part in the Project for Orthodox Renewal. In particular we would like to express our gratitude for the efforts of:

Charles Moskos, Ph.D., Professor of Sociology at Northwestern University, and a distinguished scholar in Greek American studies and military sociology, for his work as Chair of the Commission and author of the study in Faith, Language and Culture.

George Matsoukas, Director of Grants Programs at Palm Beach Community College for his work as chair of the Commission and author of the study on Spiritual Renewal, fund raiser and editor of this publication.

Eva Topping, a distinguished scholar and author of many books and articles on women's roles in the Church, for her work as chair and author of Women and Our Church.

Fr. Mark Arey and Fr. Steven Vlahos for their work as the Commission and authors of the study of Mission and Outreach.

George Karcazes, partner in the Chicago law firm of Martin & Karcazes, as chair, co-author with **Leon Marinakos**, retired engineer for General Electric, of the study of the Selection of Hierarchs.

Sotiri Tsoutsouras, former President of OCL, for his work as chair and author of the study of Administration and Accountability.

Andrew Kopan, Ph.D., Professor of Education at DePaul University and noted author of scholarly and popular studies of the Greek American community and of the Greek Orthodox Church, for his work as chair of the Commission on Orthodox Unity.

Stephen J. Sfekas, a partner in the Baltimore law firm of Weinberg and Green, who served as General Chairman of the Project for Orthodox Renewal of the Orthodox Christian Laity and editor of the Commission Papers.

THE PROJECT FOR ORTHODOX RENEWAL OF THE ORTHODOX CHRISTIAN LAITY

TABLE OF CONTENTS

---

1. All reference works are cited by Author throughout the book. For complete information refer to the Bibliography.

ORTHODOX CHRISTIAN LAITY

ORTHODOX CHRISTIAN LAITY, INC.
30 NORTH LASALLE STREET, SUITE 4020
CHICAGO, ILLINOIS 60602-2507

RECOMMENDATIONS
OF THE
ORTHODOX CHRISTIAN LAITY
FOR THE RENEWAL OF ORTHODOXY[1]

SEVEN STUDIES OF KEY ISSUES
FACING ORTHODOX CHRISTIANS IN AMERICA.

THE RENEWAL OF THE CHURCH COMMUNITY

Language and Culture. The Greek Orthodox Archdiocese is in the midst of dramatic demographic change. There are approximately 900,000 Greek Americans in the United States, of whom 200,000 were born in Greece, Cyprus or other Greek speaking areas. Because of the decline in immigration in the 1980's and the low birth rate of Greek Americans, the Greek American community has probably shrunk in the last ten years.

Based on Gallup surveys, census data, subscriptions to the Orthodox Observer and other data sources, it is likely that only 400,000 to 600,000 people in the United States belong to the Greek Orthodox Archdiocese. There is a significant problem of retaining the allegiance of persons of Greek descent to the Church, particularly among 3rd, 4th and 5th generation Greek Americans, and of attracting non-ethnic Greeks to the Church. The persistence of the use of Greek as the primary liturgical language even in the overwhelmingly English speaking parishes is a major barrier both to holding the allegiance of American born Orthodox as well as to attracting new members. The use of English, therefore, is a fundamental spiritual issue in the Church.

---

1. By Stephen J. Sfekas, partner at the law firm of Weinberg and Green, Baltimore, Maryland.

To the extent that the Church focuses its attentions and resources on promoting the secular Greek ethnic identity at the expense of Orthodox religious identity, the Church will fail in its primary function.

Accordingly, Orthodox Christian Laity recommends the following:

1. Orthodoxy in America must evolve into an indigenous and American faith drawing on the best aspects of the American tradition while recognizing and respecting its ethnic roots.

2. The Greek Archdiocese should commission a comprehensive translation of the liturgy into contemporary English as spoken in the United States and Canada. The members of this Commission should include theologians, skilled translators, experts in Church music and poets.

3. However, in the interim, the Archdiocese must move definitively to the use of English in the liturgy as the standard. Parishes in which the majority of the parish speak a language other than English as the native language such as Spanish, French, Greek or Native American languages, may continue to use such languages with the permission of their bishops.

4. The preservation of Greek ethnic identity is the proper function of Greek ethnic organizations such as AHEPA, regional associations, and folklore groups. These groups should establish programs including:

   a. A high school year in Greece for Greek-American youth.

   b. A college year in Greece or a "fifth year" in Greece following a bachelor's degree.

   c. A summer language and culture course for high school or college students. The pilot program of the University of Aegean is one model to emulate.

d. A continuing education program in Greece for Greek-American adults and their spouses.

e. A lecture series and seminar program geared to weekend attendance. Such a program could involve traveling lecturers and seminar organizers visiting local communities.

f. A fund to subsidize a journal of commentary and literature on Greek-Americana.

g. Preservation of Greek-American culture.

5. The governments of Greece, Cyprus, the United States, and Canada have a legitimate role to play in preserving secular Greek identity.

6. However, the Greek Orthodox Archdiocese should separate itself from any influence, direct or indirect, of any governmental agency of any nation.

Spiritual Renewal and Religious Education. An OCL survey of members of the Greek Orthodox Archdiocese found substantial dissatisfaction with the status of the spiritual life of the Church and in particular with the status of religious education. The first priority of the Church for clergy, laity and hierarchy should be lifelong, religious education, said 85% of the respondents to the OCL Spiritual Renewal survey. Active involvement in all aspects of church life was the seemed priority stated by 75% of the respondents.

OCL believes strongly that the spiritual vitality of the Church requires the active involvement of the laity in a relationship of syndiakonia with the clergy and hierarchy.

Accordingly, OCL recommends the following:

1. A properly educated clergy is fundamental to the life of the Church. Seminarians must receive a thorough theological training coupled with a well-rounded program of secular studies. Regular programs of continuing education must be required of all clergy.

2. The laity have an equal responsibility to learn their faith, practice their beliefs and support programs in their parishes for Spiritual Renewal, including study groups, organized retreats, and charity work.

3. The Holy Cross Seminary and in particular its library and publishing activities must become a high priority of the Archdiocese in commitment of resources and attention. The school must be held to the highest academic standards of comparable American colleges and universities.

4. Holy Cross Seminary should organize extension programs and continuing education programs to facilitate both continuing education for clergy and lay education. The seminary should seek formal academic accreditation of these programs.

5. Formal education programs should be established to welcome and educate converts into the Orthodox faith.

6. The seminary and the Archdiocese should encourage active scholarship in Orthodoxy in the seminary, but also in non-Orthodox universities. Foundations and private donors should be encouraged to fund such scholarship.

7. Special efforts must be made to encourage scholarship by and about women in the Orthodox Church.

8. There should be organized training and educational programs for the orientation of Parish Council members.

9. The laity should be encouraged to take an active role in the liturgical life of the community rather than be passive observers of the Liturgy. The parish should be encouraged to sing the responses in the Liturgy.

10. The use of English in the liturgy and in instruction is necessary for the spiritual growth of the community.

11. There needs to be special emphasis on the spiritual growth of persons in mixed marriages and of their children.

Women's Roles. From ancient times, the life of the Church has been enriched by the dedication, work, love and courage of the faithful women of the Church. However, women have often faced obstacles to their participation and spiritual growth in the Church. OCL strongly supports the elimination of all such barriers to the full participation of women in the life of the Church.

Accordingly, OCL recommends that:

1. A Commission should be established composed of hierarchs, priests, lay women and men to organize and oversee a long-range plan of investigation and discussion of all aspects of Orthodox women's roles and status in the Church, including the re-establishment of the female diaconate.

2. The Church must show greater sensitivity in the use of language. The use of inclusive rather than exclusive language in traditional liturgical phrases would help reduce the marginalization of Orthodox women while at the same time give due recognition to the historic role of women in the Church.

3. The diaconate of women should be re-instituted in our Church, according to the ancient, New Testament model.

4. Women should be welcomed to participate in the Liturgy as members of the choir, as chanters and readers. Women should be tonsured for these roles in the same manner as are men.

5. Tonsured women should be welcomed to serve in the Sanctuary as are men.

6. Both male and female infants should be Churched in the same way, within the Sanctuary.

7. The Church must make it clear that natural bodily functions should in no way bar anyone from participation in the sacraments.

Mission and Outreach. Historically, Orthodoxy was a powerful force for evangelizing the world. The Church in America must recapture this tradition and establish active programs of mission and outreach.

Accordingly, OCL recommends:

1. A national program of evangelism should be organized to attract new members to the Church regardless of ethnic background. The order of catechumens should be re-established. The use of contemporary American English in the liturgy is essential to this effort.

2. A nationwide education program for Catechists should be organized. Hellenic College/Holy Cross Greek Orthodox School of Theology must become a nationwide school of faith.

3. There should be a new emphasis on philanthropy and social and human improvement. Each parish should take on projects in its own community, as a witness to its love for Christ.

4. Social Service Committees should be formed to assist the clergy in meeting the pastoral and social service needs of the community.

5. Fellowship events, which often attract rarely seen members (Sacraments, memorials, festivals, etc.) should be an occasion for outreach to unchurched members.

6. Catechism must be implemented through classes, lectures and homilies. Too often, converts are received without proper instruction, preparation and understanding.

7. As often as possible, the reception of converts should be at well attended services, with some community event following.

8. As the monastic tradition is a **LAY** tradition and the source of much spiritual food, converts and "cradle" Orthodox alike should work for the establishment of the monastic tradition in America, to bring emphasis again to the wealth of our spiritual tradition.

9. Although the future of Orthodoxy is to become an indigenous American faith, the Church will retain a special role in the life of immigrants from traditional Orthodox countries.

10. Language schools in English should be organized to assist immigrants in making a transition to American life.

11. Language schools should have enough diversity to warrant "cultural exchange" programs within their own walls. More homogeneous parishes may want to have exchanges with nearby communities of different ethnic origins.

12. In affirming that contemporary American English should be the liturgical standard of our Church, the needs of the newly arrived, as well as the beauty and integrity of the historical liturgical tongues should not be neglected. A selection of hymns, such as the Trisagion and Cherubikon, sung in these historical languages, can give the feeling of "home" to

many immigrants, without compromising the comprehension of the Liturgy.

13. Local/traditional customs from native Orthodox countries should be encouraged.

14. The Sunday Cathechetical School must be conducted either before or after the Divine Liturgy, thereby enabling the youth to participate in the worship of the Church. The educational program of the local parish must have a unified effort towards **educating** and **involving** the parents.

15. Parishes should organize special programs for the elderly. Such programs should include an oral history project to preserve the memories and wisdom of our elderly.

16. Our Church needs a complete restoration of the Diaconate. Deacons could be prepared through study courses which would be (1) sanctioned by the Hierarchs, (2) formulated by the faculty of the Theological School and (3) administered by the local parish priest. These Deacons would serve at the Sunday Liturgy; particularly invaluable would be their assistance in the administration of Communion and other liturgical and pastoral functions. They would continue to function "in the world," but must be understood to be full clergymen.

17. There should be pan-Orthodox cooperation in developing ministries that can prepare our people for marriage. Non-Orthodox or non-Christian brides or grooms-to-be should be invited to become Orthodox Christians.

18. The process of Ecclesiastical Divorce must be opened up to the understanding of the Faithful. Conferences to deal with the differences of approach between jurisdictions in this country should be called.

19. In the local community, Orthodox support groups should be available for persons going through separation and divorce.

20. Our people need to be aware of the spiritual implications of divorce, the necessity of Ecclesiastical Divorce. The Church should not excommunicate 'en masse' those who may not yet have obtained it.

21. For those married outside the Church, there should be an effort to instruct them as to why the Orthodox blessing is so important. This should be seen as a complement to whatever marital relationship exists, even if there were only a civil ceremony. It is time to recognize the social validity of these marriages. This goes as well for Orthodox married to non-Christians. We should encourage participation in the full sacramental life of the Church as an enhancement to the existing marriage, not as a denouncement of "living in sin."

22. If it is not possible for an Orthodox blessing to occur (either due to family pressure, the refusal of a spouse of a heterodox, or because one is married to a non-Christian) the Church should admit to Communion those who have sought an entry to the Sacrament through Confession.

Renewal of the Institutional Church

Selection of Hierarchs. Given the importance of bishops in the theology of the Church, the proper selection of bishops is fundamental to the life of the Church. In Orthodox tradition and practice, the laity and lower clergy have always played a role in the selection of bishops. Indeed, lay involvement prevails throughout much of the Orthodox world. Many bishops, such as the Patriarch of Moscow and the Archbishop of Cyprus, are elected in whole or in part by lay members. Lay participation in the election of the Patriarch of Constantinople was terminated by an oppressive Turkish government in 1923. The Archbishop of North and South America formerly was nominated by the Clergy-Laity Congress.

Lay participation in the selection of bishops would assure that the bishops stay close to the needs of the people.

Accordingly, OCL recommends that:

1. Lay participation in the selection of the bishops of the Greek Orthodox Archdiocese be restored.

2. The role of the clergy in the selection of the bishops of the Greek Orthodox Archdiocese must be restored.

3. Married clergy should be eligible for elevation to bishop.

4. After the re-establishment of the participation of lower clergy and laity in the selection of bishops, the American Church should be reorganized into a larger number of smaller dioceses so that bishops will be closer geographically and spiritually to the bulk of the parishioners.

Administration and Accountability. The Greek Orthodox Archdiocese faces a major crisis in administration and accountability. The finances of the Archdiocese are in disarray, and questions have been raised as to the propriety and prudence of various land transactions. A bishop of the Church has been accused in a national magazine of personal misconduct. Questions have been raised as to the conduct of the Clergy-Laity Congress.

One fundamental problem is that Diocese and the Archdiocesan Council are not elected by the laity, but are rather appointed by the bishops and can be dismissed at will. Thus, there is no independent source of advice or oversight at the top levels of the Church. Finally, the parish clergy in many areas are suffering from burnout and low morale. The Church needs to take immediate action to improve the lives of the clergy.

Accordingly, OCL recommends that:

Parish Level

1. The Archdiocese establish policies to assure a level of economic and professional security for parish clergy, including salary guidelines for priests, and professional management of pension and benefits funds.

2. Parish clergy must not be removed from a parish in an arbitrary manner either by the laity or by the hierarchy.

3. The Archdiocese should take aggressive steps to recruit seminarians, to reestablish the active diaconate, and to encourage adult laymen to seek ordination, in order to reduce stress on full-time priests and to extend the Church's ability to minister to the faithful.

4. Although the priest is the primary authority on theological issues, the laity are entitled to reasonable explanation as to theological issues which may arise.

5. In the matters of administration the responsibility must be shared by both laity and clergy.

6. Standing Committees should be established in parishes for each of the major parish functions. Their chairpersons should be selected by the combined judgment and efforts of Priest and Council.

Diocesan Level

7. Each Diocese should have a standard date for its meeting to take place, and be announced by the bishop "no later than ninety days in advance" as the regulations stipulate.

8. The Diocese Assembly should be a working conference with a minimum emphasis on social and ceremonial activities.

9. Conference officers must be elected by the delegates.

10. The Diocese Council should be comprised of fifteen persons, five clergy and five lay persons elected by the delegates; and five additional persons, appointed by the Bishop.

Clergy-Laity Congress

11. As the Congress is the primary national working group of the Church, all social functions should either be removed or minimized drastically.

12. Schedules should be adhered to strictly.

13. The Archdiocese should consider moving the Clergy-Laity Congress to conference centers more suited to the Congress's work.

14. Workshops should be held on topics of religion, interfaith marriages, liturgical music, social issues, senior citizens, missions, outreach, youth program, fund raising, funding of our institutions, and administration and management of the parish and its components, etc.

15. Clergy-Laity Congress officers must be elected in the same manner as they are elected to the Diocese conference.

16. The staff of the Archdiocese must distribute the final agenda three months before the Congress. Input and suggestions from the parishes must be incorporated into the agenda.

17. Secular political figures and governmental figures, whether Greek or American, should not be invited to the Congress, other than the mayor or governor of the host city or state, or a public official of the Orthodox faith, who may participate as any other Orthodox lay person.

18. The Archdiocesan Council should be comprised of at least two elected laypersons and at least one elected clergyman from each Diocese, all the

Bishops of the Church, the elected president of the Presbyters' Council, the elected president of the Retired Clergy, and ten more qualified individuals (either clergy or laity) appointed by the Archbishop. Council members should serve for a term fixed in time.

19. A full accounting of the Church's financial position should be performed by outside auditors and be published regularly in the Orthodox Observer.

20. A thorough review of the Archdiocese's financial affairs should be performed by a firm of independent financial consultants to review the financial management of the Archdiocese, to recommend improved practices, and to create a financial plan.

21. Given the persistent questions relating to specific land deals involving Church properties in New York state, one of which resulted in a write-off of $5,000,000 of funds owed to the Archdiocese by a former employee, the Archdiocese should retain independent counsel and auditing firms to investigate the circumstances of these transactions and render a report to the Archdiocesan Council. The verbatim text of the report or its executive summary should be published in the Orthodox Observer. If appropriate, suit for recovery of the funds should be instituted by or on behalf of the Archdiocese.

22. The Orthodox Observer must become the voice of the entire Church community. The newspaper should print articles about the problems of the Church in a fair and objective manner. The newspaper should not censor critical commentary by members in good standing in the Church. In particular, the current editorial ban on all mention of OCL should be dropped.

23. The Church must adopt procedures by which its Spiritual Courts resolve matters in a fair, just and open fashion, and which are comprehensible to the laity. In particular, investigation into charges of impropriety directed against clergy or hierarchs should be conducted in a manner

which will do justice to both the victim and the accused. Although OCL expresses no opinion as to particular cases, no bishop accused of impropriety should be restored to full status without a public disclosure of the results of any formal proceedings.

POSSIBLE MODELS FOR ACHIEVING UNITY[2]

Autocephalous: Unification of all canonical jurisdictions into an autocephalous (self-governing) Church with its own elected primate independent of all other world Orthodox jurisdictions without particular reference to ethnic identities.

1. Canon law provides for it (2nd canon of Carthage).

2. Part of natural process of evolving Church as reflected in the establishment of modern Orthodox autocephalous churches of Europe.

3. Need for indigenous American Church to reach out to unchurched Americans as in the Great Commission of Pentecost.

4. Need to remove foreign aura of Church in America by adopting English language as vernacular of the Church to reach its youth and those who are unchurched.

5. The Ecumenical Patriarchate is a captive institution in a hostile environment subject to continuous constraints of the Turkish Government. As such, it is not an independent agency and cannot perform its religious obligations as the Great Church of Christ — center and front of world Orthodoxy.

6. The Ecumenical Patriarchate is no longer located in a Christian environment but in a nation that is overwhelmingly Muslim , whose

---

2. Written by Nicholas E. Nicholaou for THE FORUM, Spring, 1993.

immediate flock has been reduced to less than 5,000 souls. As such, Constantinople has ceased to be a major metropolitan see and is unworthy of being a center for world Orthodoxy.

7. It is for these reasons that the modern autocephalic churches evolve not wishing to be subject to a patriarch under Turkish political control, namely Greece, Serbia, Romania and Bulgaria.

8. America is not a diaspora; it is home to millions of Orthodox Christians, more so than in the ancient patriarchates of Alexandria, Antioch or Jerusalem. Hence, there is a need to form an independent Church.

Autonomous: Unification of all canonical jurisdictions into an autonomous (semi-independent) Church under the tutelage of the Ecumenical Patriarchate of Constantinople without particular reference to ethnic identities.

1. Upheld by canon law (3rd canon of 1st Constantinople and canon 28 of Chalcedon).

2. The Ecumenical Patriarchate is recognized by all Orthodox churches as *the first among equals* and final court of appeal for all Orthodox churches.

3. Despite restraints imposed by Turkish authorities, the Ecumenical Patriarchate is recognized by international law.

4. The Ecumenical Patriarchate has a worldwide multi-national jurisdiction in Europe, Asia, North and South America, Australia and New Zealand, and despite its "Greekness," is the only supra-national Church stemming from antiquity.

5. The concept of "first bishop," a prerogative of the Ecumenical Throne, is a vital and necessary principle for the preservation and stability of the worldwide church and for the fulfillment of its mission.

6. Despite its harassments by Turkish authorities in Istanbul, the Ecumenical Patriarchate has been able to administer and service its universal jurisdiction by virtue of its Orthodox Center of the Ecumenical Patriarchate at Chambesy (Geneva), Switzerland.

7. The weight of nearly 2,000 years of tradition and history of the Ecumenical Patriarchate necessitates its survival as the premier church of Orthodoxy.

Transitional: The establishment of an "assembly of Bishops" to a diocese in the "diaspora" initially based upon ethnic identities and the determination of the primatial See. Bishops would preside at all common meetings and report to the Ecumenical Patriarch. This would prevail until the Great and Holy Council would convene and approve the restructuring of multi-ethnic dioceses by the "Assembly of Bishops" into fullfledged canonical autocephalous Orthodox jurisdictions.

FAITH, LANGUAGE AND CULTURE
Charles Moskos

An assessment of the Church's contemporary situation in the United States must be anchored to the eternal truths of the Church. These truths stand independent and apart from the social currents of particular historical eras. Our purpose here is to advance the universal faith and tradition of Orthodoxy by examining certain sociological realities of the Church in America.

First and foremost, we must seek to disentangle wishful thinking from social reality. We must look at ourselves honestly and realistically. It is commonly accepted that the American environment has had a powerful socializing influence on the members of our Church. As an institution as well, the Church clearly reflects some adaptation to major aspects of the cultural, political, and economic contours of American society. None of this need imply any contradiction between Holy Tradition and the advancement of Orthodoxy in an American milieu. Our mission, rather, is to build upon the foundation of our immigrant forebears who laid the basis for an Orthodox Church in the new world.

The Church in America is not a national Church, in which Orthodox correligionists make up the large majority of the population. Nor is it a diaspora Church, which means that its members hark back to some kind of emotional, if not physical, return to an ancestral homeland. Neither is it any longer an immigrant Church, whose members were born in the old country. Rather, the Church is evolving into an indigenous and American faith whose promise is limited only by the vision of its congregants.

As the Church in America approaches the end of the twentieth century, one way to convey recent developments is to contrast the older generation of Greek immigrant church **builders** with the later generations of church **inheritors**. The 1980s marked the end of three decades of widespread church construction in the United States. Most of the builders of the post-World War II generation were motivated by the desire to establish a

Greek Orthodox presence in what was then mostly an alien environment. By the time the churches were standing, however, American society had changed. Greek Orthodoxy was no longer so alien, a reassuring sign of the success of the builders' intentions.

Yet the inheritors did not accept the bricks-and-mortar mentality that equates the success of Greek Orthodoxy with the construction of more churches and community halls. They had less of an emotional stake in the outward presentation of their religion and were inclined more toward an inward Orthodoxy. In the 1950s the Greek Orthodox were struggling with the question of what it means to be an American; in the 1990s, comfortably American, they struggled with a more fundamental question: what it means to be Greek Orthodox.

The plan of this paper is straightforward. First, we discuss certain demographic realities. Second, we look at the issue of language and liturgy. Third, we turn to the question of Greek ethnic identity in this country and the relationship of such identity to the Church in America. We conclude with a look toward the future.

Demographics
To understand social changes within the Greek Orthodox Church in this country is ultimately to grasp trends in Greek-American demography. To a large degree Greek Orthodoxy reflects changes in the numbers of new arrivals, the proportion born in the old country versus the proportion born in the United States, reproduction rates, the frequency of intermarriage, the age and generational distribution, converts from and losses to other denominations, and so on.

Immigration
First readings on the Greek-American population come from immigration statistics. We can divide Greek immigration conveniently into seven distinct periods.

18

Early Migration: 1873-1899. A trickle of Greek immigrants began to arrive in the 1870's, but by the end of the nineteenth century only some 15,000 Greeks had entered the United States. The approximate annual average was 500.

Great Wave: 1900-1917. The great wave of immigration, when 450,000 Greeks came to these shores, started at the turn of the century and ended in 1917 when the U.S. entered World War I. The approximate annual average was 25,000.

Last Exodus: 1918-1924. The final phase of the earlier immigration of 70,000 Greeks lasted from the years following Wold War I until the doors of immigration closed in 1924. The approximate annual average was 10,000.

Closed Door: 1925-1946. The two-decade "closed door" period lasted through the end of World War II. Only some 30,000 Greeks came to this country. Many of these were brides of immigrants already settled in America. The approximate annual average was 1,300.

Postwar Migration: 1947-1965. After World War II the doors opened somewhat, especially under provisions for displaced persons. Some 75,000 Greeks arrived here. The approximate annual average was 4,000.

New Wave: 1966-1979. Starting in 1966, when the immigrating laws were changed to allow easier entrance for the relatives of persons already here, a new wave of 160,000 Greeks came to the U.S. The approximate annual average was 11,000.

Declining Migration: 1980-present. For over a decade, immigration from Greece has tapered off considerably. Only 25,000 Greeks came to these shores during the 1980s. The approximate annual average is 2,500. But with returnees, the net growth rate is probably, under 1,000 annually.

The end of immigration from Greece is the first demographic reality for a contemporary understanding of the Church in America.

Fertility Rates

One other important remark must be made about the Greek-American population. For at least two decades, the American-born generations have not been replacing themselves. In terms of economic and educational status, Greek-Americans have done well, but certainly they are fewer in number than if they were not so well educated and so well off. With no renewal of immigration in sight and with little likelihood of a rise in the birthrate, the Greek-American population will shrink somewhat in the years to come.

The Greek-American and Greek-Orthodox Populations

Our numbers in the United States are much lower than inflated public relations statements. The U.S. census remains the best source of data on the Greek-American population. In the 1980 census, persons were asked to identify their ancestry in terms of national origin or descent. An identical item was included in the 1990 census, but the tabulations from that census are not yet available. Most likely, the numbers of Greek-Americans to be reported in 1990 will be smaller than those of 1980.

The 1980 census reported that 615,000 Americans identified themselves as being of purely Greek ancestry and that another 345,000 identified themselves as having some Greek ancestry.[1] Thus, under one million persons can be considered Greek-Americans on the basis of national origin. Of course, all of those who acknowledge Greek origins do not necessarily identify themselves with the Greek community or even have personal feelings of Greek ethnicity.

By using available census and immigration figures and by making some assumptions about the ratio of births to deaths since 1980, we can calculate the generational distribution of Greek-Americans in the early 1990s. An informed estimate would be as follows:

First generation (immigrants)	200,000
Second generation	350,000
Third generation	250,000
Fourth generation	100,000
Total	900,000

In other words, about a quarter, or slightly less, of all Greek-Americans have Greek as a mother tongue. The Greek language competency of the later generations is unknown, but realism dictates that English is the preferred language for virtually all of the American born. A large number of the second generation (children of the immigrants), to be sure, have some fluency with the Greek language. For the vast majority of the third and later generations (the grandchildren and great-grandchildren of the immigrants), if truth be told, Greek language competency is meager to nonexistent. We examine ways of improving Greek language capabilities later in this paper.

Religious affiliation is not tabulated by the census. A 1975 Gallup poll of American religious preference found .031 who identified as Greek Orthodox (Reinken). If the Gallup figures are extrapolated to the total U.S. population, there were approximately 670,000 self-identified Greek Orthodox in this country in 1975. A 1990 survey, however, reported only about 550,000 self-identified Greek Orthodox (Kosmin). Let us, for the sake of argument, then, say there are some 600,000 identifying Greek Orthodox in this country. The Archdiocese has approximately 130,000 dues-paying family units, which would come to approximately 400,000 individuals.

In broad terms, then, about two out of three persons with Greek ethnicity identifies as Greek Orthodox, and about the same proportion of these self-identified Greek Orthodox are formally affiliated with the Greek Archdiocese.

The Archdiocesan figures are not designators of active membership in Church life, of course. A tendency exists among even **bona fide** Orthodox Church members to limit their religious participation to occasional Church attendance. Such casual Church membership often leads to a movement away from the Church, not so much in a sense of renunciation or joining another denominational body, but in the sense that Orthodox Christianity is no longer a prime definer of one's religious identity. The danger is not that the Greek Orthodox suffer discrimination, much less persecution, in the United States, but that in the tolerance of American society, no Orthodox identity is maintained. The "drifting away" phenomenon is often accentuated by the growing likelihood of marriage with a non-Greek Orthodox.

Intermarriage

By the early 1990s, over two out of three marriages occurring in the Greek Orthodox Church involved a partner who was not Greek Orthodox. Furthermore, some number of the marriages in which both partners are reported as Orthodox include converts, thereby reducing the proportion of intra-Greek marriages even more.

The Greek-American community has had to change its position on intermarriage in the face of its frequency. The initial edict of the immigrant parents was to tell their children that all Greek potential marriage partners were better than all non-Greek. The next line of defense, typical of the second generation, was to acknowledge that there are equal measures of good and bad in all nationalities, but the sharing of a common Greek background makes for a better marriage. (Interestingly enough, the available Archdiocesan data, though not conclusive, show a somewhat **lower** divorce rate among couples in which one of the partners was not Greek Orthodox.)[2] The final argument, a common recourse for the third generation, is that if one does marry a non-Greek, one must be sure that the spouse is able to adapt to the family kinship system and be willing to become Greek Orthodox.

22

At present, the non-Greek spouse usually plays a minor role in Church functions, but there is a discernible trend for some such converts to become more actively involved in Church organizations. Non-Greeks, in fact, have been elected to Church Boards. Converts — a very, very few who learn to speak Greek — have become a new element in the impetus toward a permanent Greek Orthodox presence in this country. Now that intermarriage has become the rule rather than the exception, its meaning has also been transformed. Outmarriage no longer carries a stigma of deviance in the community; thus it is much easier for exogamous Greek-Americans and their spouses who marry in the Church to continue an active membership in the Greek community.

Without frontal recognition of the increasing likelihood of intermarriage, there can be no long-term answer to the viability of the Greek Orthodox Church in this country. The battle against intermarriage is over. The focus now must be on how to retain the non-Greek spouse and the children of the intermarried.

The Children of Mixed Marriages

What happens to the children of intermarried couples? There is no firm answer to this question. But there is good reason to think that a substantial proportion of children of mixed-marriages will have less identity as Greeks than those who are the offspring of two Greek-American parents. More salient, for our purposes here, intermarriage will reduce the number who identify themselves as Greek Orthodox in future generations **unless measures are taken to incorporate non-Greek spouses into the Greek Orthodox community.** (We do have data for Jewish-Gentile marriages. Among such marriages, only one-quarter are raised as Jews) (Jewish Federation).

It is revealing to examine the religious patterns of our five most prominent Greek-American political figures: Spiro Agnew, John Brademas, Michael Dukakis, Paul Sarbanes, and Paul Tsongas. Agnew and Brademas were children of mixed marriage and not raised in the Greek Orthodox faith. Michael Dukakis, although raised as Greek Orthodox and a member of the Church, did not marry in the Church and did not raise his children as Greek

Orthodox. Indeed, a leading American commentator described Dukakis as "the first truly secular candidate we had ever had for the presidency" (Wills, 60). Paul Tsongas and Paul Sarbanes married non-Greek women in the Church and baptized their children as Greek Orthodox. Tsongas, who has addressed OCL gatherings, states his wife and children found themselves uncomfortable with the Greek ethnic overtones of the Church and found themselves attending the Episcopalian Church (Tsongas, 40). Only Sarbanes's children have a Greek Orthodox identity.

With such experience among our most prominent Greeks, it behooves the Church to consider ways to maintain or, perhaps more accurately, even create a Greek Orthodox identity among its children. Consideration must be given to instituting some kind of focused instruction in Church doctrine and history beyond the Sunday School level. Such instruction should be directed toward adolescence, a time when young people are most likely to drift away from the Church and a time when young people are forming an adult religious identity. At present, the knowledge of Orthodox traditions and beliefs even among our observant youth is often deficient. Simply ask our young people, for example, what is the significance of such major Orthodox holydays as January 6 and August 15.

Language and Liturgy
Once upon a time, a generation ago, to be Greek-American usually meant to know something about the Greek language. Even today, there is little doubt that if we could have instant Greek, if we could by some Brave New World method learn Greek in our sleep with little effort, nearly all Greek-Americans would be glad to do so. But learning and using Greek requires conscious effort, and the effort by and large was not being made by American-born parents for their children, much less for the children of mixed marriages. Increasingly Greek Orthodox affiliation rather than Greek language has become the defining trait of Greek ethnic identity in America.[3]

The issue of the language and liturgy in the Greek Orthodox Church in this country is a vexing one. Orthodox Christianity clearly adheres to a tradition

24

of coterminous liturgical and indigenous languages. But we must recognize that many native Greek speakers (though not all by any means) and some American born have a strong and understandable desire to perpetuate the mother tongue in this country. This stance in turn disaffects many of those for whom Greek is an alien language.

What aggravates the language question is that the liturgy has unique importance in Eastern Orthodoxy. The laity's presence and participation is indispensable in the liturgy. An Orthodox priest cannot celebrate the Eucharist without lay participation. The Churchgoer wants to find his or her faith adequately, indeed inspiringly, embodied in the words and acts of the liturgy, that part of the religious experience which makes the most pervasive and persistent public manifestation and moves most hearts. It is through the liturgy that Orthodox Christians, more so than Occidental Christians, are formed in their Christian allegiance.

As early as 1927, a Boston bishop held that the Greek Orthodox could be considered faithful even if they did not know Greek (Papaioannous, 151). But this was a cry in the wilderness at the time. Archbishop Athenagoras was a conservative on the language issue, probably to avoid conflict with community lay leaders (Papaioannous, 142-43). Even Sunday schools were required to use Greek as the language of instruction up through the 1940s. Proposals for an English liturgy were seriously advanced in the 1950s, but Archbishop Michael authorized English only in sermons. During the 1950s, a major transmission of Greek Orthodox commitment to the American born occurred through the lay-directed Greek Orthodox Youth of America (GOYA). Significantly, Michael allowed English to be GOYA's official language. GOYA served as the incubator for a generation of lay leaders in the Greek Orthodox community.

In 1964, the clergy-laity congress allowed certain readings and prayers in the liturgy to be repeated in English. In the important clergy-laity congress of 1970, following the personal appeal of Archbishop Iakovos, an English liturgy was permitted, depending upon the judgment of the parish priest in consultation with the bishop. The progression to English would have been inevitable and relatively smooth had it not been for the large influx of new immigrants from Greece in the late 1960s and early 1970s. With the arrival of the new immigrants, older traditionalists could join forces with a younger constituency committed to the Greek language. The Greek Orthodox Church was more ready, in effect, for English in 1965 than it was in 1980. During the 1980s, however, the long-term movement toward English was clearly reascendant. In fact, even some of the newly ordained priests had only a shaky mastery of the Greek vernacular.

The tide of Americanization that began to lap at the feet of the Church in the post-World War II era has continued to rise in each succeeding decade. Despite resistance, the Church has begun to adapt to linguistic change. By the early 1970s, most liturgies were predominantly, but not exclusively in Greek. By the early 1990s, language use varied widely. Churches in the immigrant neighborhoods of the larger cities offered their services entirely in Greek. Churches in the metropolitan suburbs and in the West and South, those most likely to be attended by the American born, had services increasingly in English. By the early 1990s, in a manner of speaking, a kind of local option system had evolved.

The language issue to some degree solves itself outside of the liturgy. Language use in Church meetings, formal affairs, and informal conversation comes close to reflecting prevailing usage among those present. With a little give and take, no one is seriously at a language disadvantage. But the liturgy remains a source of linguistic contention. None of the various accommodations — singing parts of liturgies in both languages, a service partly in Greek and partly in English, alternating language use on various Sundays — is entirely satisfactory. The Church's policy of "flexible bilingualism," a mixture of Greek and English, dependent on the parish's linguistic makeup can only be regarded as temporary expediency. Indeed, it is inherently contradictory for the sermon and announcements in most of our churches to be in English while the bulk of the liturgy is in Greek.

The adaptation of an English liturgy in the Greek Orthodox Church in this country is handicapped by the fact that no authorized translation of the liturgy exists. Equally pressing, there has been no concerted effort to synchronize an English-language liturgy with liturgical music. The time is overdue for a commission consisting of those well versed in theology, liturgical history, the intricacies of both the English and Greek languages, and Church music.

However, the lack of an authorized liturgy in the Greek Orthodox Archdiocese should not serve as an excuse for inaction. The Antiochan Orthodox Archdiocese (1938) and the Orthodox Church in America (1971) have successfully used English as the primary liturgical language for decades, and there is no reason to believe that the Greek Archdiocese could not do the same.

Fostering a Greek Identity

To argue that the Church must come to recognize and nourish its new roots in America does not mean to forsake Greek ethnic identity. Celebration of Greek national holidays, classes in the Greek language, Greek cooking, Greek dancing and music, all have a place in the Church community — if this suits a community's needs and desires. But it is to say that preservation and encouragement of Greek ethnic identity need no longer be an overriding responsibility of the Church. We might even argue that to some extent the Church has been distracted from its fundamental mission by seeking to become the prime, if not sole, conservator of Greek ethnic identity.

The time is ripe for serious consideration of long-range programs to foster ethnic identity by a multiplicity of groups. With the advent of inexpensive mass air transit, travel to Greece becomes an increasingly available option. Also certain programs could fit in rather nicely with the growing emphasis on education abroad for young people and continuing education for adults. The possibilities merely listed here await further discussion and modification:

1. A high school year in Greece for Greek-American youth. Such a policy could be modeled after the exchange program of the American Field

Service. Each year thousands of overseas students come to the United States and an equal number of Americans go abroad.

2. A college year in Greece or a "fifth year" in Greece following a bachelor's degree.

3. A summer language and culture course for high school or college students. The pilot program of the University of Aegean is one model to emulate.

4. A continuing education program in Greece for Greek-American adults and their spouses. Such a program would foster both language and culture learning. The *ulpan* schools in Israel, where Hebrew is taught as a second language, is one such model.

5. A lecture series and seminar program geared to weekend attendance. Such a program could involve traveling lecturers and seminar organizers visiting local communities.

6. Some kind of fund to subsidize a journal of commentary and literature on Greek-Americana.[4]

The above is only a first-draft listing. Readers can think of other concepts. Some of these programs could be self-sustaining by tuition or fees paid for by participants. Others might need supplementary financial support from foundations, Greek-American donors, Greek-American associations, and, in some cases, the Greek government. Everything appropriate to Greece applies equally to Cyprus.

Such courses and programs must be tailored to the capabilities and needs of the participants. What works for someone immersed in a Greek background will not work for someone coming to his or her Greek ethnicity afresh. We stress especially that such programs could also contain material on Greek Orthodoxy, thereby bringing some secularists closer to the faith.

Toward the Future

Serious questions, not all with definitive answers, can be raised against the argument that the Church should gradually release itself of primary responsibility for maintaining the Greek ethnic heritage in America. Here are three of the most serious, in ascending order of difficulty.

If not the Church, who will represent the interests of Greece and Cyprus in the American policy? The simple answer is that the Church in America cannot be the political arm of Hellenic interests. Indeed, for the Church to try to play such a role in American politics is counterproductive. On non-religious issues, the Church should stay clear of political involvements. The causes of Greece and Cyprus are best represented by secular leaders and groups in the Greek-American community and, as much as possible, by non-Greek ethnics in the American political system. The proper conception of political activism should be in accord with the strong American tradition of separation of church and state.

If the Church sheds its ethnicity, will not Greek identify disappear in this country? In point of fact, Greek ethnic identity is already disappearing. As we have sought to demonstrate in this paper, present trends augur the possibility of a virtual extinction of an identifiable Greek-American community in another generation. A variety of groups and multifaceted programs drawing upon varying constituencies promises to be the best way for Greek identity to flower in this country.

Will not a de-emphasis of our Greek ethnic heritage lead ultimately to the creation of an American Orthodox Church? Such a question must be addressed on its own terms and in due time, if and when it arises. Some view an autocephalous Greek Orthodox Church in America with alarm, others with joy. For the present, we can state that there is nothing that either forecloses or inevitably moves toward an autocephalous Church. At the minimum, pan-Orthodoxy must be high on the agenda of the Church in America. In any event, the Church must keep clear a sense of priorities. In these straitened times, resources should be directed toward those institutions that are the seed corn of our future. Of these, the Holy Cross School of Theology stands out as most worthy.

Looking at Greek Orthodoxy in the United States, we can offer the following generalizations. For the immigrant generation, Orthodoxy was Hellenism — the two were virtually synonymous. For the second generation, Orthodoxy was found in Hellenism. To be a Greek in America meant to be a Greek Orthodox. For the third and later generations, Hellenism is to be found in Orthodoxy. This is to say that rather than viewing the increasing Americanization of the Church as antithetical to Greek identity, it will be only with an indigenous Greek Orthodox Church that we can expect any kind of Greek identity to carry on into the generations to come. Paradoxically enough, the more the Church reaches out and accepts non-Greeks, always without compromise of its doctrinal tenets, the more it will insure its own flowering and, therefore, guarantee some form of Greek-American ethnic survival into the indefinite future.

To conclude, it may be useful to distinguish between secular ethnicity and sacred ethnicity. Secular ethnicity will slowly erode, despite rearguard actions by the diasporists. Sacred ethnicity, on the other hand, can strike roots in the new world — a Church adaptable to changing social conditions and changing generations, while not deviating from its traditions and transcendental truths. If the Greek Orthodox Church in America were to emphasize secular ethnicity over sacred ethnicity, it might well end in a situation in which the descendants of the immigrants are neither Greek nor Orthodox.

NOTES

1. Bureau of the Census, <u>Ancestry of the Population by States: 1980</u>, PC80-S1-10 (Washington: Government Printing Office, 1983). A comprehensive 1977 survey found that only .3 percent of Americans self-identified as being of Greek origin, a number lower than reported in the 1980 census. See Stephan Thernstrom, ed., <u>Harvard Encyclopedia of American Ethnic Groups</u> (Cambridge: Harvard University Press, 1980, p. 965.

2. Divorce statistics by the faith composition of the couple are found in yearbooks of the Greek Orthodox Archdiocese of North and South America.

3. For sociological studies on Greek-American ethnic identity, see Evan C. Vlachos, <u>The Assimilation of Greeks in the United States</u> (Athens: National Center for Social Research, 1968); George A. Kourvetaris, <u>First and Second Generation Greeks in Chicago</u> (Athens: National Center for Social Research, 1971); Alice Scourby, <u>The Greek Americans</u> (Boston: Twayne, 1984); Michael C. Christopher, "Cultural Continuity Among Second Generation Greek-American Student in a Greek Community," unpublished doctoral dissertation, Florida State University, 1985; Chrysie M. Costantakos, "The Greek American Subcommunity," in eds. Spyros D. Orfanos, Harry J. Psomiades, and John Spiradakis, <u>Education and Greek Americans</u> (N.Y.: Pella, 1987), pp. 35-71; the special issue on "The Greek American Experience," <u>Journal of the Hellenic Diaspora</u>, Vol. 16, Nos. 1-4 (1989); Gary A. Kunkelman,. <u>The Religion of Ethnicity</u> (N.Y. Garland, 1990); Andrew T. Kopan, <u>Education and Greek Immigrants in Chicago, 1892-1973</u> (N.Y.: Garland, 1990).

4. The classic work is Theodore Saloutos, <u>The Greeks in the United States</u> (Cambridge: Harvard University Press, 1964). For a recent social history, see Charles Moskos, <u>Greek Americans: Struggle and Success</u> (New Brunswick, N.J.: Transaction, 1989). Also Dan Georgakas and Charles Moskos, eds., <u>New Directions in Greek American Studies</u> (N.Y.: Pella, 1991).

SPIRITUAL RENEWAL
George Matsoukas, Chairperson/Author[1]

*And we all, with unveiled face, beholding the glory of the Lord,
are being changed into his likeness from one degree of glory to
another; for this comes from the Lord who is the Spirit.*

2 Corinthians 3:18

The Topic

The third annual meeting of Orthodox Christian Laity (OCL) held in Chicago, October 1990, approved the formation of seven study groups to explore seven topics that were identified as critical to moving the Church ahead into the twenty-first century. The topic developed in this paper is Spiritual Renewal as seen in the context of the Church and by Orthodox Christians living in the United States. Understanding Spiritual Renewal is basic to developing the OCL "Project for Orthodox Renewal" because all the other topics relate to our understanding of Spiritual Renewal.

Summary of Spiritual Renewal Task Force

The task force paper defines spiritual renewal by understanding how it is seen in the tradition of the Church. This was accomplished by examining recommended books and interacting with select clergy. The perceptions of the living body of the "royal priesthood" on their understanding of spiritual renewal are examined through a survey instrument developed on the topic. The survey sample included 300 select members and the response rate exceeded 35%.

Spiritual renewal can be defined as the process of growth and transformation into the image of God. The spiritually alive are in a kinetic state because

---

1. A special thank you to Rev. Stavroforos Mamaies, Rev. Dr. Frank Marangos, Rev. Dr. George Neofotistos and Rev. Emmanuel Vasilakis for their guidance in the preparation of this task force paper.

they constantly strive to approach God, become united with God by grace. God became human so we humans could become divine. He truly is in our midst! We learn to cooperate harmoniously with God and repeatedly renew our covenant with Him through the Eucharist. Through the synergy of working together with God by His grace we become obedient to His will. We are drawn to the Light. We are pure in heart. We are able to love and forgive. This transformation is accomplished through divine grace, human freedom, and the gift of the Holy Spirit, given to each of us at baptism through the Father when we are chrismated, anointed with holy oil.

We need to live the sacramental life in order to win the struggle of transforming our nature. The Church is the divine instrument through which we journey into God's time, place, and presence. The Church was established at Pentecost and is historic and apostolic. The process of learning about Orthodox spirituality and renewal is through the liturgy. Christ resides in the community of the Church. He is our living presence through His resurrection. The Holy Spirit is our guide. The Bishop, who is also the image of the Lord, is our teacher. The Bishop, through his teaching, preserves the message of the Apostles, baptized members of the body are participants in God within the Church and are to participate freely and responsibly in the life of the Church.

According to the tradition of the Church and the response of the laity, the task force on spiritual renewal concludes:

1. Life-long learning for clergy, laity and hierarchy needs to be the first priority of the Church. Christians have an insatiable natural urge to acquire spiritual knowledge because they are created in the image of God, and the Fathers teach that the image of God resides in our intellect which is the highest aspect of human nature. It is therefore natural for us to want this spiritual knowledge. Presently spiritual education is not the priority of the Church. Lay persons have not been educated nor encouraged to understand the spiritual life of Orthodoxy, because of a combination of factors including: too few formal educational experiences

available to them; major church writings not translated into English; and no official English liturgy available to the faithful.

2. Spiritual vitality in Orthodoxy can be restored only as the ministry is shared and the divine liturgy becomes participatory. We are all responsible for the spiritual life and vitality of the Church as we act together — hierarchy, clergy and laity. Laity must once again find their place, know their duty to become aware of the traditions of the faith and then to actively assume their roles as guardians and participants in the faith. The Very Reverend Eusebius Stephanou has asked the direct questions:

> *Why the need for Orthodox spiritual renewal, when all the while the Holy Eucharist, which is celebrated every Sunday and on Feast days, is supposed to renew the Church both as a body of believers and as individual believers? Is there a missing ingredient? Every divine liturgy is, in a sense, a renewal conference. Why is it not meeting the need?* (Stephanou).

Could it be because we are Christian spectators?

The obstacles that impede spiritual renewal can be lessened through developing a systematic process of spiritual education.

Elements of Spiritual Renewal
Duty of the Laity: Be Aware; Be Guardians
Orthodox Christians have a responsibility and duty in the Holy Tradition of the Church to be fully aware of the faith. Vladimir Lossky states "that . . . each member of the Church is called to confess and to defend the truth of tradition. A Christian who has received the gift of the Holy Spirit in the sacrament of the Holy Chrisma must have a full awareness of his faith! He is always responsible for the Church!" (Lossky, 10).

Baptized, chrismated members become the body of the Eucharistic Community of the living Christ and as the body are the guardians of the faith. This is our responsibility.

> *Among us, neither patriarch, nor councils could ever introduce*
> *new teaching, for the guardian of religion is the very body of*
> *the Church, that is, the people itself.* (Patsavos, Art. 2)

Members of the Church are called to know, to preserve and to defend the truths of the faith. The Holy Spirit makes truth manifest and inwardly plain, in greater or lesser degrees, to all the members of the Church. George Florovsky further states in quoting Metropolitan Philaret, "All the faithful united through the sacred tradition of faith, all together and all successfully, are built up by God into our Church, which is the true treasury of sacred tradition . . . ." (Florovsky 1:53)

Shared Ministry

Syndiakonia, shared ministry, is what makes the Church Holy, Catholic and Apostolic. Lossky says that since the Church is catholic in all her parts, each one of her members, clergy, laity, hierarchy, is called to confess and defend the truth (Lossky 16). The religious vitality of Orthodoxy rests on an intensive spiritual life which permeates the whole mass of believers, united in the awareness that they form a single body with the hierarchy and clergy of the Church (Lossky 17). Religious vitality got lost in the Greek Orthodox Church in North and South America when barriers were placed between the clergy and the laity that would not let them share the ministry of Christ.

Florovsky states emphatically that in the tradition of the Church, authority in the Church is a shared authority — the sharing and working together of clergy, laity and hierarchy because the Holy Spirit moves through all of us. "The whole body of the Church has the right . . . of verifying, or to be more exact, . . . the duty of certifying the truth" (Florovsky 1:53).

Spiritual Renewal will become a more vital part of our Church and be seen as a priority when laypersons once again realize their place in the Church. It is their duty to become aware of the traditions of the faith and then to actively assume their roles as guardians and participants in the faith. Clergy have a responsibility to help the laity discover their own unique duty within the Church. The truth of the matter is that laypersons do not know their duties and obligations. They have not been educated nor encouraged to understand the spiritual life of Orthodoxy, which includes active participation in the ministry of the Church, and they remain in a state of spiritual adolescence. The Christian education program of our Church is inadequate. The laity already discern this, as the survey included in this study indicates. We will mature in the faith when we assume our proper roles as individuals and members of the Body and allow Syndiakonia to become a reality in the Church.

As practicing Orthodox Christians we are Holy, we are reflections of God's Glory, we are the affirmation of God's Word. We must have the confidence to be spiritually aware and involved in the syndiakonia, shared ministry, of all aspects of the Church.

> *And his gifts were that some should be apostles, some prophets, some evangelists, some pastors and teachers, to equip the saints for the work of ministry, for building up the Body of Christ, until we all attain to the unity of the faith and of the knowledge of the Son of God, to mature manhood, to the measure of the stature of the fullness of Christ.*
>
> *Ephesians 4:11-13*

What is Spiritual Renewal?

Spiritual Renewal is the process for growth and transformation into the image of God. Therefore, the Orthodox Church and the spiritually alive members of the body are in a constant state of movement. This is so because the goal of our lives is striving to approach God, becoming united with God by grace. Orthodox Theology describes this process as Theosis/Deification. Christ is in our midst because God became human so we humans could become divine. "The perfection of the human person and the very substance of human spiritual life is to partake of God's nature and to share in His life. And in this world this means always and of necessity to share in His sufferings, joyfully and gladly" (Hopko, Fullness 47).

Indeed God created us in His image and after His likeness. We strive to be like God. Likeness is the dynamic and not yet realized potential to be with God (Mantzarides 17-21). We choose to be like God. We are already in God's image. All of us start in His indistinct image and we share His image as common property as baptized humans. Being in the image of God, Gregory Palamas teaches, "resides not in the body but in the intellect, which is the highest aspect of human nature" (Mantzarides 17). Man fashioned in His image exhibits an inherent conjunction of intellect, intelligence (logos) and spirit. This is why man has an insatiable natural urge to acquire spiritual knowledge (Mantzarides 19).

Cooperation Between Man and God

To become like God we must cooperate with God. Our "spiritual life is the result of a harmonious divine-human action" (Stylianopoulos 32). Orthodox theologians define the cooperation between God and man as synergy. But in this relationship we depend entirely on the love of God. The Kingdom of Heaven is a gift of the Lord (Grace) prepared for His faithful servants. We are responsible for fulfilling His commandments. We need to fully respond to God, both in faith and works, if we are to share in the fruits of salvation. While God's part in salvation is decisive, and always assured in Christ, each person's part is also indispensable for his or her own individual salvation. One's relationship with God remains free and personal. Our willingness to accept Christ and to follow His ways pleases God. What is the disposition and direction of our hearts? Are we willing to cooperate with God? What and where are our treasures?

The basis of the harmonious cooperation of God and humankind is the New Testament agreement (covenant) affirmed and renewed in each Eucharist which is the redemptive death and resurrection of Jesus for the forgiveness of our sins. The New Testament covenant implies the commandment of love (John 13:34) which is a personal and mutual relationship between God and humankind. The covenant is accessible to us through the mystery of the Resurrection and the presence of the spirit (Meyendorff, Living Tradition 30).

> *He who has my commandments and keeps them, he it is who loves me; and he who loves me will be loved by my Father, and I will love him and manifest myself to him.*
>
> John 14:21

We are obedient servants.

We achieve theosis by subjecting our will to God's will. "Thy will be done" (Matthew 6:10). We are invited to become like "God by grace" to become one with God, as we cooperate with God for our personal salvation (Stylianopoulos 38). Let God draw you in; God takes us.

> *For every one who does evil hates the light and does not come to the light, lest his deeds should be exposed. But he who does what is true comes to the light, that it may be clearly seen that his deeds have been wrought in God.*
>
> John 3:20-21

The pure in heart and the faithful see and know God. Orthodox theology holds that rediscovery and uncovering our pure heart is the way we come to be with God. "God's gracious action through His word and His spirit . . ." is the means of rediscovery of our spiritual being (Hopko, et al. God and Charity 5)

"The pure in heart see God everywhere, within their own nature and in everything that God has made. The pure in heart know that 'the whole earth is full of His glory' (Isaiah 6:3). The pure in heart are capable of seeing and believing, of believing and coming to know" (Hopko, et al. 6).

39

"The knowledge of God is given to those willing to know" (Hopko, et al. 7). Christ helps us put on the new nature which is being renewed in knowledge after the image of the Creator (Colossians 2:3-10). The Orthodox writer, the Elder Silouan wrote, The Lord is not made known through learning, but by the Holy Spirit. "Jesus Christ renews the nature of man by sanctifying and sealing it with the spirit of God. It is by the Holy Spirit, the spirit of truth who proceeds from the Father and is sent into the world through the Son, that human beings come to know and exalt God" (Hopko, et al. 12).

Spiritual renewal is the process for growth and transformation into the image of God. We focus on the Trinity as we go up and down the spiritual ladder. As we move from Glory to Glory, we move closer to the image of God. This transformation is accomplished through divine grace, human freedom and the gift of the Holy Spirit given us at baptism, Chrismation and through the Father. The Holy Spirit is never lost to us. "The sacramental life — 'The Life in Christ' — is thus seen to be an unceasing struggle for the acquisition of that grace which must transfigure nature . . . . As we aspire to be united with God, the gift of grace shifts and varies according to the fluctuations of the infirmities of the human will" (Lossky 180). The climb upward on our spiritual ladder is sometimes shaky.

The Church

"The Church of the living God exists on earth . . . ." It is a sacramental and Eucharistic community. "It is one Church, with the unity of God, holy with the thrice Holy Lord, catholic with the boundless fullness of His divine being and life, and apostolic with His own divine mission. It is eternal life, God's kingdom on earth, salvation itself" (Hopko, et al. 20). God invites us to ascend our spiritual ladder from Glory to Glory through His Church. The Liturgy is the process through which we learn about orthodox spirituality and renewal. The Church brings us into God's time, God's place, and God's presence. The Church gives us daily and yearly liturgical cycles in order to relate to God. The Church sets forth practices: "prayer, worship, fasting, attentiveness, struggle, temperance, confession of sins, participation in the sacramental life particularly the Eucharist" all leading us toward the transfigured life (Harakas 37). We grow whole in Christ within the cycles of the Church.

Christ and His Church are the answer to the crying needs of the world. We are the witness of this conviction through service, ministry and love. Our actions and energy demonstrate to the world how the needs of the world are satisfied by Christ and His Church "not in words and speech, but in deeds and in truth" (Hopko Fullness 72).

As members of the Body of Christ, our participation in the Church is communal because the Triune God is present in the community through the Holy Spirit. We the Body have renewed the seal of the Spirit (Ephesians 1:13) and are taught in the spirit (1 Corinthians 2:3).

Our absolute, unique human person is guaranteed and perfected through communal existence with others. We become more and more ourselves as we become more and more an incomparable and externally valuable member of the community which is the Body of Christ (Meyendorff, Living Tradition 184). True community is achieved only by the abandonment of self to love for others. A person discovers himself and others by forsaking his or her self and by living for others, with others, and even "in" others, with compassionate, co-suffering love. We are whole in community. We are closer to the image of God in community. Our world needs this understanding.

Authority in the Church

The Body of Christ is directed by the authority of Christ who teaches us to follow His commandments through love (Matthew 22:35-40). Because the living presence of the risen Christ is in our midst, there is no authority over the community. Christ and the community are identified together. Authority in the Orthodox Church is established and confirmed at Pentecost by the guidance of the Holy Spirit and the apostolic witnesses to the historical events of the life of Jesus. The community, the Body, preserved the apostolic

41

message in its original purity and continues the missionary and pastoral ministry with the Bishops.

In the Church everything occurs within the sacramental framework of the Eucharistic assembly whose president, the Bishop, is an image of the Lord and is called to express the will of God. The Bishop expresses the nature of the community. The continuity of the episcopal office in each community preserves the message of the apostles (Meyendorff, Living Tradition 32).

The Bishop's ministry is to be in charge of defining the historical continuity and consistency of the Christian Gospel and tradition. He defines the unity of the faith and sacramental communion. Only he has the full authority and power to speak in the name of the Body. The Body speaks through the Bishop. The Bishop never speaks for himself, he speaks in the name of the Church.

Christ through Apostolic Succession gives the Bishop the full power to teach, to witness the catholic experience of the Body of the Church. The Bishop of the Church is a teacher.

But the whole Body is the Guardian of the Church. (Therefore the "royal priesthood," laypersons, also have a role and responsibility for judging the teachings of the Bishop.) The spirit makes the community the Body of Christ. Inside the Body, God not only speaks to us, but He also makes us speak out His will. Baptized members of the Body are participants in God within the Church and are to freely and responsibly participate in the life of the Church. The teaching of the Bishop finds its limits in the expression of the whole Church (Florovsky 1:54). The Church is called to witness this experience, which is a spiritual vision.

The clergy, laity and hierarchy have different functions and gifts within the Church. They are the gifts within the Church. They are the gifts of the same Spirit given for the glory and unity of the Church. The ecclesiastical conscience includes the clergy, laity and hierarchy. The Church works in a conciliarly way.

Religious Education

The purpose of religious education is to impart upon the laity, clergy and hierarchy the truths, continuity, unity and patterns of our faith, so that we can grow in the Image of God. Religious education helps us grow in His Image by developing our sensitivities to receive God's love, to be open to His self-manifestation and revelation which strengthens our faith. Through faith and religious education we learn how to pray, to be obedient to God's way and to have integrity. With these elements in hand, we can actively serve our fellow human beings and overcome evil. Clergy, laity and hierarchy are truly servants of the Lord.

The first conclusion of the commission for an Archdiocesan Theological Agenda states, "We must focus resources and attention upon the developing of a spiritually formed membership. This means much more attention to all aspects of Church life as it touches personal, ecclesial and outreach dimensions of our existence. It means priority attention to education and spiritual formation on all levels" ("Commission" 34:3:305). The laity must insist that these task force conclusions be implemented. Spiritual renewal is why the Church exists. In order to cope with the secular world forces around us it is imperative that the Archdiocese make its priority "Extending the Benefit of Theological Education Beyond the Ordained Ministry to the People of God" (Harakas, qtd.in Patsavos).

What Do We Think About Spiritual Renewal In Our Time And Place?

In order to connect with and understand what other brothers and sisters think about Orthodox Spiritual Renewal, a questionnaire on the topic was prepared and mailed to a select group of 300 Orthodox Christians. A questionnaire enables one to see consensus and involves others in the process, which is a conciliar approach and within the tradition of the Church. It also enables us to see how those of us living in the United States today, in the two thousand year old tradition of the Church, fit into the context of the Church's understanding of Spiritual Renewal, which is outlined in the first half of this discussion.

A response rate of 10-15% to a questionnaire is considered good. Our response rate was 35%! The quality of responses and vigilant consideration given to each answer is a witness to the Holy Spirit working with the Orthodox church. Two responses are reprinted in their entirety with the approval of the authors. These two, in particular, capture what the others were saying, but these authors chose to be more complete in their responses. They represent the discernment used by all the other respondents. Thank you to all who responded!

Overview of Results
A few generalizations gleaned from the responses are presented.

1. The responses came from all geographic areas of the United States: Oregon, California, Illinois, Wisconsin, Maryland, Minnesota, Michigan, Missouri, Connecticut, Massachusetts, New York, North Carolina, Ohio, Virginia, Florida, Texas, Utah, District of Columbia, and other states too.

2. Three percent (3%) of the respondents were clergy.

3. Sixty-eight percent (68%) of the respondents demonstrated an understanding of Spiritual Renewal in the tradition of the teachings of the Church. A representative sample of the meaning of Spiritual Renewal follows.

Spiritual Renewal Means:
*   "[A] rebirth of love for Christ and our Orthodox Christian faith in the hearts and minds of all our people, clergy and laity"

- "[C]ontinued growth to attain "Theosis" through the Church, which is the vehicle"

- "Christ-centered contemplation"

- "[B]ut we all . . . are being transformed (renewed) . . . by the Spirit of the Lord (2 Corinthians 3:18). A personal experience/relationship with God's Holy Spirit, bringing Spiritual Renewal."

- "Thy will be done . . . for me personally it was similar to the story of the prodigal Son's repentance when He returned to His Father"

- "[O]ffering our people incentives and stimulation to re-evaluate their commitment to our Church and to Christ"

- "[A]ctive participation in the full sacramental life of the Church. For the baptized Orthodox Christian, this means full participation in Holy Confession, Holy Communion and an active personal prayer life. The motive for the Christian would be just one — Jesus commanded this and I believe and love Him."

- "[L]earning to live more fully with Christ at the center of life and family"

Consensus on Education and Involvement
The questionnaire revealed an overwhelming consensus on two points:

1. Eighty-five percent (85%) believe that lifelong education in our Church should be the number one priority for clergy, laity and hierarchy. Spiritual Renewal is directly related to religious education. At the end of the twentieth century, Orthodox Christians in the United States still have an insatiable natural urge to acquire spiritual knowledge as Gregory Palamas taught.

2. Seventy-five percent (75%) believe that the laity need to be actively involved in all aspects of the Church. They decry the passivity in our churches. They write about reinvolvement in the Church. They want to recapture religious vitality! They want to be active participants in the ministry of the Church.

Education for clergy, laity and hierarchy and syndiakonia — shared ministry in all aspects of the Church are the means of reinvolvement and revitalization of the Church.

Education

- "My people are destroyed for lack of knowledge" (Hosea 4:6).

- "Seminarians are to receive full, complete thorough Theological training in addition to a well-rounded education of secular studies" (The library at Holy Cross needs to be the concern of all of us who care about the Church).

- "Train our priests in a legitimate seminary with Orthodox views with the intent to be priests rather than academicians and/or businessmen."

- "Some Bishops are very strong in their personal views". (Bishops speak for the Church. They should not speak personally.)

- "Educate the laity and serve them . . . ." Do not be "arrogant and try to dictate to them."

- "The hierarchy seems to have lost touch with the individual Church member."

- "Priests need continuing education."

- "Educate converts"

- "Teaching all the things that Jesus taught, in English." (40% of the respondents volunteered that the use of English is an educational issue and essential to Spiritual Renewal. "You can not be spiritually involved in services you cannot understand.")

- "The people need to hear more than the 52 Gospels and 52 Epistles repeated century after century."

- "The laity have a responsibility to learn their faith, practice their beliefs and support parish programs that promote Spiritual Renewal, through Bible studies, charity work, etc. Their role is to their Church more than a Greek social club."

- "Teach Christ above human categories (language, ethnicity, culture, etc.)"

- "[T]o educate the laity about the Theology and traditions of the faith."

- "Adult education should be stressed because it helps us clarify the beliefs that lead us to Spiritual Renewal."

- "We should encourage writers to prepare Orthodox literature." (utilize and pay retired clergy to translate sacred texts into English) "This encouragement includes both the purchase of literature by Churches and grants for new literature."

- "[E]ncourage women Orthodox writers since there is a lack of this type of literature."

- "Religious literature should be easily available and cover a wide range of subjects."

- "[W]orkshops for parish council members so they can be Church leaders."

- "Organize study/seminars to train lay teachers."

- "The role of the laity is to avail themselves of . . . opportunities to learn and worship and develop a personal prayer life."

Involvement — Shared Ministry

- "Laity have an equal claim in the Holy Spirit."

- "Laity want to share in full responsibilities in the life of the Church at all levels."

- "We have one master, Jesus Christ. All others must serve in unity, compassion and understanding to renew a faltering Church."

- "Expressing a genuine concern for each other and our feelings in the name of Christ."

- "We cannot assume that everyone shares the same concept of what ministry is. Therefore, a clear and concrete definition has to be established before we enter into the idea of syndiakonia/ shared ministry. Ministry needs to be defined in generalized terms so that all of God's People can be part of it. I suggest that ministry is the concrete and constructive expression of Christ when two or more people gather in His name. I believe the real issue is developing ministry, rather than education."

Liturgical Involvement

- "Meaningful, active participation in the full sacramental life of the Church . . . ."

- "Liturgical participation — laity need to learn and be encouraged to participate in the Liturgy — to me, this means less reliance on formal choirs and more emphasis on simply sung responses by the entire congregation. The difference in feeling the liturgy or just being a spectator is tremendous."

- "Parishes should be instructed by clergy to sing the responses in the liturgy. Passive sitting and watching a performance should be eliminated from Orthodox Churches."

- "Women should be allowed to chant." (Young women should serve in altar and be lay readers.)

- "Clergy should share the ministry."

- "Laity need to take on ministries."

Community Involvement

- "Develop strong outreach programs that get parishioners involved in helping others, thereby giving them a chance to practice what their religion preaches."

- "Reach out into the peripheries of our congregations to bring people in, and together to make them feel a part of the whole . . . ." "More participation in the community outside the Church."

- "Act jointly in support of member needs and problems."

Administration

- "[S]taffing of parishes — we need paid staff to meet the needs of the community. One person can't do everything."

- "Participation of professional and volunteers in parish life."

- "First we need administrative renewal. We have a crisis of leadership. Bishops must be elected by the people, clergy and laity . . . from the most qualified candidates, celibate or married." (Laity need to participate in election of archbishop and participate in synods and councils.)

- "[N]ew church leadership, to set the tone."

- "[A]dministration is not elected . . . it does not rotate (stagnation). Money is the primary reason for appointment."

- "Real legislative authority for clergy-laity conferences. Greater lay input in the selection of archdiocesan council members."

- "Presently only one voice is heard — no chance of many voices contributing to make the one."

- "Hierarchy is now dominating with advice only from an appointed cadre . . . if all are the Body of Christ, the ultimate authority is the people. The historic Church is conciliar — all working harmoniously together for the Glory of God." (Seventy-five percent (75%) believe the Church administration from parish, diocese, archdiocese needs to use conciliar approaches.)

- "Providing honest information to all concerned about Church matters . . . honesty is a spiritual matter."

- "Establish an American Orthodox Church on conciliar basis with a clear commitment to renewal . . . empower parish clergy and laity to act."

Summary
The OCL survey shows that there is overwhelming agreement on the part of the laity concerning what the priorities of the Church should be:

1. Lifelong religious education should be the first priority;

2. Reinvolving the laity in the Church — sharing the ministry should be the second priority.

OCL will use its resources to make these priorities a reality in the Orthodox Church of the Twenty-First Century!

Response to Questionnaire
from Nancy C. McNeil — Waco, Texas

Nancy is a full-time mother. She has been an art teacher and graphic artist. She sings in her Church choir.

1. I received this questionnaire on Holy Wednesday — an appropriate time to reflect on spiritual renewal. I pray that I will be spiritually and physically renewed this evening as I participate in the Holy Unction. I believe that I am spiritually renewed each time I prepare and receive Holy Eucharist. I think that on a personal level spiritual renewal is an ongoing discipline involving prayer, education and participation.

    For the church as a whole, the concept of spiritual renewal takes on a corporate view of this set of disciplines. It involves the Christian community actively renewing its life in Christ or the living faith. The Church should be involved in providing guidance and education for living one's faith and activities in which to participate in the life of Christ. It must also engender a spirit of participation.

    In talking about spiritual renewal of the Church, I also include spiritual renewal of the clergy and hierarchy both on an individual and corporate level.

2. My list seems to focus more on elements of the Church that need to be reviewed rather than just renewed.

    First and foremost, I see a great need for more and better education of our laity — and some priests. In many places, the need exists for basic education e.g., reading and using the Bible, understanding the Liturgy and other services of the Church, understanding the Sacraments of the Church. In all places we need to make available the wonderful resources of the Orthodox faith. It was through my non-Orthodox husband that I was introduced to the Philokalia! What an incredible source of spiritual guidance. Through the book store run by the Y.A.L. in Houston I came to know Mother Maria of Normandy and Father Schmemann. On a Y.A.L. retreat I was introduced to the work of Father Florovsky. All parishes need access to this type of material whether by library, exchange library, book store, classes, etc.

Secondly, I think we need to review some of the social activities within the Church. I have a hard time sensing spiritual community when I see things like trips to horse races, casino nights, etc. advertised by different groups in the Church bulletin. In fact the plethora of raffles in the church these days bothers me. I do not mind groups loosely associated with the Church community doing these activities e.g., AHEPA, Daughters of Penelope. I do not believe they have a place at church or in Church publications. Likewise I don't think it is helpful when church organizations engage in activities that promote or allow excessive behaviors such as drunkenness (as at a Food Festival) or $100 per plate dinners. I enjoy social events at church, yet I think they must be held within the context of living our faith and therefore they must attempt to be an outstanding example of, if you will, "good clean Christian fun!"

Finally, I see a need to renew or, in some instances, establish sources for spiritual enrichment. By this I mean retreats, Bible study groups, prayer groups/breakfasts, conferences. Annunciation Church in Houston holds an annual winter retreat for the women of the parish. They bring in a guest speaker and spend two nights and one full day in a retreat center. Here the participants have a wonderful opportunity to reflect on, learn more about, grow in and share their faith. I would propose that retreats of this type should be available to all parishioners, perhaps provided through cooperation and organization on a regional basis. Within each parish, I think that many opportunities should be available for spiritual growth and renewal. These could include Bible study groups, adult "Sunday School" classes, one day retreats, etc. On a larger scale each region of the U.S. has a choir federation and most of these, if not all, hold an annual conference. I would like to see these organizations raise the level of spiritual awareness within their conferences or organize retreats for their members.

In short, in almost every aspect of Church life there are elements that need to be reviewed and renewed.

3. Causing spiritual renewal is an interesting idea. As a group, as an institution, we can engender a desire for spiritual renewal, but I don't believe we can effectively cause spiritual renewal to happen. As I noted in my response to a preceding question, I think the corporate church needs to provide the instruments, activities, guidance to engender and aid personal spiritual renewal.

Father Florovsky speaks of the necessity and appropriateness of "fixed formularies of worship" in his article The Worshipping Church. I think what he has to say can apply to Church activities as a whole not merely the liturgical aspects. He states that it is "spiritually dangerous to neglect the 'books,' . . . . The settled formulae not only help to fix attention, but also feed the heart and mind of the worshippers. . . ." This is how the Church can "cause" spiritual renewal. By providing "food" for the hearts and minds of its members, the Church can "set the table" of spiritual renewal.

4. I think the laity has the greatest role and responsibility in the spiritual renewal of our church. Without each individual commitment to spiritual renewal, i.e. without individual participation in prayer, confession, communion, there is no renewal of the Church at large. I pass on the following in support of lay involvement and responsibility.

In talking about the mission of the Orthodox Church, Father Alexander Schmemann calls for a "movement" of the laity to "fulfill the tasks that institutions alone cannot and must not fulfill." He further discusses the spiritual profile of this movement and notes that he sees it based upon three specific vows. This is what he says in elaboration:

Prayer: The first vow is to keep a certain well-defined spiritual discipline of life, and this means a rule of prayer: an effort to maintain a level of personal contact with God, what the Fathers call the 'inner memory of Him.' It is very fashionable today to discuss spirituality and to read books about it. But whatever the degree of our theoretical knowledge of spirituality, it must begin with a simple and humble decision, an effort, and — what is the most difficult — regularity. Nothing indeed is more dangerous than pseudo-spirituality whose unmistakable signs are self-righteousness, pride, readiness to measure other people's spirituality, and emotionalism.

What the world needs now is a generation of men and women not only speaking about Christianity, but living it.

Father Schmemann's second vow is obedience, which he sees as the antithesis of hysterical individualism. Finally, the third vow of the lay movement should be acceptance or accepting precisely what God wants us to do. He notes that "It is very significant that ascetic literature is full of warnings against changing places, against leaving monasteries for other and 'better' ones, against the spirit of unrest, that constant search for the best external conditions."

Father Schmemann then discusses the goals of this lay movement and he states,

The first goal would be to help people . . . to experience and to live their Orthodox faith. We all know there exists today a real discrepancy between the Orthodox ideal of the Church . . . of liturgical life — and reality. There must be a place, a situation, where this ideal can be tasted, experienced, lived, be it only partially and imperfectly. Here the experience of other Orthodox movements is conclusive. It is because their members experienced — at their conferences, retreats, study groups — the joy and the meaning of Church life that they could witness to it and call to the Church "at large."

5. I see the role of the clergy and hierarchy as empowerers, assistants, guides and examples.

6. a. As I have previously noted, I see the laity's role and responsibility in spiritual renewal as most important. Therefore, they need to be able to work in conjunction with and in harmony with the clergy and hierarchy. Without involvement of all three entities — laity, clergy and hierarchy — I don't believe a true and complete spiritual renewal of the Church can be achieved.

   b. When, within a monarchial administration, there is only direction from the top down and there is no inclusion of all entities within administrative functioning, then the model doesn't seem to work. In parishes where the laity seek all solutions and answers from the priest or other hierarchy, there seems to be a rather lifeless sense of community as opposed to those parishes where the laity take an active role in problem solving and resolution making.

(How would you restructure the Church to encourage Spiritual Renewal?)

7. I am not sure of my answer here. I think I see not so much a need for restructuring as a need for reinvolvement. My problem here is that I am not particularly well-versed in the "structure" of the church. My response comes from having seen parishes within the present structure that can and do encourage spiritual renewal while others seem to lie spiritually comatose. So my question becomes what is it that makes some parishes "work" spiritually while others do not? My experience seems to dictate that it is not the structure *per se* but the parish's particular view of the structure. And most importantly it is, again, the lay involvement in the "structure."

Response to Questionnaire:
Joint effort of Albert Alexander and Dr. Susan Alexander.
Albert and Susan coordinated the Feeding the Hungry Program at St. George Greek Orthodox Church, Bethesda Maryland. Albert is a career civil servant. He is a foreign trade specialist at the International Trade Administration, U.S. Department of Commerce. Susan is a professor of sociology and is presently writing a book on attitudes in the popular press concerning immigrants and immigration.

1. Spiritual renewal means commitment to actions which strengthen and emphasize the primary role of the church as an instrument of religion and spirituality. While strong fellowship among parishioners is desirable and should be encouraged, fellowship should stem primarily from bonds of common religious belief. The Church should not be misused as a vehicle for maintaining ethnicity or as a locus for social activities to the extent that it overwhelms and distorts the Church's dominant spiritual character.

2. Most parishes include elements of Church life that (1) provide activities for men, women, young adults, and teenagers; (2) administration and finance (Parish Council and supporting committees); (3) education (Sunday School, discussion groups, Bible study, etc.) Too often these elements are focused primarily on the business affairs of the parish (fund raising, building and maintenance) or activities that are purely social or ethnic in character. Such activities are important and necessary but they should not be allowed to be the core of parish life.

   To attain the full meaning of Church life, all parish activities should aim to encourage regular attendance (and participation) at the Divine Liturgy and other religious services, community/charitable service to the community at large both within and outside the Orthodox community, and increased efforts to spread knowledge and understanding of the Orthodox Christian faith to the non-Orthodox.

3-8. With regard to structure, roles and responsibilities, I would like to offer some general observations.

Both the laity and the clergy (including the hierarchy) have roles to play in the spiritual renewal to the Church. I do not have an opinion on what structure works best but an essential ingredient in any successful organizational relationship is that the participants have democratic opportunity to express opinions and views and that the organization has the flexibility to change when it is clear that the majority desire change and it would be of benefit. There must be opportunity for dialogue and the structure must be responsive to the views of the individuals and groups that make up the Church. I am not well-informed enough to judge what that structure should be.

Spiritual renewal is best achieved through "grass roots" and spiritual renewal of each individual Orthodox Christian. Currently, there is a good deal of holiness in the Church. But its potential for being a greater spiritual force is hindered by the tendency of traditional, born-in-the-faith Orthodox to regard the Church as a closed club for ethnically-correct persons who make a nominal appearance at Christmas and Easter.

The surest way to cause and achieve a spiritual renewal in the Church as a whole is for each individual to live his/her Orthodox Christian faith in a manner that sets an example that others cannot resist following. We cannot reform a body unless the individual members of that body reform themselves first. The most efficient organization is empty if it is not at base true to its ideals and is made up of persons who gain the respect of others and thereby influence others far beyond their numbers. This is what I perceive what OCL is attempting to do.

Conclusion
OCL and Commission: Archdiocesan Theological Agenda
The "Committee on Spiritual Renewal, Decisions of the 22nd Clergy - Laity Congress, Chicago, Illinois, June 30 - July 7, 1974" left us a list of

recommendations for renewal. The recommendations were not implemented as policy. The insights and findings of the commission titled "Archdiocesan Theological Agenda," published in 1989 in the Greek Orthodox Theological Review, are excellent. Why did it take so long to circulate this study to the Body of the Church? Could it be that the Orthodox Observer decided to print the study, Winter, 1991, because OCL has raised similar issues? Nevertheless, the laity need to become familiar with the findings of the Commission so that clergy, laity and hierarchy can work together for their implementation.

Orthodox Christian Laity supports the study as a blueprint for Spiritual Renewal and reordering priorities within the Orthodox Church. OCL has advocated these priorities since its founding in 1988 and the enclosed survey also reinforces the commission study. The challenge is how can we work together to translate these insights and truths into Church policy? If we don't work together, the findings will go the way of the Orthodox-Catholic Commission on Marriage — nowhere!

We reprint the Commission's conclusion because our survey demonstrates there is a consensus on priorities. We have a take-off point for entering the Twenty-First Century. It should be noted that the OCL survey reinforces the commission's first priority, i.e. implementing syndiakonia.

"Our survival and growth as a Church depends on lifting up four major concerns and opportunities for future policy direction."

- "First, we must focus resources and attention upon the developing of a spiritually formed membership. This means much more attention to all aspects of Church life as it touches personal, ecclesial, and outreach dimensions of our existence. It means priority attention to education and spiritual formation on all levels." The OCL task force reinforces this conclusion and it is our number one priority along with redefining the role of the laity in the life of the Church.

- "Secondly, we must focus resources and attention upon the parish, the focus of the religious, cultural and spiritual life of our Church. Vigorous, informed, participatory parish life is a key to the future of the Church."

- "Thirdly, the leadership of our Church especially the hierarchy and the presbyters, need to find ways to understand their roles in ways which focus resources and attention on the conciliar understanding of the life of the Body of Christ, and to emphasize their facilitative role in building up the people of God. Inevitably this will demand changes in role expectations in regard to the laity and lead to increased concern with Pan-Orthodox cooperation and unity." This is the second priority of OCL based on the enclosed survey information.

- Finally, an honest assessment of our number and the realities of intermarriage demand serious reflection and reorientation of basic assumptions about our identity and the future course of our Archdiocese. A firm, clear and unequivocal acceptance of the social realities in which we live need not mean an abandonment of our ethnic heritage, but like many other ethnic groups in America, it will be preserved only within the framework of a larger commitment to the Orthodox Christian faith (Review 34:305-06).

Call to Action: Implementing Priorities

The OCL task force on Spiritual Renewal concludes with a call to action! The laity can help restore Orthodox tradition and vitality by getting reinvolved and working to implement the priorities outlined in the task force studies. Our grandparents were involved. They established the Church in this country before there was a Greek Orthodox Archdiocese. They struggled, uprooted from their homeland and families, overcoming material obstacles, to establish the faith here. Three generations later in our overwhelming affluence the Church has been reduced to a social club and lobby of disjointed interests — more secular than spiritual — under the direction of the Archdiocese. This state of affairs is the result of inadequate religious education and misguided priorities.

The Church will once again become a vital spiritual force in the United States of America when the laity re-establish the harmony of shared ministry in the Church as expressed by respondents from the questionnaire.

- "Pray to God continuously for renewal. Begin with oneself — true repentance. Witness the Orthodox way of life with love and humility."

- "The distorted notion of separation between clergy and laity must be completely rejected."

- "Renewal process will never occur as long as the laity are left out of the process as is now the case."

Priorities Recommended
By Spiritual Renewal Task Force:

1. A properly educated clergy is fundamental to the life of the Church. Seminarians must receive a thorough theological training coupled with a well-rounded program of secular studies. Regular programs of continuing education must be required of all clergy.

2. The laity have an equal responsibility to learn their faith, practice their beliefs and support programs in their parishes for Spiritual Renewal, including study groups, organized retreats, and charity work.

3. The Holy Cross Seminary and in particular its library and publishing activities must become a high priority of the Archdiocese in commitment of resources and attention. The school must be held to the highest academic standards of comparable American colleges and universities.

4. Holy Cross Seminary should organize extension programs and continuing education programs to facilitate both continuing education for clergy and lay education. The seminary should seek formal academic accreditation of these programs.

5. Formal education programs should be established to welcome and educate converts into the Orthodox faith.

6. The seminary and the Archdiocese should encourage active scholarship in Orthodoxy in the seminary, but also in non-Orthodox universities. Foundations and private donors should be encouraged to fund such scholarship.

7. Special efforts must be made to encourage scholarship by and about women in the Orthodox Church.

8. There should be organized training and educational programs for the orientation of Parish Council members.

9. The laity should be encouraged to take an active role in the liturgical life of the community rather than be passive observers of the liturgy. The parish should be encouraged to sing the responses in the liturgy.

10. The use of English in the liturgy and in instruction is necessary for the spiritual growth of the community.

11. There needs to be special emphasis on the spiritual growth of persons in mixed marriages and of their children.

ORTHODOX WOMEN AND OUR CHURCH
Eva C. Topping

As many of you as were baptized into Christ have clothed yourselves with Christ. There is no longer Jew or Greek, there is no longer slave or free. There is no longer male and female.

Galatians 3: 27-28

Introduction

However ancient its roots and however powerful its traditions, no church is today an island unto itself. This is no less true of the Orthodox Church than of its sister churches. From its apostolic beginnings to the present day the Orthodox Church has profoundly both shaped and been shaped by history. It cannot be otherwise.

Like other Christian communities of faith, the Orthodox Church exists in time and space. It owes its location on earth and its temporal existence to Christ, the founder. In order to establish the Church, God descended from heaven to earth, became human (as proclaimed in the Creed) "and lived among us" (John 1:14). God and the Church thus entered the history of humankind. Through two millennia Orthodox Christians have never escaped from the here and now. Nor can we today. Modern technology has turned our country of two hundred and fifty million souls into a single neighborhood, our planet into a global village.

Our Church, the Body of Christ, moreover, does not consist of robots. Rather, it is composed of women and men made of flesh and blood, each generation of which lives in a particular time and place. In each generation, therefore, the Church faces challenges and changes imposed by a particular historical and cultural context. In one way or another, it is inevitably affected and compelled to respond, whether negatively or positively. The Church does not exist in a vacuum.

From the new experiences of men and women arise new questions, demanding answers. Frequently, old answers are inadequate, sometimes even useless. What is then required of our Church is the open minded re-examination and creative use of its historical experience and sacred traditions.

Located in the United States in the closing decade of the twentieth century, our Church cannot and dares not ask for whom the bell tolls. To ask this question is to put the future and welfare of Orthodoxy in this country at risk in the third millennium.

The woman's movement is now universally recognized as a dominant sign of our times[1] (Behr-Sigel 106-11). In most of the Christian *oikoumene* feminists are ringing the bell inside the Church itself. Once raised, the issue of women's place and role in the ecclesial body cannot be laid aside, stonewalled, unanswered.

That this bell tolls today as loudly for the Orthodox Church as it does for other churches can no longer be denied. As recently as a decade ago it was deemed extraneous to Orthodoxy. Like the "evil generation" of Pharisees and Sadducees, however, we too must heed the Lord's warning to "interpret the signs of the times" (Matthew 16:1-4).

Orthodox women have ears that hear and eyes that see the changes around them. Better educated and living in a more open egalitarian society, they have choices undreamed of by their grandmothers and mothers. Outside their Church they are experiencing an equality and a sense of personhood new in the history of humankind. Once upon a time it was not possible for Orthodox women either to express alienation or to leave their Church. Thanks to enormous economic, political and social changes, that time no longer exists. For our Church to pretend otherwise will prove dangerous.

More and more Orthodox Christian women are questioning their present subordinate status, their restricted participation in the rich liturgical and sacramental life of our Church. Each day their number increases. Their voices grow stronger. One Orthodox woman theologian writes of the "mental anguish" and "spiritual crisis" endured by women of our Church because of ancient traditions which marginalize them. Another refers to the "gap" that separates the "theoretical" Orthodox Church from the "real" Orthodox Church. Orthodox women of faith are asking whether or not our Church really believes that women are created in the divine image. The Scriptures and Orthodox theology answer their question with a "yes." But when Orthodox women here and now attend our Church, they experience a "no" which causes them pain and alienation.

The empirical reality of women's lives in the Church thus exposes a serious contradiction between what the Church *proclaims* and what it *practices*. Nor can it any longer be hidden under a mystifying bushel of obfuscations or justified by newly-minted theologies which lack biblical and patristic pedigrees.

In 1982, Metropolitan Meliton of Chalcedon (second only to the Ecumenical Patriarch in the hierarchy of the ecumenical throne) confessed publicly that within the Orthodox Church "internal dialogue" on the question of women in the Church was deficient (Behr-Sigel 162). In the nine years since then the situation he described has not significantly changed. It is therefore time to encourage and broaden this much-needed "internal dialogue." That is the hope and purpose of this paper.

It is, of course, not possible to discuss here all aspects of the contradiction between Orthodoxy's theology and its *praxis* in regard to women. This contradiction is now almost two thousand years old. Nor is it possible to answer all the questions involved in the issue of women in the Orthodox Church. Our history is too long, our traditions too many, our theology too complex, our experiences too varied.

To produce even a general overview of "Orthodox Women and our Church" presents daunting challenges. One pen can hardly do more than raise some questions, suggest a few answers and make some recommendations. This may, however, prove useful as the Orthodox Church in the United States prepares for the third millennium. Guided always by the divine light of the Holy Spirit, we can succeed in transforming our Church into a "spiritual house" of "living stones" (I Peter 2:5), female and male.

Informed discussion followed by action is imperative. Orthodox women will not forever wait silently and patiently for the "new creation" (II Corinthians 5:17) in which discrimination based on gender has been abolished. At stake is not only the equality and full humanity of women within the *ekklesia*. Beyond this, the spiritual and sacramental wholeness of the Body of Christ is also at stake.

Diakonia

> *Now there are varieties of gifts, but the same Spirit, and there are varieties of services, but the same Lord, and there are a variety of activities, but it is the same God who activates all of them in everyone.*
>
> *I Corinthians 12:4-6*

The record of women's service or *diakonia* in the Church provides a useful perspective for discussing Orthodox women's roles and status. This splendid record ought to be better known.

Orthodox women belong to an ancient sisterhood. For two thousand years it has honorably and sacrificially served the Church. Not only have the gifts of women always been varied, historically, their roles have been far more diversified than at present. This is a very important point.

Women have been disciples, apostles, evangelists, deacons, miracle-workers, missionaries and prophets.[2] They have preached, composed hymns, taught and healed. Women have built and endowed churches and monasteries. They have established and maintained countless philanthropic institutions everywhere in the Orthodox *oikoumene*. Essentially an extension of women's domestic responsibilities, philanthropy has always been considered a proper "feminine" activity for women of the Church.

In times of ecclesiastical crises, women always proved to be defenders of Orthodoxy. Powerful, "Christ-loving" empresses of Byzantium convened and dominated three important ecumenical councils (Ephesus 431; Chalcedon 451; and Nicea II 787). Empress Theodora "restored" Orthodoxy in 843. Imperial defenders of the faith, Pulcheria, Irene and Theodora added immortal haloes to their bejeweled crowns.

For almost two millennia, women have served the Church as monastics, unceasingly praying for the salvation of humankind. In fact, the first Christian monastics were women. Among them are the "desert mothers" whose ascetic achievements and wisdom matches those of the celebrated "desert fathers."

Finally, from the time of Nero to Stalin, whenever the Orthodox Church was persecuted, women paid blood tribute for the faith. Orthodoxy's liturgical calendar is sanctified by numerous female martyr saints. For martyrdom knows no gender.

Since the Orthodox Church has apostolic roots, the record of women's *diakonia* is as old as the *ekklesia* itself. It begins in the historic community that gathered around Jesus. This first part of women's history in the Church is little known. At the same time, it is of utmost significance.

Mary's son, the young, charismatic rabbi from Nazareth, called women as well as men to "follow" Him. The verb *akoloutho* (follow), with its special New Testament meaning of "to become a disciple," is used of women (Mark 15:41) and men alike. Among others, women like Mary Magdalene, Joanna and Susanna (Luke 8:1) received and accepted the call to discipleship. They belonged to Jesus' intimate circle.

Authentic Orthodox tradition recognizes these women as *mathetriai* (disciples). In Byzantine sermons and hymns these remarkable foremothers are repeatedly identified as *mathetriai* of Jesus. Being His disciples, they shared Jesus' early ministry (Luke 8:1-3). Enrolled singly among the saints of Orthodoxy, these women disciples are also celebrated collectively after Easter on the Sunday of the Myhrrbearers.

The equal discipleship of women, their public presence and participation in Jesus' itinerant mission, represents a radical and scandalous break from traditions of Jewish culture in the first century. At that time, discipleship was restricted to men only. Rabbis were prohibited from teaching women, either privately or publicly. Jesus did both. How He abolished this gender-based discrimination is related in Luke 10:38-42.

Once when Jesus was visiting His friends in Bethany, Martha busied herself with preparations in the kitchen. Her sister Mary, however, "sat at the Lord's feet and listened to what he was saying" (v.39). A rabbinic phrase, "to sit at someone's feet" meant "to study with a person, to become a disciple." On her own, Mary had assumed a traditionally "male" role. What she was doing was a new experience for women.

Martha then asked the Lord to send Mary back to the pans and pots, to the proper "place" for all females. But He refused, telling Martha, "Mary has chosen the better part, which will not be taken away from her" (v.42).

The Lord of our Church thus rejected the idea of a single "special" role for women. Recognizing women as persons, He validated their autonomy. Christ offered them new roles, new spaces outside the home. Empowered and encouraged by her Teacher and friend, Saint Mary of Bethany (June 4) claimed a new role for herself. The choice was unconditionally hers alone.

Furthermore, according to the unanimous witness of the four Gospels, it was the women disciples alone who proved to be the true "followers" of the Lord.

Unlike James and John (Mark 10:36-40), no *mathetria* ever asked for status and power. Unlike Judas (Mark 14:43-46), no *mathetria* ever denied her Teacher. And unlike all the male disciples who "fled, every one of them"

(Mark 14:50) when Jesus was arrested, all the women disciples stayed with Him. They alone went all the way to the Cross and beyond.

Having shared the agony of the Crucifixion, the women disciples were the **first** to experience the joy of the Resurrection. The Easter story thus belongs to women.

They were the **first** to see the Risen Lord. From women's lips fell the first triumphant "Christ Is Risen" (*Christos Aneste*). The women disciples were thus the **first** to proclaim the good news (*evangelion*) that Christ had indeed trampled on death by death. The frightened, runaway male disciples first heard the "good news" of the Resurrection from the women.

Orthodox tradition names these faithful women disciples the "first evangelists," thereby acknowledging the primacy of their *diakonia*. Saint Mary Magdalene (July 22), their leader, is given the unique title of "Apostle to the Apostles." (Topping, Saints 246-55). Without the valid witness of the faithful women disciples there would be no Gospel to preach. The truth of the Christian message ultimately depends on the words of women. With the women's proclamation of the Empty Tomb the Church was born, and this at a time when a woman's word was worth less than nothing.

The four Gospels reveal that discipleship, membership in the community gathered around Jesus, was not gender-prescribed. Open equally to men and women, it depended only on individual commitment to Jesus' liberating vision of a new world order. In it, mutual love and service replace old structures of power and hierarchy: "whoever wishes to be first among you must be your slave, just as the Son of Man came not to be served but to serve. . . ." (Mark 10:44-45).

As seen in Acts and the genuine Pauline epistles, Christ's vision of a new order, in which women and men were equal, guided the Apostolic Church, inspiring its communal life and work.

The *diakonia* of women was unrestricted in the first decades of the Church. Although the whole story is not known, it is nevertheless clear that women participated on equal terms with men in the Church during the first century. It is likewise clear that leadership in the first Christian communities was exercised by women as well as men. If we are to believe the testimony of the New Testament, our Church has founding mothers as well as fathers.

The names and activities of some of the prominent women in the primitive Church were fortunately recorded in the writings of the Evangelist Luke and Saint Paul. They provide evidence that the most important positions of authority and leadership in the fledgling Church were not prohibited to women.

In each church, the apostle exercised the greatest authority (I Corinthians 12:28). Some were women. The greatest of all apostles (not one of the "Twelve"), Saint Paul mentions a number of women whom he valued as co-workers (*synergoi*, Romans 16:3). Nowhere does Paul ever suggest that they were in any way subordinate to him or that their apostolate differed from his.

Paul calls Jounia an "outstanding apostle" (Romans 16:7). Sharing Paul's admiration for Jounia, Saint John Chrysostom wrote, "Oh, how great is the devotion of this woman that she should be worthy of the title of *apostolos*" (Migne 60-669).

True to the historical record, the Orthodox Church in fact recognizes a number of women saints as *apostolos*. These includes Paul's co-workers, Jounia (May 17), Prisca (February 13), Apphia (November 22) and Nympha (February 28).

To these should be added Saints Mary Magdalene (July 22), commissioned by the Risen Lord Himself on the first Easter morning (John 20); Mariamne and Photeine (February 17 and 26 respectively); Thekla (September 24), commissioned by Paul to preach the gospel (in Byzantine art she is depicted holding a book, the attribute of the apostle); and Horaiozele, commissioned by Saint Andrew, the first Patriarch of Constantinople, to continue his apostolate.

(Hagioreites 277-78). Accustomed as we are only to the twelve male apostles, the existence of women apostles comes as an unexpected revelation.

In sacred stories and songs, Orthodox tradition preserves and cherishes the memory of women apostles who evangelized the Roman Empire. Like their male colleagues, they traveled, preaching the Word, converting and founding churches. Women apostles performed miracles. Like their male colleagues, they healed the sick, cast out demons and resurrected the dead.

The women apostles feared nothing, not even torture and death. Like Saint Thekla, some were martyred. By their sacrificial deaths they insured the life of the Church and its final triumph over paganism.

Other women received the charism of prophecy and exercised leadership in the primitive Christian congregations. According to Saint Paul (I Corinthians 12:38), prophets ranked second only to the apostles.

At the birth of the Church at Pentecost, fire touched the heads of the women who had gathered with the male disciples in the "upper room" (Acts 1:13-14). Free of gender-bias, the Holy Spirit did not stop first to see whether a male or female body housed a soul: "It allots to each one individually just as the spirit chooses" (I Corinthians 12:11). The biological category of sex has no relevance to the granting of spiritual gifts.

Thus, women as well as men were empowered to prophesy and to speak with authority for God. In Acts 21:8-9 Luke mentions the four famous prophesying daughters of Philip the Evangelist. In them and other women was fulfilled God's promise to "pour out my Spirit on all flesh, and your sons and your daughters shall prophesy" (Acts 2:17). Women spoke publicly the word of God.

Women also served the primitive church as deacons. The first of a long line of women-deacons in our Church,[3] Phoebe, lived near the city of Corinth. She was a *diakonos* (Romans 16:1-2), deacon, **not** a deaconess of the large church at Cenchreae. Entrusted with leadership responsibilities at home and with important missions abroad, Saint Phoebe (September 3) was a church official held in high regard by Paul.

From this and similar evidence, we may conclude that charisms, status and roles in the primitive church were not defined as "male" or "female." Women and men alike practiced Christian *diakonia*. The role of apostle, prophet, teacher, and deacon, each was open equally to women and men of faith. The Pauline corpus thus presents the luminous image of a vibrant Church which used all the varied gifts of women in a variety of roles to further its salvific mission and to spread the Gospel in a hostile world.

In the beginning, the Church was faithful to the vision of its divine founder. Then it was a *koinonia* (community) of believers in which distinctions based on class, nationality and sex did not exist. It was for women a rare springtime of promise and fulfillment.

In its deliberations on the question of women's place and participation in the Church, Orthodoxy must look to the model of equal discipleship and *diakonia*, which Christ established and which the apostolic Church followed.

Full participation of women in the life of the Church, however, did not last long. Restrictions based on gender began to appear already at the end of the first century, as ancient patriarchal patterns, structures and traditions reasserted themselves in the Christian community.

By the fourth century women had been effectively excluded from leadership and authority in the Church, their *diakonia* greatly circumscribed. Since then the ecclesial situation for Orthodox women has remained basically the same. A few recent cosmetic changes have not in any way altered traditional structures and practices which discriminate against women.

This, however, is not to say that women's service to the Church ended in the fourth century. Far from it. Women's love of God and loyalty to Orthodoxy has to this day never diminished. Nor has their desire to serve ever wavered. On the contrary. Orthodox women today ask the Church to expand their *diakonia*, to open to them other ministries that they might use **all** their many gifts to serve God and God's people.

Tradition/s

> So God created humankind in his image, in the image of God he created them; male and female he created them.
>
> Genesis 1:27

> The male must always command and the female must everywhere be in second class (**en deutera taxei**).
>
> Saint Cyril, (qtd. in Migne 68:1068C)

When Orthodox Christian women ask for symmetry between their *diakonia* and that of their brothers, they are told that "tradition" has made arrangements which cannot be altered. This answer acts as a stone wall. It prevents discussion. The "tradition" appealed to is seldom, if ever, identified. The premises on which it is built are never explained. This answer also implies that there is one monolithic "tradition" concerning women in the Church. This, however, is not the case.

The Orthodox Church is uniquely blessed with magnificent traditions of spirituality, theology, liturgy, and art. Through its long pilgrimage through history, however, it has also adopted ideologies and practices which are alien to its basic beliefs and dogmas. In time, these also became accepted as "tradition," sacred and eternal. Some of them, "leftover beliefs of a neolithic age," (Behr-Sigel 8) are still operative in the closing decade of this millennium.

As indicated by the above quotations from Genesis and Saint Cyril, there is more than one tradition relative to the nature and "place" of women. One affirms the equality and symmetry of female and male, both created in the divine image and likeness. The other proclaims universal male supremacy and female subordination.

At this point, our Church has to decide which of the two represents Orthodoxy's authentic, sacred Tradition (spelled with a capital "T"). In the process of making the decision, clergy and laity alike must bear in mind Christ's warning against abandoning the "commandment of God" (*entolen tou theou*) and keeping "human tradition" (*parpdosin ton anthropon*) (Mark 7:8). These words of Christ imply a conflict between the two.

Enunciated in the fifth century by Saint Cyril, Patriarch of Alexandria, second-class status has for too long been the living reality for Orthodox Christian women. It is their experience today.

Were the Alexandrian patriarch to pay us a pastoral visit, he could quickly ascertain that an all-male clergy and hierarchy still rule the Church. Women do not hold positions of authority and decision-making. In more ways than one, women remain "in second class." Begun early, when Orthodox females are only forty days old, their subordinate status, determined by their sex, lasts a lifetime.

Still in place, this powerful tradition assigning Orthodox women to permanent second-class rests on two premises. (Topping, <u>Mothers</u> 44-45) Bolstered by selected biblical texts and androcentric exegesis, it justifies women's subordination in the Church on two grounds. Through Eve, their "first mother," women are **second** in the order of creation and **first** in the order of sin.

According to Genesis 2:21-22, God created Eve out of a rib removed from Adam. Man preceded woman. The Greek (and Latin) Church Fathers interpreted this text as proof of women's inferiority. The all-wise Creator of the universe had designed women to be lesser than and inferior to men. The text in itself does not support this interpretation.

The inferiority of women, however, was not an idea derived solely from scriptures. It had roots deep in classical Greek culture. For example, Aristotle had taught that every female born was a "deformed male" (<u>De</u>

Generatione Animalium 782A, 17ff). Accepted as scientific fact in ancient and medieval times, this anti-woman theory was elevated by Christian thinkers into divine law, everlasting and immutable.

Inferiority inevitably implies "weakness." A text from the New Testament provided the proof. A second-century presbyter in Asia Minor described women as the "weaker vessel" (*to asthenosteron skeuos*) (I Peter 3:7). The alleged "weakness of the female" (*to asthenes or he astheneia tou theleos*) thereafter became a stock motif in patristic references to women. Femininity was synonymous with weakness.

Time and again in Byzantine hymnography, even the most heroic of Orthodoxy's women-martyrs are reminded that they are genetically the "weaker vessel." (Topping, Mothers 61-65) (Their sex was sometimes also described as "rotten" (*sathron*)). To call a woman a "man" was to give her the highest possible praise. Of all women, the Theotokos alone was spared "feminine" weakness.

The voluminous writings of the Greek Church Fathers amply document their reductionist, negative and demeaning image of women. Women are described as physically, morally and intellectually weaker and inferior to men. It is revealing that Saint Gregory of Nyssa (330-395) hesitated to apply the word "woman" to Makrina, his beloved sister and teacher (Migne 46:960b). (She had transcended the failings common to her sex.)

Chosen at random out of many, a few examples will serve to illustrate the dominant patristic view of women. Saint Epiphanios of Cyprus (315-403) attributed to women instability, weak-mindedness and frenzy (Migne 35:800). Saint Cyril (+444) believed "the whole species of females is somewhat slow of understanding." (Migne 74:689B, 691C-692D). This prestigious dogmatic theologian combined fervent devotion to the Theotokos with contempt for all other women.

This phenomenon was not peculiar to Saint Cyril. Orthodox theologians and scholars have commented on it. "The spectacular development of the veneration of the Mother of God was accompanied by a growing and concomitant scorn for Mary's sisters who were condemned to silence and relegated to an inferior place in the ecclesial community." (Behr-Sigel 36).

Although his best friends were women, Saint John Chrysostom (347-407) characterized the female sex as fickle, garrulous, servile, and lacking the capacity to reason (Migne 47:510-511, 59:346, 61:316). He concluded therefore that women are justly confined to undemanding domestic roles, freeing men to manage the important affairs of church and state. (Migne 62:500).

Given this derogatory view of "female nature," it does not surprise that this golden-tongued patriarch of Constantinople categorically excludes all women from the sacramental priesthood. This exclusion, he states, is in accordance with "divine law" (*theios nomos*). (Jurgens 17, 38).

In the same treatise, Chrysostom alludes to the second premise of the tradition which denies woman equal participation and *diakonia* in the Church. It is this: women occupy first place in the order of sin (*hamartia*). That being so, Chrysostom advises priests and bishops that women require greater pastoral care because of their "propensity to sin." (Jurgens 102).

Genesis 3:1-18 provides the proof of women's "primacy" in sin. When Eve ate the forbidden fruit, she became the first sinner. In this anti-woman tradition, Adam is generally exonerated from any responsibility for the disaster in Eden. I Timothy 2:14 identifies Eve as the only sinner: "Adam was not deceived, but the woman was deceived and became a transgressor." Accepting this verdict against Eve, the Church Fathers repeatedly call her the "author," the "instrument," and the "mother" of sin. Because Eve is named the single parent of sin, all her female descendants have been sentenced to eternal submission, silence and subordination to the superior, stronger sex. (Again, the Theotokos is the lone exception.)

According to this male-centered tradition, in contrast to all women, all men do not have a "propensity to sin". Consequently, **some** men can enter the priesthood, but **no** woman. The exclusion of women is total, categorical. In the blunt words of Saint John Chrysostom, "let the whole female sex retreat from such a task" (the priesthood)." (Jurgens 17).

Such are the premises of an entrenched androcentric ideology which stereotypes half of the Body of Christ as weak, inferior and sinful. As a result, women are judged unfit to participate fully in the "royal priesthood" (*basileion hierateuma*), to which **all** baptized Christians are called (I Peter 2:9). (Topping, <u>Mothers</u> 102-21) Because of their sex, women are considered to be less "royal" and less "priestly" than their fathers, brothers and sons.

Sanctified by certain biblical texts, interpreted with a bias against women and buttressed by the immense authority of the Church Fathers, this tradition has, from the fourth century to the present, prevailed over the one which reflects Christ's teachings and *praxis*. Consequently, Orthodox women today are where Saint Cyril long ago put them, "in second class."

Nevertheless, despite the remarkable staying-power of this sexist ideology, Orthodoxy's authentic tradition remains in place. Asserting women's dignity and equality, it invalidates the traditional superior male/inferior female, ruler/subject model. In contrast to the tradition which was made by men (to preserve power and privileges), the Sacred Tradition of our Church projects a positive image of women.

Two fundamental teachings of the Orthodox Church undergird this Tradition.

First, at the spiritual core that distinguished Orthodoxy from other branches of Christianity is the unshakable belief that the divine "image and likeness" (Genesis 1:26) exists within every person, female and male, without exception. This belief has biblical foundation: "So God created humankind (*anthropon*) in his image (*kat'eikona Theou*) . . . male and female He created them." (Genesis 1:27). The divine image and likeness which God stamps on human beings is thus the same for male and female. God transcends all human categories, including sex. Likewise, the divine image immanent in women and men lacks gender specificity.

Their misogynist discourse notwithstanding, the Greek Church Fathers of the fourth century placed Genesis 1:27 at the center of their dynamic theology and anthropology. Saint Gregory of Nazianzos the Theologian (329-389) expressed the passionate and "revolutionary" (Behr-Sigel 91) conviction of the Cappadocian Fathers that women and men share a single, God-given nature and destiny: "There is only one Creator of man and of woman, one dust from which both have come, one image [of God], one law, one death, one resurrection." (Migne 36:289-292). Orthodoxy's authentic tradition has never repudiated this theology.

Saint Basil of Caesarea (330-379) likewise confirms the image of God in women. In his encomium of Saint Joulitta the Martyr (July 30), Basil assigns to her these self-confident words:

> We women are taken from the same matter as men, we were created in the image of God like them. Like the masculine sex, the feminine sex is capable of virtue, and this by the will of the Creator. (Behr-Sigel 90).

The great archbishop of Caesarea so completely rejects the assumption that the male represents the norm for humanity that he chooses a woman to proclaim the equal worth and dignity of her sex. It is as if Saint Basil, himself the grandson, son and brother of strong women, wants women to know who they really are. Elsewhere he writes, "Let no woman say, 'I am weak'" (Behr-Sigel 88).[4]

Both of these influential Cappadocian Fathers emphatically reject the patriarchal notion that women have a "special" nature, that they are something "other." In their view, women share one nature (*physis*) with men.

The Church Fathers, however, were unable to move beyond prevailing patriarchal structures and ethos. Christendom's most brilliant, creative theologians though they were, Saints Basil, Gregory of Nyssa and Gregory of Nazianzos, were captives of the traditional androcentric mind-set of their era. On the one hand, they preached the spiritual equality of women. On the other hand, accepting inherited cultural stereotypes, they did nothing to change the unequal status of women, even in the Church.

The three Cappadocian Fathers could not conceive of men and women holding identical positions and sharing identical functions either in society or the Church. However, what was inconceivable to them in the fourth century is both conceivable and realistic to Orthodox Christians standing on the threshold of the twenty-first century.

Theosis (deification) is the second passionately held belief undergirding Orthodoxy's sacred Tradition.[5] God, who assumed "human flesh and dwelled among us" (John 1:14) calls humankind to become "partakers of the divine nature" (*theias koinonoi physeos*) (II Peter 1:4). Greek patristic tradition understands the message of deification to be the message of salvation. The message is the same for both genders.

From the third century on, the Greek Fathers time and again repeat what was classically stated by Saint Athanasius of Alexandria (296-373): "The Word of God (*Logos tou Theou*) became human (*enanthropeo*) that we might be deified" (Migne 25:1928). Through divine grace and love (*philanthropia*) it is possible for Christians of both genders to become god.

In patristic discussions of *theosis*, women are never treated separately. Believing that women as well as men are created in the "divine image and likeness," the Greek Church Fathers do not apply categories of gender to deification. Their vision of human nature and destiny is inclusive. Female persons are not excluded from the divine image. Together with men they receive from the Creator the calling to become god and to achieve holiness:

"I said, you are gods." (John 10:34). Like God, holiness is characterized by neither hierarchy nor gender.

By canonizing women, the Orthodox Church does in fact acknowledge that holiness knows no gender. The Church grants the title "holy" (*hagia*) to countless women, famous and anonymous.[6] From September 1 to August 31 hardly a day of our liturgical calendar exists which is not hallowed by a female saint. Female saints indeed form half of the golden chain that binds Orthodox Christians of all times and places into one living, undivided *koinonia*.

No Orthodox Christian needs to be reminded that it is a woman who stands pre-eminent among all the saints. Many are holy (*hagia/hagios*). But only the Theotokos is "All-Holy" (*pan-hagia*). The Orthodox Church indeed exalts Mary precisely because she is *Panagia* (All-Holy). (Ware, Orthodox Church 263 n.19).

Through the ages, countless women have been transfigured into living icons of Christ. The haloed heroines in Orthodoxy's pantheon of saints refute the patriarchal image of women as the inferior, weaker and more sinful sex. One has only to read the saints' lives to marvel at women's strength and goodness, their love of God and loyalty to the Church. Shining paradigms of holiness, these women are models to be imitated by all Orthodox Christians, women and men alike.

In the persons of our many "holy mothers," Orthodoxy's authentic Tradition has long since confirmed that the daughters of Eve share equally in the divine image and that they reflect equally the glory of God. The sexist assumptions and conclusions used to maintain women's subordinate status in the Church fail to stand up in the light of Orthodoxy's Tradition of saints.

Finally, Orthodox Tradition embraces the apostolic church which Orthodoxy claims as its origin. In that Church women were not only numerically significant. Sacred history records that they also contributed significantly to the Church as leaders, apostles, deacons, prophets, missionaries and teachers. The equal discipleship of women in the apostolic church therefore has relevance to the quest of today's Orthodox Christian women for greater participation in all the ministries of our Church. To ignore this is to falsify church history, in effect, erasing women from the record.

Reflections/Recommendations

Rejoice always, pray without ceasing, give thanks in all circumstances. . . . Do not quench the Spirit . . . but test everything; hold fast to what is good.

I Thessalonians 5:16-21

The above verses come from a letter sent by Saint Paul to the new church in Thessalonike. Written in 50 A.D., it is the oldest extant piece of New Testament writing. In it the apostle gives the troubled congregation some good advice. As we reflect on Orthodox women and our Church, it will profit us to keep in mind the words of Saint Paul, especially to heed his warning not to "quench the Spirit." With glad hearts and minds open to the Holy Spirit, we are sure to receive life-giving grace.

Thus far, discussion of the critical issue of women and the Orthodox Church has been inadequate and superficial. Metropolitan Anthony of Sourozh regrets the "many fearful spirits that are afraid of rethinking ideas that have been accepted without reflection." (qtd.in Behr-Sigel, p.xii). The discussion, according to Father Thomas Hopko, is at a "primitive state." (p.x) Dr. Elisabeth Behr-Sigel correctly emphasizes the "necessity of a creative reflection." (p.4) The need for such discussion is obvious.

Beginning with the "timid and stammering" (Behr-Sigel 18) conference of Orthodox women held (1978) at Agapia[7] in Roumania, there have since been several others. (Rhodes, 1988 and Crete, January, 1991). Having minimal resonance in the community, these conferences have not significantly advanced the discussion. From accounts in the press, it seems that generally the participants are the same persons, that they draw the same conclusions, make the same recommendations. The time has come to widen participation in the discussion and to advance the arguments of both sides in a more constructive manner.

These objectives could be furthered by the establishment of a broadly based commission, composed of hierarchs, priests, laywomen and men, to organize and oversee a long-range plan of investigation and discussion of all aspects of Orthodox women's roles and status in the ecclesial community. (Such commissions and programs already exist in a number of churches in this country, including the Roman Catholic.) Diocesan and local commissions, also broadly based, could have the responsibility for arranging lectures, study-groups and meetings. This could then afford all the people of the Church, clergy and laity alike, the opportunity to hear and discuss various points of view, to ask questions and express opinions.

The opportunity to speak and be heard is especially important for Orthodox women, who "for nearly 2,000 years had been invited to keep silent." (Behr-Sigel 10). It is time to let them speak of and for themselves, openly and freely. It is likewise time for the Church to listen to what its faithful women have to say. They deserve a respectful hearing. The Church ought not imitate the eleven male disciples and dismiss the words of women as female "foolishness" (*leros*) (Luke 24:11).

The agenda for a program of meaningful discussion should at least include the following issues.

Liturgical Language. All language communicates, carries messages. Words convey thoughts. (The Greek *logos* has multiple meanings, including "word" and "reason.") The language used in the liturgy about human beings carries to Orthodox women a painful message of subordination and non-existence. Some familiar examples will serve to illustrate.

Traditional phrases like the "God of our fathers" and the "faith of our fathers" suggest two things: either our mothers had no God and faith or they had another God and faith. Yet nothing could be further from the truth!

References are made to the "brotherhood in Christ." Is there not a sisterhood in Christ, the untold millions of pious Orthodox Christian women? Prayers are offered for our "fathers and forefathers." All Orthodox Christians have mothers and foremothers. Should we not also remember them in our prayers.

Likewise, Orthodoxy's many canonized "holy mothers" are routinely forgotten. The Divine Liturgy of Saint John Chrysostom concludes with the words, "Through the prayers of our holy fathers, Lord Jesus Christ our God, have mercy on us." And yet our numerous "holy mothers," the female saints, including the Theotokos, also hear our prayers and intercede for us in heaven. Surely, their *presbeia* (intercession) is no less powerful than that of the "holy fathers."

Phrases like the "brethren of this holy Church" or the "sons of God" are frequently heard. They completely ignore the existence of at least half of the Body of Christ. The congregation includes women, sisters, wives, daughters, mothers of the "brothers." Even as women sit in the pews and worship God, such androcentric, exclusive language denies their very presence. Does not God have daughters as well as sons?

The Church must show greater sensitivity in the use of language. The remedy is not at all difficult. The addition of words like "women," "daughters," "sisters," "mothers" to traditional liturgical phrases could help reduce the unnecessary marginalization of Orthodox women through language.

In this connection, it is pertinent to note that Christ made such an addition, altering Judaism's liturgical language which referred to the Israelites as the "sons of Abraham." A poignant story, it is told in Luke 13:10-17.

When Christ healed the crippled woman who had been bent over for eighteen years, the "leader of the synagogue" accused Him of breaking the Sabbath. Christ then "shamed" His opponent, asserting the priority of the woman's welfare over man-made traditions of the Sabbath. He not only enabled her to stand up straight, by calling her "a daughter of Abraham," Christ was also the first to recognize the woman's personhood and human dignity. Previously, only males, the "sons of Abraham," were recognized as persons in the Jewish community of faith.

The Uncleanliness of Women. The Orthodox Church does not teach that women are "unclean" and "ritually impure" during menstrual periods and for forty days after giving birth. Nevertheless, it tolerates practices (based on Leviticus 12 and 15) which define females as "unclean" and "ritually impure during" these times. According to this tradition, females are prohibited from taking communion, from baking bread for the Church, and even from attending services when there is "an issue of blood."

In effect, this primitive tradition of the "blood taboo" excommunicates Orthodox Christian women, not because they are guilty of any, sin but because certain natural processes are taking place in their female bodies. This and similar traditions deeply offend women. Metropolitan Anthony has correctly called them "an insult to women." (Behr-Sigel 9).

Yet, this taboo is still officially maintained by the Church and defended by some churchmen. Not long ago, a prominent Orthodox theologian explained that "uncleanliness" describes the "biological condition" of a woman who has just given birth. He further stated that she needs forty days to "normalize" before she can return to normal social and Church life." This explanation raises the question, is the giving of a life "unclean" and "abnormal"? Furthermore, what is the sin or stain that requires a new mother to be "purified"?

Without violating any of its teachings and doctrines, the Orthodox Church should disclaim and discard all manifestations of this tradition which demeans women. The Church could thereby bring its praxis into harmony with that of our Lord.

The three synoptic gospels (Mark 5:21-43, Matthew 9:18-26, Luke 8:40-48) tell how Jesus ignored Jewish tradition when He healed the hemorrhaging

84

woman who touched Him. Jesus did not shrink from her, in fear of pollution. He considered her neither defiled nor defiling. Instead, with infinite tact and love, Jesus restored the woman to health and to the community from which the "blood taboo" had socially and ritually isolated her for twelve years. Orthodox Christian women today ask why our Church holds to a tradition which Christ Himself abolished.

Access to the Altar. Orthodox females are from infancy denied access to the altar. There appears to be no theological justification for the denial. It is probably connected with the idea that females are agents of pollution because they menstruate. Thus is created another tenacious tradition which discriminates against Orthodox Christians who are born female.

The discrimination begins when forty-day old baby girls are **churched**. Unlike baby boys, they are not carried around the altar. (There are today only a few priests who take all infants around the altar.) At 40 days, baby girls are mercifully unaware of the discrimination. But they experience it soon enough, at the critical age of their physical and emotional development. We have altar boys, but no altar girls.

How do we explain to adolescent girls why only boys are allowed to serve God at the altar? Whatever the explanation, the message they get has to be that in some mysterious, unspoken way, girls are not as "good" as boys. Hurt feelings at this time in the life of an Orthodox girl can lead (and it often does) to permanent alienation from the Church.

In adulthood, Orthodox females, no matter how pious and faithful, are still denied access to the altar. The irony of their exclusion is not lost on them. The imposing figure of a woman, the Theotokos, dominates the sacred space from which all her sisters are barred. Only men are allowed to stand at the altar, close to Mary. Ecclesially invisible, women watch silently from a distance.

Resolution of this issue does not mean violation of Orthodox teachings. Sacred Tradition does not present obstacles. Given Orthodox belief that both males and females are created in the image and likeness of God, that both are called to become God, why is access to the altar available only to males?

The Diaconate of Women. The ecclesial visibility of Orthodox Christian women could be promoted by tonsuring women as readers and chanters. But more importantly, the diaconate of women should be re-instituted in our Church. From Agapia (1976) to Crete (1991), conferences on women and the Church have consistently recommended its renewal. However, despite these repeated recommendations and almost a decade of sporadic discussion, no action has been taken on this matter.

The Tradition of women's diaconate is well established and documented. It begins with Paul's co-worker Phoebe, "deacon of the church at Cenchreae" (Romans 18:1) in addition to her, Orthodoxy recognizes a number of women deacon saints. Among them are Susanna, ascetic and martyr; Nonna, the mother of Saint Gregory the Theologian; Olympias, deacon of Hagia Sophia, the trusted friend and associate of Saint John Chrysostom.

Until well into the twelfth century women were **ordained** deacons in the Orthodox Church. Almost a millennium later, in the twentieth century Metropolitan Nektarios (+1920, canonized 1961) ordained several women deacons in Greece.

The ancient ordination service is included in the Euchologion. (It is there, ready to be used once again.) Women were ordained after the Anaphora during the divine Liturgy. Recognized as part of the sacramental priesthood (*hierosyne*), they wore the orarion and took communion at the altar.

During the long history of the women's diaconate, their roles varied, liturgical, pastoral, catechetical, philanthropic, according to the needs of the Church. When the order is renewed, it "must not be simply an archaeological reconstruction". (Behr-Sigel 225). If it is to have meaning and to be a true diakonia after the model of Christ, the women's diaconate should be based on authentic Orthodox theology. And it should also be creatively structured to serve the needs of the contemporary world and Church.

Women and men must share equally in the dignity and responsibility of service to God and the people of God. The Holy Spirit does not discriminate according to biological categories. Nor should the Church so define its ministries.

The Priesthood. In any discussion of women and the Church, the question of women priests cannot be avoided. In ecumenical discourse it has displaced the filioque as the burning issue of our time. It cannot be ignored.

Given the fact that there is no biblical or historic precedent for women priests in the Orthodox Church, the issue is considerably more complex than that of the diaconate.

The idea of ordaining women priests has encountered resistance. Ultimately, however, this is the issue that will test Orthodoxy's allegiance to the ecclesial ideal proclaimed in the ancient baptismal formula. "As many of you as were baptized into Christ have clothed yourselves with Christ . . . there is no longer male and female" (Galatians 3:27-28).

Through the sacraments of baptism and chrismation Orthodox females receive the same heavenly illumination (*ouranion ellampsin*) and the same gift of sanctification (*hagiasmou doron*) as do males. Why then is an iron clad line drawn to bar all Orthodox women from the sacramental priesthood?

At present, this critical question is being answered in two ways. First, the exclusion of women from the priesthood is defended by appeals to the dominant tradition (the one which defines females as inferior, "weak and sinful") and to certain Biblical passages taken out of context. Second, the exclusion is justified by new theories, the "iconic image" and "complementarity," both of which lack Scriptural and patristic bases.[8] Since these answers have proved theologically inadequate, intensive theological reflection and critical re-examination of all Church traditions are imperative.

We cannot here present the arguments on both sides of the issue. They are the subject for extensive and honest dialogue between clergy and laity, between women and men, between theologians and lay persons. All members of the "royal priesthood" have the privilege and responsibility to help form the mind of the Church. The process will take time and will not be easy. It will undoubtedly cause pain. But the Church can no longer postpone a serious response to this serious question.

Prejudices, fears and passions will have to be laid aside. In this connection, the advice of Saint Isidore of Pelusium to Saint Cyril of Alexandria still holds: "Prejudice does not see clearly" antipathy does not see at all. If you wish to be clear of both these affections of the eyesight, do not pass violent sentences, but commit causes to just judgment" (Migne 78:361C).

History now presents Orthodoxy with a "cause" to "commit to just judgment," the issue of women's place and participation in our Church. For fallible human beings to judge this cause justly will be difficult. But given the promise of divine grace, it can be done. The Holy Spirit will not fail us.

Christ Himself made us the promise: "When the Spirit of truth comes, he will guide you into all the truth; for he will not speak on his own, but will speak whatever he hears, and he will declare to you the things that are to come" (John 16:13).

Once the search begins, the truth shall be found.

With "faith, hope and love" (I Corinthians 13:13) these reflections are offered for your consideration and prayers.

NOTES

1. This work of the noted French Orthodox theologian advances the discussion of our present subject.

2. For details see Eva C. Topping, <u>Holy Mothers of Orthodoxy: Women and the Church</u> (Minneapolis, 1987) <u>Saints and the Sisterhood: The Lives of 48 Holy Women</u> (Minneapolis, 1990).

3. See the names given in the useful work of Matushka Ellen Gvosdev, <u>The Female Diaconate: An Historical Perspective</u> (Minneapolis MN, 1991), pp. 11-19.

4. Basil's view is analyzed by Maryanne Cline Horowitz, "The Image of God in Man—Is Woman Included?" <u>Harvard Theological Review</u> 72 (1979), pp. 195-199.

5. A readily available commentary can be found in Timothy Ware, <u>The Orthodox Church</u> (London, 1987), pp. 236-242.

6. See, for example, the 48 women saints whose lives and deeds are related in <u>Saints and Sisterhood</u>.

7. Elisabeth Behr-Sigel was the keynote speaker at this meeting.

8. For criticism of these views see Elisabeth Moberly's review of <u>Women and the Priesthood</u> edited by Thomas Hopko (New York, 1984), in <u>Sobornost</u> 6 (1984), pp. 86-89; <u>Holy Mothers</u>, pp. 124-125; Behr-Sigel, pp. 175-179.

ORTHODOX
CHRISTIAN
LAITY

MISSION AND OUTREACH
The Reverend Father Steven J. Vlahos
The Reverend Mark B. Arey

Summary
Mission
We live in a time of the decline of the Christian consciousness in our country, the world, and within the walls of our own Churches. We have a great task to renew that consciousness. What is our Mission? Go baptize and teach! Clergy, laity, and hierarchy are called upon to spread the good news.

How are we to fulfill our mission?

We must know what it is to be an Orthodox Christian. We have to prepare ourselves to be able to have others experience Christ. This can be accomplished by:

- Restoring the order of the Catechumens
- Developing a nationwide program of catechism/evangelism
- Developing a nationwide program of continuing education
- Speaking in "truth and love"
- Using contemporary American English as the norm in Church life, and
- Emphasizing philanthropy

Outreach
It is not enough to bring souls into the church through our mission, we must nurture and care for them by constantly reaching out to all of the members of the Body. Outreach seeks to draw Christians into the fourfold life of the church:

- Apostles Doctrine — Education
- Fellowship — Community Involvement
- Breaking of the Bread — Divine Liturgy

- Prayer — Spiritual Life

The ten outreach concerns:
- The Unchurched
- Converts
- Immigrants
- Youth
- Senior Citizens
- Modern Day "Captives" (homebound, prison, nursing home)
- Marriage and Divorce
- Those Married Outside the Church —
  - Orthodox and Heterodox Spouses
  - Orthodox and non-Christian Spouses
  - Children of These Marriages
- Homosexuals and the Church
- Women and the Church —
  - Liturgical Roles for Women
  - Purity Issues
  - Ordination

This list is not inclusive. It is a beginning. The world and our faithful await the Orthodox Christian mission and outreach for the Glory of God.

It is in the hope that we will all be inspired to walk in that newness of life, that we present these thoughts and recommendations on Mission and Outreach for our Church and our world today.

Mission

And Jesus came and spoke to them saying, 'All authority is given to Me in heaven and in earth. Go therefore and make disciples of all nations, baptizing them in the Name of the Father, and of the Son, and of the Holy Spirit: teaching them

to observe all things which I have commanded you: and,
behold, I am with you always, even to the end of the age.'

St. Matthew 28:18-20

What is our Mission? It is our response to this command of Christ. By His authority, we are enjoined to preach the Gospel to every person, to make them His disciples by baptism, and to teach these new followers of Christ all of His commandments. This is the *KERYGMATIC* aspect of the Church, the Preaching of the Gospel of Christ in word and deed.

"Make Disciples Of All Nations"

We know the commandment of Christ, to **GO, BAPTIZE,** and **TEACH**; how are we to fulfill it?

There must be a new commitment by our whole Church, Hierarchs, Priests **and** the Laity, to the evangelizing of our own country, as well as missionary projects overseas.

It is not only the clergy who must preach the Gospel.
Our Church has been sorely lacking in spreading the Good News of Jesus Christ, as if we were going to offend other Christian communities by our preaching. Evangelism is not proselytizing, emotional pressure, or threats of eternal damnation. It is the invitation to a life in the Body of Christ, incorporation in the Church that Jesus Christ founded, and against which the gates of hell will not prevail.

But we should make no mistake. There are individual and corporate implications for this new life in Christ. If we are serious about preaching the Good News and calling people into the fellowship of the Orthodox Church, we must consider what kind of life we are offering. The life of a Christian Disciple begins with self-denial. The Lord's call is a call to sacrifice and self-denial.

> *If any one will come after Me, let him deny himself, and take*
> *up his cross daily, and follow Me. For whoever would save his*
> *life shall lose it; but whoever shall lose his life for My sake, the*
> *same shall save it.*
>
> St. Luke 9:23,24

In an age when society at large expects Christians to indiscriminately authenticate nearly every lifestyle, the ascetic message may be difficult (if not delicate) to communicate. But Orthodoxy is called to transform the world, not be conformed to it.

Our daily cross is the cross of self-crucifixion, the cross of self-sacrifice. Through it, we are able to extend beyond ourselves and live for others.

We must remember that the "Sin of the Progenitor," (usually referred to as "original sin") was self-love. The Cross of Christ has taught us "a more excellent way," as St. Paul has admirably described in I Corinthians, chapter 13. The call to be a Christian is a call to this kind of love.

> *This is My commandment, that you love one another, as I have*
> *loved you. Greater love has no man than this, that a man lay*
> *down his life for his friends.*
>
> St. John 15:12,13

It is only when we have denied ourselves, and taken up our cross, that we can truly be followers of Christ.

The invitation of the Gospel is an invitation to discover our true self, a painful and often difficult process. There are many who would gladly accept the Gospel, if it would not interfere with their personal agendas, which often have no point of reference in the faith and teaching of the Church.

In calling others to Christ, we owe it to them to be honest about the Christian vocation. To become new, to become what and who God has created us to be is not an easy task. Even the Lord admonished us to "count the cost" (see St. Luke 14:27,28).

The fact is, we live in a time of the decline of the Christian consciousness in our country, the world, and within the walls of our own churches. We have a great task to renew that consciousness. Our responsibility is great. Our opportunity is even greater.

We have many places to **GO**; many people to **BAPTIZE**; many more to **TEACH**. We have the challenge of inviting the human family to become the "NEA KTISIS" - the New Creation. The invitation is Christ's own.

> *Wisdom has built Her House, She has hewn out Her seven pillars; She has killed her beasts; She has mingled Her Wine; She has also furnished Her Table. She has sent forth Her maidens; She cries out upon the highest places of the city, 'Whoever is simple, let him turn in here;' to the one that lacks understanding, She says, 'Come, eat of My Bread, and drink of the Wine Which I have mingled.'*
>
> *Proverbs 9:1-5*

Recommendations
Restoration of the Order of the Catechumens

> *Repent and be baptized, every one of you, in the Name of Jesus Christ, and you shall receive the gift of the Holy Spirit.*
>
> *Acts 2:38*

As people respond to our preaching, we need to **prepare** them for their New Life in the Christ. In the case of families who are Orthodox already, we need to spend time preparing the sponsors and parents of infants who are to be baptized. The restoration of the Order of the Catechumens will meet these needs.

We all require an introduction to Christ, someone to lead us to Him. As it is written of St. Andrew the First-called, "first he found his own brother . . . and brought him to Jesus" (St. John 1:41,42).

As a Catechumen, adult converts have a role and responsibility in the Community. Sponsors and parents have an opportunity to reacquaint and recommit themselves to their Faith.

The Service of Chrismation, as part of Christian Baptism, must be given its rightful context and meaning. As we prepare converts from heterodox Christian communities, we must affirm that our Church accepts only a complete Orthodox Baptism, and that if Chrismation alone is used, this is only by *oikonomia*.

In all things, our goal is to receive souls into the Faith, and that they may have an appreciation and initial understanding of the great commitment and joy of the Christian calling. Let our response be that of the Deacon and Apostle Philip to the Ethiopian Eunuch (see Acts 8:26-39).

This is a great challenge for the Church today. As the Lord said:

> *The harvest truly is plenteous, but the laborers are few. Pray, therefore, to the Lord of the harvest, that He will send forth laborers into His harvest.*
>
> St. Matthew 9:37,38

Support Parish Catechists

> *How, then, shall they call on Him in Whom they have not believed? And how shall they believe in Him in Whom they have not heard? And how shall they hear without a preacher? And how shall they preach except they be sent?*
>
> Romans 10:14,15

The Apostles once complained that they did not have enough time to commit to the "word of God" (Acts 6:2). Many of our Hierarchs and Priests are in

96

the same circumstance today, and yet, this is their principle function in the Church.

It is time for our Clergy to commit a greater part of their ministry to Catechesis/Evangelism and to form a corps of lay co-workers to assist them in spreading the Gospel and teaching the Faith. This is nothing more than the restoration of the order of Catechists who, in the first centuries of our Church, prepared individuals for Baptism.

Parishes should support these Catechists, full-time or part-time ministers of the Gospel and see this as part of the integral life of the Parish.

The **UNIFORM PARISH REGULATIONS**, which govern our Communities, speak to this issue: "The diakonia (work and ministry) of the Parish consists of proclaiming the Gospel in accordance with the Orthodox Faith. . . ." (Chapter 1, Article 2, Section 2).

The Priest has the responsibility of "proclaiming the Kerygma of the Apostles and Dogma of the Fathers, preaching the Word, teaching the commandments of the New Life, . . ." etc. (Chapter 4, Section 1). And not only on Sunday morning!

> *Preach the word; be diligent in season, out of season, exhort*
> *with all patience and teaching.*
>
> *II Timothy 4:2*

We need **LITURGICAL PREACHING**, at every Mysterion and Service of our Church. Call it **MISSION**, or call it **OUTREACH** — the fact is that we must **evangelize** our own people, many of them for the first time.

Our Faithful must first hear the Gospel themselves; then they will "cooperate in every way towards the welfare and prosperity of the Parish and the success of its sacred mission" (Article 6, Section 6).

There are tremendous resources in our community-at-large, mass media, radio, television, as well as the printed word. We must harness these resources for the spreading of our own faith and fit these methods to our own message. That message can only be defined by the Faith of the Apostles, the Faith of the Fathers, the Faith of the Martyrs, the Faith that sustains the Universe.

A catechism/evangelism program in the local parish can spark new and invigorated enthusiasm. Our people are hungry. They are thirsty. Let us set aright our goals.

> *Labor not for the food which perishes, but for that food which endures to life everlasting . . . .*
>
> St. John 6:27

Continuing Catechetical Education

> *And daily in the temple and in every house, they ceased not to teach and to preach Jesus Christ.*
>
> Acts 5:42

What a description of the first clergymen of our Church! So it should be today. At Hellenic College/Holy Cross Greek Orthodox School of Theology, we have more than a center for the academic and theological training of our priests. It must become the source for a nationwide school of faith. We cannot afford to leave the preaching, catechizing, educating and living of Christ's Gospel to the self-appointed and self-ordained.

Within the present structure of the Archdiocese, with Cathedrals and major parishes in every state, the means to establishing such a "school without walls" is already in place. Consider the impression this ministry would have on the Faithful.

A national program would not only facilitate the training of Parish Catechists, it would also help prepare seminarians to become Preachers, as well as provide ongoing education for Priests. It would encourage our clergy, Bishops and Priests alike, to hone their skills at preaching; both in substance as well as style. Our message is too important. Without vision and conviction our people will perish.

> *The lion has roared; who will not fear? The Lord God has spoken; who can but prophecy?*
>
> Amos 3:8

"Speak the Truth in Love"

> *And other sheep I have, that are not of this fold; them also I must bring, and they shall hear My voice; and there shall be one fold, and one Shepherd.*
>
> St. John 10:16

It is time for our Church to incorporate Evangelizing as part of Her ecumenical dialogue with heterodox Christians. His All-Holiness, Patriarch Joachim III of Constantinople expressed, as early as 1902, the following viewpoint to his fellow Orthodox Patriarchs, "on the subject of our present and future relations with the two great growths of Christianity, *viz.* the Western Church and the Church of the Protestants:"

> *Of course, the union of them and of all who believe in Christ with us in the Orthodox Faith is the pious and heartfelt desire of our Church and of all genuine Christians, who stand firm in the evangelical doctrine of unity, and it is the subject of constant prayer and supplication . . . . It is a truism that the Holy, Catholic, and Apostolic Church is founded upon the Apostles and preserved by the divine and inspired Fathers in the Oecumenical Councils, and that Her Head is Christ, the Great Shepherd, Who bought Her with His own Blood, and that according to the inspired and heaven-bound Apostle [Paul] She is the pillar and ground of truth and the Body of Christ: this Holy Church is indeed, one in identity of faith with the decisions of the Seven Oecumenical Councils, and She must be one and not many, differing from each other in dogmas and*

fundamental institutions of ecclesiastical government. (Letter
in The Orthodox Church in the Ecumenical Movement).

We need to return to the spirit of these early ecumenical pioneers, who saw their responsibility to their fellow Christians as a responsibility of love and truthfulness.

We have a prophetic role to fulfill, as a watchman to the house of Israel (see Ezekiel 33:7-9). This requires purity of heart and sincerity of intention.

> *How will you say to your brother, "Let me pull the speck out of your eye;" and, look, there is a log in your own eye? You hypocrite, first cast the log out of your own eye, and then you shall see clearly to pull the speck out of your brother's.*
>
> *St. Matthew 7:4,5*

Speak and Listen with Understanding

> *We hear them speak in our own language of the wonderful works of God.*
>
> *Acts 2:11*

The miracle of the Day of Pentecost was **not** that the Apostles spoke in marvelous languages; it was that the Good News they preached was understood by everyone who heard them.

For too long, our Church has fought and argued about which language to use. The historical languages of the Liturgy, Greek, Slavonic, Arabic and others, have a place in the Church today, but **not** at the expense of the understanding and nurturing of the Faithful, much less of the Catechumens.

Contemporary American English is the language of the Orthodox peoples of America. It should be the language of their Services as well.

Where there is need, by all means, let there be divergence. We seek unity, not uniformity. What is appropriate for one situation may not be for another. But at all times, the moving force behind our decisions should be the edification of the Church. As St. Paul has written:

> There are, it seems, so many kinds of languages in the world, and none of them is without significance. But if I do not know the meaning of the language, I shall be like a barbarian speaking. . . . But you, since you are zealous for spiritual gifts, strive to excel in gifts that edify the Church.
>
> *I Corinthians 14:10-12*

Philanthropy . . . . Again!

> Let your light so shine before men, that they may see your good works, and glorify your Father Who is in Heaven.
>
> *St. Matthew 5:16*

Our Lord said that a sign of the coming of the Kingdom of Heaven would be that the poor would have the Gospel preached to them (St. Matthew 11:5). He also said that we would always have the poor. Why? Not because He isn't merciful, but because He wants us to participate in His mercy.

We hear many today say that the Church has not proven to be a good steward of these gifts of God; that money is wasted on excess and vainglory.

And so we have the poor with us, so that we may learn again to be merciful, as God is merciful with us.

Who are these poor? Just look around. The homeless, the hungry, the illiterate, people with AIDS, the helpless, the hopeless, the prisoners, the sick. They wait for us in every generation to bring the Gospel to them, not with high-sounding words, but with humble and patient acts of compassion and love. This is the Everlasting Gospel, "that God so loved the world, that He gave His Only-begotten Son."

101

We have the potential for great social and human improvement right in our own backyard. Each Parish can take on projects in their own community, as a witness to their love for Christ. It is a message delivered in silence that speaks louder than any words.

> *My little children, let us love not in word, neither in tongue, but in deed and in truth.*
>
> *I John 3:18*

These are our recommendations. Not just words that may or may not sound good to the hearer, but what we feel our Church is called to today.

- A Restoration of the Order of the Catechumens
- A Nationwide Program of Catechism/Evangelism
- A Nationwide Education Program for Catechists
- A New Ecumenical Approach of "Truth in Love"
- Contemporary American English as the Norm in Church Life
- A New Emphasis on Philanthropy

It's time. It is later than we think.

> *Do you not say, There are yet four months, and then comes the harvest? Behold, I say to you, Lift up your eyes, and look on the fields; for they are already white, way past the time of harvest. And he that reaps receives wages, and gathers fruit unto life eternal: that both he that sows and he that reaps may rejoice together.*
>
> *St. John 4:35,36*

Outreach

> *And they continued steadfastly in the Apostles' Doctrine, and in Fellowship, and in The Breaking of The Bread, and in Prayer.*
>
> *Acts 2:43*

What do we mean by Outreach? It is the **continual incorporation of the Body of Christ**, the creative and multiform *diakonia* which makes the new life in Christ available to every Orthodox Christian, in accordance with their measure of faith.

Becoming New Creations in Christ is a process, which requires our cooperation, with God and with each other. It is the nurturing process of maturation which St. Paul speaks of in the Epistle to the Ephesians:

> *[F]or the perfecting of the saints, for the work of the ministry, for the edifying of the Body of Christ: until we all grow, in the unity of the Faith, and in the knowledge of the Son of God, into a complete person, unto the measure of the stature of the fullness of Christ.*
>
>

Ephesians. 4:12,13

This is the **DOGMATIC** aspect of the Church, the continuous teaching of the Gospel of Christ in word and deed.

The Fourfold Nature of Outreach

As Christ reached out on His Holy Cross to the four corners of the world, so does our **OUTREACH** seek to draw all Christians into the fourfold life of the Church.

- The Apostles' Doctrine
- Fellowship
- The Breaking of The Bread (Divine Liturgy)
- Prayer

It is not enough to bring souls into the Church through our Mission, we must nurture and care for them by constantly reaching out to all of the members of the Body. St. Paul makes this clear in his teaching:

*God has set each member in the Body as it has pleased Him.
If everyone were the same, what would the Body be? Now
there are many members, but one Body. The eye cannot say
to the hand, "I don't need you;" neither can the head say to
the feet, "I don't need you." . . . God has fit the Body
together, giving a greater abundance of honor to those members
that seem lacking, in order that there should be no divisions in
the Body; and that the members should all care for one
another. If someone is suffering, the other members should
empathize, and if someone is honored, let all the others rejoice.*

I Corinthians 12:18-21, 24-26

Our task is to examine how we may relate every member of the Body to the
whole, bringing them into the fullness of the Church, with real participation
and inclusion. Based on the Apostolic model, we can see the four essential
areas are:

- Education (Apostles' Doctrine)
- Community Involvement (Fellowship)
- Liturgical Participation   (The Breaking of the Bread)
- Spiritual Life (Prayer)

What follows is a list of ten concerns. It is by no means exhaustive and we
hope that others may follow as a result of this paper. (A special insert on
human sexuality, **"Male And Female Created He Them,"** will preface the
last four).

- The Unchurched
- Converts
- Immigrants
- Youth
- Senior Citizens
- Modern Day "Captives" (homebound, prison, nursing home)
- Marriage and Divorce
- Those Married Outside the Church

- ○ Orthodox and Heterodox spouses
- ○ Orthodox and non-Christian spouses
- ○ Children of these marriages
- Homosexuals and the Church
- Women and the Church[1]
  - ○ Liturgical roles for women (chanter, reader, choir)
  - ○ Purity issues (presence and/or service in the Altar)
  - ○ Ordination

Our recommendations will be based on the Apostolic model for Church life. Some will call for renewal according to the mind of Christ, others for the restoration of ancient practice; but in either case, the dominant principle will be that of Christ:

> *Every scribe, who is learned in the Kingdom of Heaven, is like*
> *a man who is a householder, who brings forth both new and*
> *old things out of his treasure.*
> St. Matthew 13:52

The Unchurched

> *Even so, it is not the will of your Father, Who is in Heaven,*
> *that one of these little ones should perish.*
> St. Matthew 18:14

So concludes the parable of the ninety-nine sheep and the one who went astray. Today, it would be fair to say that the ratio has increased in favor of the latter. There are literally tens of thousands of Unchurched Orthodox, with as many reasons why they no longer practice their faith.

---

1. Although there is another paper on this topic; we also address it here, as it relates to the wider issue of human sexuality.

Recommendations

1. In every local parish, let there be a campaign to seek out and search for those who have dropped out or have not been seen for a long period of time. Follow up with a reintroduction to the Faith and a welcome back.

2. Fellowship events, which often attract rarely seen members (Sacraments, memorials, festivals, etc.), should be occasions of encouragement and warm welcome. Special committees must be formed to follow up on attraction and instruction of Unchurched members.

3. At Great Feast Days (e.g. Palm Sunday, Holy Friday) clergy should make it a point **not** to preach sermons castigating those who have "shown up." Rather, let us give them something to come back to!

4. Let there be prayer in the Church at every Liturgy, public and pronounced, for those who are absent.

Although we cannot force anyone to live their Faith, we can lift up Christ in our own lives. Do our brothers and sisters see the love of the Christ in us? If we are bearing our cross, they will. It is love that draws us to God.

> *And I, if I be lifted up from the earth, I will draw all people to Myself.*
>
> St. John 12:32

Converts

> *I will bring them to My holy mountain, and make them joyful in My house of prayer; for My house shall be called a house of prayer for all peoples.*
>
> Isaiah 56:7

The first great issue of the Orthodox Church was whether the Faith was meant for Greeks (Gentiles), as well as Jews. Even some of the Apostles were not certain at first! The tables have certainly turned since then, but have we changed?

From clergy who discourage mass conversions to parishioners who tell seekers that their ancestry is wrong, we still struggle as a Church with being Catholic (*kath olous*) — for all people. We still make it difficult for others to join our Church. If we are serious about preaching the Gospel, we should be ready for people to respond to it.

Recommendations

1. Catechism is essential. It is an understanding of our Faith that we seek to impart. There must be classes, lectures and homilies. Too often, converts are received without proper instruction, preparation and understanding.

2. As often as possible, the reception of converts should be at well attended Services, with some community event following.

3. To put to rest a misconception — not all converts prefer the Divine Liturgy in English, but most are in the same boat as the rest of our members; they do not understand any of the historical languages of the Liturgy. English or the vernacular, is the only path to a worshipping Church that fulfills the Apostolic model, to pray and sing with understanding (see I Corinthians 14:15).

4. Far from the popular notion, the monastic tradition is a **LAY** tradition and the source of much spiritual food. Converts and "Cradle" Orthodox alike should work for their establishment and increase, to bring emphasis again to the wealth of our spiritual tradition.

Whether we were born into an Orthodox family, or we have created our own through a conscious decision, the fact is, we all must make a beginning in our faith; we are all converts to Christ.

Our Church calls all mankind to the knowledge of the love of God. We must learn to embrace all those who embrace the Faith, regardless of their ethnic origin, color, or cultural tradition. The Lord Himself observed that it is not only those born with the privilege of faith, but those that choose, who shall find a place in His Kingdom.

> *And they shall come from the east, and from the west, and from the north, and from the south, and shall sit down in the Kingdom of God.*

St. Luke 13:29

Immigrants

> *The stranger who dwells with you shall be to you as one born among you, and you shall love him as yourself.*

Leviticus 19:34

Immigrants, simple men and women, brought the Orthodox Faith to the Americas. It would be a great shame if our Church were to forget those origins. How especially grateful should converts be to this memory, and how supportive should all of us be to those who are **still** arriving in this land of opportunity. What are we offering these fellow Orthodox when they arrive on our shores?

Recommendations

1. Where appropriate, let us have English Schools, as well as Greek (or whatever) Schools to perpetuate native tongues. Let there also be religious instruction in Greek, Russian, Arabic and any other language that is spoken by the Faithful.

2. The ethnic language schools have often become isolated fellowships within the larger community. Many Parishes have enough diversity to warrant "cultural exchange" programs within their own walls. More homogeneous Parishes may want to have exchanges with nearby communities of different ethnic origins.

3. In affirming that contemporary American English should be the liturgical standard of our Church, let us not forget the needs of the newly arrived, as well as the beauty and integrity of the historical liturgical tongues.

A selection of hymns, such as the Trisagion and the Cherubikon, sung in these historical languages, can give the feeling of "home" to many immigrants, without compromising the comprehension of the Liturgy.

4. Those who come from native Orthodox countries often bring many local/traditional customs. These should be encouraged and not ignored.

Differences of culture, language, race and ethnic origin are not obliterated by Christ; they are sanctified. Hospitality to strangers is a good beginning towards this holiness.

> Let brotherly love continue. Do not forget to be hospitable to strangers, for in this way, some have entertained Angels unawares.
>
> Hebrews 13:1,2

Youth

> Permit the little children to come to Me, and do not forbid them; for of such is the Kingdom of God.
>
> St. Mark 10:14

Again and again, we hear the cry in our Parishes, "What are we doing for our youth?" If statistics tell us anything, they tell us our programs are not doing enough. We are raising generations of young Orthodox, who neither know, nor care to know their Faith. Is it that they are not drawn to Christ, or has something been blocking their path?

Sunday School, has it worked? How many of our children know who the Saints are on their Parish Iconostasion? Religious instruction begins in the home; there is no getting around it.

Recommendations

1. The Sunday Catechetical School must be conducted either before or after the Divine Liturgy, thereby enabling the youth to participate in the worship of the Church. The educational program of the local Parish

must have a unified effort towards educating and involving the parents. Everything we do and say in Sunday School is only an affirmation of what occurs in the home.

2. Dedicated Youth Ministries with emphasis on Christian faith and action are a must for each Parish, meaning both dedication of time and money. In addition, our youth must be integrated with the rest of the Parish; an evening of GOYA with the Golden Age Club, for example.

   Nowhere is the need for English so pronounced as in our Youth. And not only on this level of understanding; there needs to be a concentrated effort to explain the **meaning** of the Liturgy in its many facets.

3. Spiritual retreats, local pilgrimages (to a monastery or wonder-working icon) and special programs must be organized to meet their spiritual needs.

Our children are full members of the Body of Christ. They may not pay on a pledge, fill the coffers of the building funds, or make donations to adorn the sanctuary. Rather, it is they who adorn the Church, in the beauty of their simplicity and trust. In these, we would do well to follow their example.

> Truly I say to you, unless you are converted and become as
> little children, you shall not enter into the Kingdom of Heaven.
>
> St. Matthew 18:3

Senior Citizens

> You shall stand up in the presence of the elderly, and honor
> them, and reverence your God.
>
> Leviticus 19:32

In a day when men and women are living longer and comprise the largest segment of active Church members, the needs of our elderly community need to be addressed. These people, who have devoted an entire lifetime of faith and service in the Church, are too often forgotten in their waning years.

Recommendations

1. As much as our Senior Citizens participate in the ongoing educational programs of the Church, they also have much to offer. Their memory of the recent history of the Church is invaluable. Oral history sessions should be encouraged, lest their wisdom be wasted on our own ignorance.

2. Many Parishes have succeeded at providing fellowship opportunities for the elderly, but we must be careful not to isolate the elderly from the rest of the Community.

3. Although many of our Senior Citizens enjoy the Services in the traditional tongues, they also enjoy having their grandchildren in Church! They, more than any other group, seem willing to make language sacrifices in favor of understanding and keeping their descendants Orthodox.

4. A long life is considered a blessing from God, but it also means a long history of spiritual struggle. Our Church must honor this struggle, especially as many prepare to face the end of this life. We must establish special ministries to serve them, particularly when one has been bereaved by the death of a spouse or a child. Many of the auxiliary groups (e.g. Philoptochos) can serve to this end.

The Youth and our Senior Citizens have many of the same needs. The way we treat the latter, may have a great deal to do with whether we shall retain the former.

> *Honor your father and mother; (which is the first commandment*
> *with a promise) that it may be well with you and you may live*
> *long on the earth.*
> *Ephesians 6:2,3*

Modern Day "Captives"

> *Whoever has this world's material benefits, and sees his brother
> in need, and shuts off his own compassion from him, how does
> the love of God dwell in him?*
>
> St. John 3:17

Christ came to set the "captives" free, and we must continue that ministry
in our own Communities. There are many modern day "captives," those in
hospitals, nursing centers, institutions, prison, and those living at great
distances from a parish. It is most certainly **not** only the clergy who have
the responsibility of this ministry.

There are many opportunities for the laity to serve, not only those in their
own Parish, but in the community at large. This is the witness to our love,
the proof of our preaching.

Recommendations

1. We cannot meet the needs if we do not know what they are. Social
   Service committees should be formed to heighten the awareness of the
   Parish and assist the clergy. Monthly updates, seminars, and Parish
   programs should be organized to expand the involvement of as many
   people as possible.

2. **Visitation** is essential. For those who cannot participate in the local
   fellowship of the Church, it must be brought to them.

3. **Our Church needs a complete restoration of the Diaconate** to serve
   the crying need for liturgical participation with those unable, for
   whatever reason, to attend. These Deacons could be prepared through
   study courses which would be (1) sanctioned by the Hierarchs,
   (2) formulated by the faculty of the Theological School and
   (3) administered by the local parish priest. These Deacons would serve
   at the Sunday Liturgy; particularly invaluable would be their assistance
   in the administration of Communion and other liturgical and pastoral

functions. They would continue to function "in the world," but must be understood to be full clergymen. The Diaconate is not a **step** to the Priesthood; rather it is **part** of it, with a full ministry of its own.

4. Those who work with the special needs of this often forgotten segment of our Communities need to have special sensitivities to their needs. There should be training and spiritual instruction in this regard.

If we are truly the Body of Christ, then we cannot afford to cut off our own limbs. How we respond to those of greatest need, yet least prominence, will one day come back to us all. Will we hear our Lord say this on the Day of Judgment?

> *I was hungry, and you gave Me food; I was thirsty, and you gave Me drink; I was a stranger, and you took Me in; naked, and you clothed Me; I was sick, and you visited Me; I was in prison, and you came to Me.*
>
> St. Matthew 25:35,36

"Male And Female Created He Them"
Before we move on to the recommendations on marriage and divorce, homosexuals, and the role of women, let us pause and reflect on the meaning and purpose of sexuality.

In the Book of Genesis we read:

> *So God created man in His own Image, in the Image of God He created him; male and female created He them.*
>
> Genesis 1:27

We may understand this passage in two ways. One, that men and women share in the same image of God, and, that our human nature is compound, both male and female. We were created by God to bear within ourselves the totality of sexuality. This does not imply a physical or biological notion of

113

gender; rather that the **fullness** of sexuality was part of the original state of humankind, before the "Fall" (it should be noted that both the word and concept "Fall" are a convention of speech — they do not appear in Holy Scripture).

If we examine the nature of this "Fall," we see that the "Sin of the Progenitor," (the "original sin") was not mere disobedience, much less the desire for the physical sexual act (as many have wrongly interpreted the eating of the forbidden fruit).

In disobeying the command of God, our spiritual ancestors failed to choose for love, love for God, love for one another. God gave them, and has given us, the ultimate freedom, the freedom to choose (Genesis 2:16,17).

Adam and Eve, who were created to be together (Genesis 2:18-25), are reported as being apart when the temptation to disobey came (Genesis 3:1-6). This was the beginning of the opposition and fragmentation in the human spirit that has plagued the world ever since (Genesis 3:16). This was the beginning of the dissolution of love. Its first offspring was murder (Genesis 4:1-8).

The consequences of this choice for self-love have been devastating to the human family. The Creator was abandoned by His creation. Communion with Heaven was lost. Paradise was removed from earth. Our human nature, created to be immortal, became subject to death and divided against itself. Our sexuality, created to be a power and force of unifying love, became misdirected and misunderstood.

Then came Christ, born of the Virgin, to heal and restore our nature. The significance of Christ's sexuality cannot be underestimated.

In the story of Genesis, we read that from the virgin body of a man (Adam) came forth woman, who was called Eve, or Zoe, because, by giving birth (by blood and water in the natural sense), she would become the source of the human race.

In the "Book of Genesis of Jesus Christ" (St. Matthew 1:1 — literal translation), we read that from the virgin body of a woman, the new Eve — the Theotokos and Ever-Virgin Mary, comes forth the **New Adam**, Who, through the Holy Blood (Eucharist) and the Holy Water (Baptism) that flowed from His Side (St. John 19:34,35), has become the source of the **New Creation**, the new human race.

Consider the similarity of both creations. Adam was put to sleep, then his side was opened to bring forth Eve. Christ was put to sleep on the Cross, then His Side was opened, to bring forth the New Creation. As if to memorialize the creation of humanity, women, to this very day, give first nourishment to children at their own breast. And where else does the Christian seek spiritual nourishment, if not at the Breast of Christ, from which flow His Most Precious Blood and the cleansing waters of Regeneration?

The process of dissolution and disintegration of our human nature and the division of our sexuality is corrected by the New Adam and the New Eve. They have turned the process upside down, reversing the sexual roles, in order to bring them together again. Instead of a perfect woman from a perfect man, we have a perfect man from a perfect woman. Nowhere is the consequence of this reunification so poignantly depicted, as in the Icon of the Resurrection, which shows our Lord bringing Adam and Eve up **together** from out of the depths of hell.

And what of this new sexuality, this new human nature? Although Our Lord lived as a virgin, we surely cannot consider Him to have been asexual. Rather, He embodied the totality of male and female and redeemed their purpose. By His Incarnation, He has re-created our sexuality. By giving up His life for the world on the Precious Cross, He has restored its purpose. And in virtue of His Holy Resurrection, He has granted us His Holy Spirit, to empower us to partake of our sexuality as New Creations in Him.

Our nature, our sexuality is restored through sacrificial love. It finds its true purpose and fulfillment only in this love.

We know the commandment. It is the same yesterday, today and forever.

> *As the Father has loved Me, so have I loved you: continue in My love. If you keep my commandments, you shall abide in My love . . . . This is my commandment, that you love one another, as I have loved you.*
>
> St. John 15:10,12

The Martyrs have showed their love in every age, giving their very life, not for fanatical convictions, but out of deep love for a person, the Divine Person, God Himself. Their love is a passionate love which testifies to their redeemed sexuality. What is the sign of a Martyr? It is not without significance that the First Martyr of our Church was St. Stephen the Archdeacon, whose name means **"crown."**

But we also call Marriage a crowning, a "*stepsis*." Is it not because those who are married are also called to that same sacrificial love which inspires the Martyrs? It is also a union with God, and our sexuality find physical expression in this context, as both a means of forging and expressing our new nature.

In the Mystery of Marriage, we return to the Garden of Eden, where they were exposed and vulnerable to each other, and not ashamed (Genesis 2:25). In this context, a physical sexual life becomes a willful commitment to another person, in whom one's nature finds fulfillment. This is the true meaning of the Epistle read at all Orthodox Marriages (Ephesians 6: 20-33).

The imagery of St. Paul, "being subject" and "above" and below" has nothing to do with the subjugation of women. He is speaking of the relationship of the heart and the head in the human body. Whereas a man brings the aspect of his sexuality as *logos* (reason — the head) to the conjugal relationship, a woman brings *sophia* (wisdom — the heart).

When a man and woman are joined in Marriage, they become "one flesh." They are one nature (male and female) and yet, two distinct persons. In this way, they glorify Christ, who, as both the *Logos*/Word and *Sophia*/Wisdom of God, was two natures (human and divine), yet One Divine Person. Sexual relations are a means of expressing this deep mystery, but they by no means comprehend its totality.

It should be pointed out that physical relations, like children, are not necessary to an Orthodox marriage. Both can be the cause of great joy and personal enrichment, but the foundational love of marriage goes deeper than either (note that the Orthodox Church is the only Christian community which considers the couple married at the altar, without the need for physical consummation — this is why there is no annulment in our Church).

Obviously, everyone cannot be married, much less, Martyrs. This is why God has given us a third way, the way of virginity, the way of celibacy — and it is no less sexual than the prior two.

We tend, in our modern world, to think of celibate persons as being strange and asexual. Rather, they are called to give full expression to their sexuality by a virginal love for all people. Monastic life is a perfect example.

In contrast to marriage, where we choose our partners, the monk does not choose the brethren of his, or her, community. But they are still called to love them, all of them, as intensely as God loves us. This is the fullness of sexuality without physical action. And it is more common than we think.

Consider our children or parents. We do not choose them (except in the case of adoption, which is considered a divine and grace-filled state, because it imitates God's choosing of us), but do we love them less strongly for that? We all know that physical sexual expressions are against nature in these relationships, but the love is passionate. Like the celibate, whether monk or in the world, these relationships call for self-denial and self-sacrifice.

It is only through this sacrifice that we find our true selves, united in the complete image of God, male and female. The Lord said: "Whoever would save his life must lose it." Part of carrying a cross is the willingness to hang on it, not as punishment, but in redemptive and sacrificial love for others.

Orthodoxy is **not** a religion; it is a way of living, a way of loving. Whether we are called to Martyrdom, or the intimacy of marriage, or a life of celibacy, we are all called to give up ourselves, and find our true selves in the Other, the other man, the other woman, the other person, the Image of God Himself.

Marriage and Divorce

Truly I say to you, whatever you bind on earth shall be bound in Heaven; and whatever you loose on earth shall be loosed in Heaven.

St. Matthew 18:18

Marriage has been given, like other Sacraments of the Church, as a provision for this world. Our Lord Himself called it an indissoluble bond (see St. Mark 10:2-12). This is the Christian ideal and any variance from it is by oikonomia, dispensation, out of love and compassion.

Although we conform to the civil laws of our land, we must recognize that it is the Church which has the authority from God to bind couples together through Marriage, as well as loose them from each other, through divorce.

The increasing divorce rate in our Church should give us pause as to whether we are preparing the Faithful for the challenge of Marriage, and ministering to them through the pain of divorce.

Recommendations — Marriage

1. Let there be pan-Orthodox cooperation in developing ministries that can prepare our people for marriage. Many do not understand the purposes of Christian Marriage, and why we try to marry within our Faith, at least someone who is Christian. If it happens to be the case, the non-Orthodox or non-Christian bride or groom-to-be should be invited to become an Orthodox Christian.

2. We need to provide the means of fellowship for couples preparing for marriage, as well as the newly married.

3. **If not the entire Liturgy, let us at least restore Holy Communion for two Orthodox partners at a Marriage.** Where there is one non-Orthodox partner, let the Common Cup remain. There are other liturgical practices that can be employed as well: the tradition of the Bride and Groom walking down the aisle together, traditional Orthodox Hymns, and the Betrothal taking place in the narthex. These lend a certain degree of variety to the service, and can involve the couple in a more active way in the planning of the ceremony.

4. Let us enhance the spiritual appreciation of Marriage, with the teaching of the unity of human nature that is so much a part of Orthodox Theology.

Recommendations — Divorce

1. The process of Ecclesiastical Divorce needs to be opened up to the understanding of the Faithful. Our Spiritual Courts often resemble either the inquisition or paper formalities. The Church should seem more interested in the souls of the Faithful, rather than the fees for the proceedings. There is also a difference of approach between jurisdictions in this country. Conferences to deal with these issues should be encouraged. The clergy and especially the Bishops should lead this effort.

2. In the local community, groups should be available for persons going through separation and divorce.

3. Very often, people do not receive their Ecclesiastical Divorces until they need to, for the sake of a new marriage or a desire to participate in one of the Mysteries of the Church as a sponsor. Receiving Holy Communion is not even discussed with the individual. We need to make our people aware of the spiritual implications of divorce, the necessity of Ecclesiastical Divorce, and not excommunicate 'en masse' those who may have not yet obtained it. Each circumstance will be different and needs to be treated as such; not that we should disregard the standards of the Church, but that we should apply *oikonomia* liberally, when it is for the salvation of a soul.

4. The spiritual needs of people going through divorce are delicate. We need to train the clergy of our Church in the demands of this particularly painful situation.

Our Lord said that divorce was given because of our "hardness of heart." But He has also promised that He would give us a "heart of flesh" for our "heart of stone." If we can deal with the pain and challenge of divorce in our Church today, then perhaps we will have a better chance of living in marriage as the Apostle calls us:

> *For the man is not without the woman, neither is the woman*
> *without the man, in the Lord. For as the woman is of the man,*
> *so also is the man by the woman; and all things are of God.*
> *I Corinthians 11:11,12*

Those Married Outside The Church
> *For the unbelieving husband is sanctified by his wife, and the*
> *unbelieving wife is sanctified by her husband. If this were not*
> *so, your children would be unclean, but now they are holy.*
> *I Corinthians 7:14*

120

There are two different problems here, but many similar solutions. Those who are married outside the Church to Heterodox Christians need only to have their marriages blessed in the Church in order to reincorporate themselves in the sacramental life of the Church.

Those married to non-Christians cannot do this, for the Church does not (and should not) marry Christians and non-Christians (II Corinthians 6:14). But it does happen that decisions about whom to marry are made at one stage of life and faith, while the recognition of and need for the truth of the Gospel may happen at another.

Recommendations
1. There should be an active effort to inform and instruct the Orthodox and Heterodox couples as to why the Orthodox blessing is so important (as well as the invitation to become Orthodox). This should be seen as a complement to *whatever marital relationship exists*, even if there were only a civil ceremony. It is time to *recognize* the social validity of these marriages. This goes as well for Orthodox married to non-Christians. We should encourage participation in the full sacramental life of the Church as an enhancement to the existing marriage, not as a denouncement of "living in sin."

   If it is possible, let the children be baptized and raised in the Church. Here we should stress the role of sponsor and the Orthodox parent as being responsible for raising the child in the Faith.

2. The witness of friendship and fellowship can be instrumental in bringing both parties into the Faith. Let there also be a mutual appreciation of the heterodox partner's devotion to their own Christian community, and a warm welcome for the non-Christian. Children must always be welcome at fellowship events, even if they have not been baptized.

3. If it is not possible for an Orthodox blessing to occur (either due to family pressure or the refusal of a spouse of a heterodox, or because of

121

marriage to a non-Christian) **let us admit to Communion** those who have sought an entry to the Sacrament through Confession. It is senseless to deprive our own people of the Eucharist for an indefinite period of time. There is no sin that excommunicates a person from the Church forever, except that it not be repented.

4. If we cannot bless the Marriage, then we must pray with the couple for mutual understanding and growth. We must remember that the children of such families are special, even if they are not baptized.

This is a difficult and delicate issue, but we must always be guided by the same principles that guided the Apostles.

> *For how do you know, O woman, whether you shall save your husband? Or how do you know, O man, whether you shall save your wife?*
>
> *I Corinthians 7:16*

Homosexuals And The Church
Be followers of me, even as I also am of Christ.
I Corinthians 11:1

One of the most controversial issues in modern religious life is the status of an emerging homosexual community. Although many may think so, this is not a new situation in world history. Homosexuals have been part of the world scene and culture from earliest recorded time (see Romans 1:26,27).

It is not our intention to speculate on the theories of homosexuality, whether there is a biological basis or predisposition, or it is a condition of environment and choice. The fact is that our Church has numerous homosexual members, and She must reach out to them in love.

While the Church should support the full civil rights of homosexuals in our free and democratic society, She is under no obligation to endorse a lifestyle inconsistent with Her own teachings. Unions of male with male, or female with female, are contrary to the meaning and purposes of human sexuality.

While it is certainly possible for monogamous homosexual relationships to manifest some of the character of marital relationships, we must emphasize that even these fail in their understanding of the nature and purpose of marriage.

Marriage is given as a sacred context for the renewal of the image of God within us, through sacrificial love, and it can be expressed in physical love.

The incompleteness of the homosexual relationship is found in this: rather than reuniting the human image (male **and** female), it becomes fixated in the affection of an incomplete nature (either male **or** female). In this way, it "misses the mark" (*amartia*) and so can be described as sin.

This incompleteness is symbolized by the necessary barrenness of such relationships, where physical sexual expression not only **does not** produce offspring, but **cannot**.

In describing homosexual relationships as sin, let us not forget that heterosexual relationships, even faithful ones, are also sinful, if they are not bound within the context and meaning of marriage. Outside of Marriage, both heterosexuals and homosexuals are called to a life of celibacy. Their response to this call is a matter of free will, even if their sexual preference is not.

Recommendations
1. There needs to be much education, counseling and teaching in this area, bringing a new understanding of self to the Christian community, based on the image of God within us, not sexual preference.

2. We need to see celibacy as a "normal" lifestyle in the Church. The fellowship in our Church must make room for the single, unmarried,

celibate and often homosexual members in the Parish, and **not** expect them to socialize with each other in order to get married.

3. Let us remember that the only thing that blocks our access to the Liturgy is our own sinfulness, and Christ is always willing to forgive.

4. In many ways, our homosexual members have a more difficult path, and very often not of their own choosing. They need spiritual support and encouragement from clergy and laity alike.

The Lord never promised us an easy spiritual life, but He stands by those with the fortitude and courage to take on the task.

> *Everyone cannot receive this saying, except for those to whom it is given. There are some eunuchs, who were born that way; and there are some eunuchs, who were made into eunuchs by others; and there are some eunuchs, who have made themselves eunuchs for the sake of the Kingdom of Heaven. If you can receive this saying, then receive it.*
>
> St. Matthew 19:11,12

Women And The Church[2]

> *For you are all the children of God by faith in Christ Jesus. All of you who have been baptized into Christ have put on Christ. There is neither Jew nor Gentile, neither slave nor free, neither male nor female; for you are all one in Christ Jesus.*
>
> Galatians 3:26-28

It would be unreasonable to assume that our Church has given women the recognition they so richly deserve, especially when one considers the inestimable importance of the Ever-Virgin Mary. Women have ministered in

---

2. A complete analysis of Orthodox Women and the Church is presented in Eva Topping's Commission Paper beginning on page 67.

countless ways, in opposition to Judaic custom, which still has many vestiges in our Church.

The consideration of our three concerns should be tempered with a sensitivity to the present needs of women. Recommendations will follow in each section, based on the content of that section.

Liturgical Roles for Women: Participation in the Divine Liturgy (or any other service) should not be judged on whether one has an active role in that Service. Remember the story of Sts. Mary and Martha (St. Luke 10:38-42). Mary received the "good part," "the one thing necessary . . . which cannot be taken away," by attentively sitting at the feet of our Lord.

Our people need to learn again the meaning of the exhortation, "Wisdom, let us be attentive!" The greatest role in the Divine Liturgy is that of Communicant, to receive the Body and Blood of Christ. Here, our gender is not an issue, only the purity and readiness of our intention and our souls.

We would consider the Apostolic injunction against women speaking during the Liturgy (I Corinthians 14:34 and I Timothy 2:11) to be a holdover out of respect for Judaism, where women had no religious function at all.

Recommendation[3]
Women may participate in choirs, as chanters, and as readers. They should be tonsured for these roles as men (should be — there are other implications for this tonsure, as will be seen below).

Purity Issues: Here again we find Judaizing elements in the tradition of the Church. These elements need to be seen in the complete light of the transfiguring Christian message, and if they are to be maintained, let it be for a holistic symbolic value, rather than any even implied denigration of women.

---

3. See Topping, E., "Orthodox Women and The Church."

Entry of Women into Church after Childbirth (40 days) — This tradition, found in Leviticus 12:1-6, is kept in our Church, but not for the same reasons that ancient Judaism practiced it. It is also part of a wider context of thanksgiving and blessing for both mother and child after childbirth. For ancient Judaism, it was an issue of ritual purity (an extensive treatment and rejection of ritual purity can be found throughout the writings of St. Paul).

For the Christian woman, it is part of the great and mystical honor of becoming a mother. In this context, we must renew the traditional blessing that precedes the 40 Day blessing. First there is the blessing after the delivery of the child. On the Eighth Day, instead of a Jewish ritual circumcision, we are to give the child its Christian name. The mother then continues to remain outside the worshipping community for 40 days as a commemoration of the 40 days spent by the Ever-Virgin Mary (St. Luke 2:22), which culminated in the Presentation of our Lord in the Temple (feast — February 2nd). The Christian woman has this time, not only for the recovery of her body, but for the consideration of the new life she has brought into the world. Far from a negative connotation, this time should be of utmost importance in the spiritual life of the family.

Recommendation[4]
Let the 40 days be a time of joy and reflection, not exclusion, which is consummated in the woman's presentation of her offspring in the Temple, and her reception of Holy Communion. If there is a good reason why the woman should be in the community before the 40 days, let the blessing be done early.

Churching of Female Infants — Along with the blessing of the mother (father and sponsors as well!), there is also the blessing of the child. It should be noted here that the official Service Books of the Church do not

---

4.   See Topping, E., "Orthodox Women and The Church."

indicate that there should be a difference between the ways male and female children should be Churched.

The common practice today, that boys are brought into the Altar, while girls are blessed in front of the Iconostasion, is not substantiated in the "Euchologia." The argument that only male children should be carried around the Altar because only they may become Priests is a non-sequitur; as we will see later, not all males may become Priests.

Recommendation
Both male and female infants should be Churched in the same way, within the Altar.

Service within the Altar (liturgical and otherwise) — There is a false notion in our Church that **only** males may go inside the Altar. This is patently false. Only those **appointed** to serve the Altar may enter it, and it is time that the clergy enforced this pious tradition.

So then we must ask: May women serve within the Altar? Of course, as they are apportioned such ministries. This service may consist of cleaning (which is not dishonorable — even a Priest must "clean" the Holy Vessels), or direct assistance to the clergy during services.

As to the question of "Altar Girls," this relates to the wider issue of tonsuring women. "*Cheirothesia*," the placing of hands, accompanied by tonsure, is the traditional means of the appointment to liturgical ministry for men and women. In the early Church, there were even deaconesses who assisted at the Baptisms of women (it should be noted that adults were baptized as children are today, naked and fully immersed — the deaconesses were used for the sake of propriety).

Recommendation
If a woman is tonsured as a reader, then she must be welcome in service to the Altar. It is time for our Church to recognize that these gifts are a normative part of Church life. Perhaps, we may see an increase in the

monastic vocations of women (almost unheard of in the Americas) if more liturgical encouragement were to be given in the local parish.

Receiving Holy Communion and Menstruation — The practice of a woman not receiving Holy Communion during the time of her menstrual cycle is rooted in the ritual purity laws of Judaism. The woman who touched the hem of our Lord's garment (St. Mark 5:24-34) was also conscious of these purity laws, and so sought her healing in secret. But the Lord brought her faith to the light of day and accepted her.

Recommendation[5]
We must affirm that natural bodily functions **in no way** bar anyone from participation in the Sacraments, but we should not condemn those who observe ancient traditions out of personal piety.

Ordination:
Unity of the Priesthood — Although there is much that could be said on this subject, we must affirm that the Priesthood, as understood in the Orthodox Church, is a unified reality, which finds its only fullness in the High Priesthood of our Lord Jesus Christ. The Priesthood belongs to Christ, not to any one person. Whether one is a Deacon, Presbyter, or Bishop, it is the same Priesthood, only a different degree of responsibility.

(It should be noted that in the New Testament, the offices of Bishop and Presbyter were so similar, that the terms are often used interchangeably.)

Even if one accepts that only males may become Priests, it should be pointed out that not all men have this opportunity. For example, a man must have all of his external bodily parts, he cannot be blind or deaf; if he is married, he must be married to his first and only wife (I Timothy 3:2; Titus 1:6). Thus

---

5. See Topping, E., "Orthodox Women and The Church."

we see the importance of the Priest as the living icon of Christ in the Divine Liturgy, for it is the celebration of the Liturgy, more than any thing else, that makes a Priest (Deacon, Presbyter, or Bishop) a Priest.

Why are there no women clergy? — This is a legitimate question, even in the light of a two thousand year old tradition, and deserves an adequate explanation.

Given the **total human nature** of our Lord, it does not seem possible, but we must consider the full historical implications of such a decision (as well as the reason it has not been decided so to this day).

Our Faith has its foundations in the **historical reality** of Jesus Christ, His Birth, Ministry, Passion, Death, Resurrection, and Ascension — all of which our Church takes to be historical fact.

The reason why the clergy of our Church are male is because He came as a male (see the insert on human sexuality). This is part of the integral historic evidence that any icon of the Church manifests, that Our Lord was a **real person** (see I John).

In the Liturgy, **the Priest, like the Icons, directly and mystically represent Christ Himself.** The Priest is no more, **but no less,** Christ than any of the Icons are. This sacred, iconographic function is as necessary to the integrity of the Orthodox Faith as the Icons themselves. In this way, the historico-iconographic role of the clergy support and confirm the decisions of the Holy Seven Oecumenical Councils. It is not without reason that the Holy Spirit has guided the Church in this way for nearly two thousand years.

The Priestly Ministry of the clergy must be understood as a provision for this world, not the world to come, where there will be no more need for Mysteries and Promise, but Christ will be all in all. Moreover, we have all been called, in virtue of our Baptism and response to it, into the Royal Priesthood of

Christ. Here there is neither male nor female, and we all have the same access to the Same Spirit of God.

Deaconesses (is there a liturgical/pastoral need?) — Since there were deaconesses in the early years of our Church (until the 4th century), it is reasonable to examine whether and under what circumstances this old treasure might bring forth new gifts.

Although the liturgical needs do not seem apparent, there may yet be pastoral needs (the affirmation of women's varied roles) which necessitate its reinstitution.

Recommendations[6]
1. Care must be taken to teach the Faithful in the **meaning** of the Holy Priesthood, that there not be any misunderstandings about **why** the Priesthood is reserved for males.

2. Consistent with Orthodox tradition and theology, the office of deaconess must be restored.

There is much that can be done to involve women in creative and new ministries in the Church. There is also much to be done to educate our Faithful to the true meaning of our purposes as redeemed women **and** men, who are called into the fullness of communion with God.

Whatever our gender, Christ has called us into relationship with Himself, and as He Himself says, there will be new roles for all of us.

---

6. See Topping E, "Orthodox Women and The Church."

For whoever shall do the will of My Father, Who is in Heaven,
the same is my brother and my sister and my mother.

St. Matthew 12:50

We hope and pray that these thoughts and recommendations will serve to inspire reflection and dialogue on the needs of our Church today, as well as encourage thoughtful exchange of the clergy and the faithful on other issues. There is so much work of the Gospel to do; the world is waiting and so are our own Faithful.

The quest to become New Creations in Christ Jesus is a difficult and arduous one, but one that He has promised to be with us in. That promise is sure; He is the Same yesterday, today and forever. With boldness let us go forward to work the "works of God," confident in a more certain hope, that the One that is in us, is greater than anything that is in the world.

For I am persuaded, that neither death, nor life, nor angels, nor
principalities, nor powers, nor things present, nor things to
come, nor height, nor depth, nor any other creature, shall be
able to separate us from the love of God, which is in Christ
Jesus our Lord.

Romans 8:38,39

+ To God be the Glory +

+ Amen +

ORTHODOX
CHRISTIAN
LAITY

THE SELECTION OF HIERARCHY

George D. Karcazes, Co-Chair

Leon C. Marinakos, Co-Chair[1]

Introduction

Membership in Orthodox Christian Laity has always been open to **all** baptized and chrismated Orthodox Christians, including priests, bishops and archbishops. The OCL ministry was initiated by a group of lay persons, with strong encouragement and support of priests, some of whom have joined as members of the ministry, and others who have offered their moral support. OCL has also enjoyed input and moral support of several bishops who share OCL's belief that our church in America is in need of renewal.

The work of this Commission was authorized by the membership of the Orthodox Christian Laity at its Third Annual Meeting at St. Basil's Church in Chicago, Illinois in November, 1990. The Commission has had the benefit of advice from a number of individuals, including priests, who have reviewed some but not necessarily all, of the sections of this Report. They have acted as consultants to the Commission, but the conclusions of the Commission as contained in this Report are not necessarily those of the priests who acted as consultants.

This Report is not intended to be the last word on the questions it deals with. It is intended to generate discussion, and hopefully, to shed some light on those questions. It is our hope and our prayer that all Orthodox Christians living and practicing their faith in America, will engage in the dialogue this and the other Commission Reports are intended to spark, so that the Church can

---

1. Members of the Commission on the Selection of Hierarchy and Consultants to the Commission are: Dr. Andrew T. Kopan, James A. Koulogeorge, V. Rev. Eusebius A. Stephanou, Katherine G. Valone, Rev. Steven J. Vlahos, and Dr. John Koumoulides.

"function as a living organism in which all its members and parts are organically related and alive."

The Objective of the Commission

One of the initially stated goals of the Orthodox Christian Laity ministry is: To restore the role of the laity in the election of the hierarchy. Our discussion will focus on the situation confronting members of the Greek Archdiocese of North and South America, but it will also consider Orthodox practice in general and as it exists in other Orthodox jurisdictions. Any discussion of this issue also raises the issues of Canonical unity of the Orthodox Church in America, Autonomy and Autocephaly, which is discussed in detail later in this book.

Scriptural Testimony and the Apostolic Pattern

The process, if not the exact procedure, of the all important matter of selecting the spiritual leaders must trace its origins to the infant Apostolic Church and the testimony of the Church Fathers. The process of ordination or commissioning a spiritual leader of the Church in a formal-structured service, such as we know today, does not appear in the New Testament. However, what is mentioned there indicates some type of ceremony, albeit a very simple one:

- The twelve "chosen" and "sent" by Christ. (Mark 3:13-19, Luke 6:12-16).

- The election of Matthias (Acts 1:26).

- The seven elected and commissioned by the "laying on of hands." (Acts 6:6).

- The commissioning of Paul and Barnabas by the Antioch church by the "laying on of hands." (Acts 13:3).

134

- And the primary source of an ordination service comes from I Timothy 4:14; and II Timothy 1:6.

As for the election of those to be ordained and commissioned, the prominent lay theologian Panagiotis Trembelas of Athens, Greece (Religious and Ethical Encyclopedia) says:

> Already from the first days of the establishment of the Church, with the question that arose to replace the fallen twelfth apostle, despite the fact that the apostolic chorus constitutes a special class in the Church, selected by the Lord directly and undertaking an extraordinary mission, the entire Church is invited to participate in the election of Peter "with the expression of public opinion and allowing the judgment of the masses. . . . Men were called brothers, by all present." This proclaimed in such a way that "none of the faithful there were split, neither male or female." (Chrysostom). Thus, women also participated in the election.

When after a while the matter arose about electing the seven deacons, "the twelve summoned the body of the disciples [i.e. the followers of Christ]" (Acts 6:2-3), and charged that body to select the seven. Chrysostom commenting on what happened says "the right to determine the number and the placing of the hands [ordination], the apostles reserved for themselves, but allow the people to elect the specific men."

The Practice in the Time of the Apostolic Fathers
In the period of the Apostolic Fathers following the time of the apostles, there are numerous references to the selection of hierarchy by the people, as well as the example being followed by the civic authorities. Some examples:

1. There is witness from the First Epistle to the Corinthians of Clement of Rome (Chapter 44,3) which proclaims that "the installed [bishops] by them [the Apostles], or the other worthy men agreed to by the whole church . . . these we believe cannot justifiably be eliminated from the

135

liturgy." This witness takes on a special meaning if it is related to another of the author Lampridius, certifying about Alexander Severi (222-225) that leaving the election of rulers to the people, was following the practice of Christians and Jews (Vita. Alex Severi, Chapter 45).

2. During those same years, Cyprian of Carthage (+258) witnesses about Pope Cornelius that on the one hand, he became bishop by the judgment of God and Christ, and on the other hand, by the witness of almost all of the clergy and the vote of all of the people present and the college of the old priests and good men (Epistle 10, Paragraph 8).

3. At the same time, there is the election of Pope Fabian, who was martyred in the reign of Decius (251-258). While all the brothers were deliberating about filling the widowed throne of Rome, he too came from his fields, at the moment when "in no one's mind did the thought exist that it was possible Fabian could be elected." But it is universally mentioned that a dove from the heights alighted on Fabian's head. "Following which the entire people as if by a single spirit divinely moved, carried him and placed him on the throne of the episcopate" (Eusebius, Ecclesiastical History VI:29).

4. Examples of elections in which it is evident that the vote of the people was victorious and prevailing, are all too numerous in church history. Gregory of Nazianzos (Homily 21 8:35, 1089) certifies explicitly the witness that the elections were by "the vote of all the people" of such hierarchs as Athanasius the Great, Nectarios, John Chrysostom, Sisinios, Germanos, and Tarasias, all of Constantinople, Eustathius of Antioch, etc. Theodoritos (Ecclesiastical History V:982, 1217) says on the subject: "the entire city voted" and Socrates (Ecclesiastical History VI:2 67, 661) states that there was "a public vote by all the clergy and the voice of the people."

The Decrees of the Holy Canons

The Holy Canons and other edicts have much to say about the election process.

1. Perhaps the oldest written monument, stipulating the election of bishops is an encyclical of the synod which convened around 258 in Carthage. It is included in the Number 67 (or 68) epistle of Cyprian in which it is stated, "The divine and apostolic tradition must be followed" so that concerning the ordination of a bishop it must be done "among the people of which the one to be ordained will be the leader, and the bishops neighboring on this diocese to assemble, and the bishop to be elected in the presence of the people, who know the life of each and witnesses about all the deeds of each."

2. Considered as contemporary is a stipulation in the Apostolic Decrees referred to earlier also in the Canons under the name of Hippolytos. There it is stated that the candidate bishop must be irreproachable in all respects with superior merits, elected by all the people. During a Sunday gathering of all, the presiding notable would ask the presbyter and the people if the candidate was the one they wanted as leader. If they would assent, there would be an examination by the bishops to ascertain if truly the proposed candidate is "witnessed by all as being worthy of the great and brilliant position." Thereafter the people once again were invited to acclaim a third time and the ordination followed. (Apostolic Decree VIII 5:1, 1069). The Synod of bishops had the right and duty to dissent in the election of the people whenever it was convinced that the proposed candidate was unworthy. However from the 18th Canon of the Synod of Antioch (314 A.D.) and the 18th Canon of the Ancyra Synod (314 A.D.), it is evident that the right of the people to elect their bishops remained strong.

3. The 4th Canon of the First Ecumenical Synod stipulates that a new bishop would be elevated by all the bishops in the province and the authority of the decision rests with the metropolitan of the province.

However that Canon, in combination with the letter of the same Synod to the Church of Alexandria, proves that the rights of the people were not being limited. The letter reaffirms the voting obligations of the people (Socrates, Ecclesiastical History I:9). "Thus also at the time of the First Ecumenical Synod, the people elected and the Metropolitan, with the Synod around him, ratified or invalidated the election" says theologian Trembelas.

4. The clever and the selfish have never been absent from the Church of Christ, and among the people, there are always the gullible and the easily deceived. Thus, very early extremes were noted, fomented, and aroused by ambitious clerics, who usurped vacant episcopal thrones by mob actions. These excesses were addressed in the 4th Canon of the First Ecumenical Council, the 16th Canon of the Antioch Synod, and the 13th Canon of the Laodician Synod. These Canons in effect say that a bishop having usurped a throne would be expelled even if "he were elected by all the people" and the mobs should not be permitted to elect those who would in the future be elevated to the hierarchy.

5. Practices involving the laity in the elevation to the hierarchy were also followed in the West. Thus, Leo the Great ordered that from all those proposed for the episcopacy, the one who would be preferred should be the person agreed to by clergy and laity (Epistle 14, 5, PL 54, 673). He also pronounced the classic: "He who is to be the superior of all should be elected by all." (Qui praefuturus est omnibus eligatur) (Epistle 10, 5, PL, 632). Also, Gregory the Great strongly espouses the right of the clergy and the laity to participate in the election of the bishop (Thomassinum, Vet. et Nov. Eccl. Discipl. H 7C 34 Paragraph 10).

Succession of the Episcopate in the Byzantine World

In Byzantine times Emperor Justinian (527-565) issued the Nearai No. 6, 123, 137 (see also the code Justinian, Book I, Title III, Law 42 about bishops). In those decrees among other provisions, it was stipulated that for the election of bishops the "clergy and the primates of the city, in which the bishop will be ordained" should come together and they should propose three individuals so that from them the best would be ordained (Neara 123, Chapter 1, In Vasilika Book III, Title I).

It is true that many extremes were perpetrated by the emperors, the kings and other rulers in the West, the mob interventions of the masses, and the coups by metropolitans and bishops. Especially in the election of the Patriarchs of Constantinople, as well as the filling of vacant thrones in the West, the emperors and kings dictated beforehand the ones they preferred, and afterwards the ones who voted were usually the simple executors of the sovereign commands. History also notes instances where synodic ordinations were not acceptable to the people, the ordinations were invalidated, and the elevated prelates were transferred to another see.

The ordination of the bishops took place usually in the widowed sees where the metropolitan would meet with all the bishops in the area and presided over the election. When the bishops were convinced that the candidate enjoyed the common approval, the first of the bishops would proclaim him officially in the church saying to the people among other things "this person, dear brethren, who has been elected as most worthy for the hierarchy, agreeing he is laudable, assist and proclaim: he is worthy. [*Axios*.]" With the proclamation of "*Axios*," the ordination ceremony **would begin**. This practice has now been reversed. The acclamation of "Axios," he is worthy, in today's ordinations is invited **after** the ordination sacrament has been completed, and not **before** as was the ancient practice. In other words, the ordination is a *fait accompli* when the congregation is asked to give its assent, rendering the role of the people a subservient, acquiescing formality. In some instances, mainly in Greece, where congregations have asserted their free judgment to proclaim the ordained bishop as "Axios," unrest, turmoil, and even riots have ensued.

This information about the historical right and practice of the People of God to express their approval or disapproval of the one who will be their shepherd is seldom, if ever, mentioned by our current shepherds, inferring that things are being done as they always have been.

There is, in fact, no disagreement in the official Church, even today, over the testimony of the ancient Church in this regard. The evidence is unmistakable and incontrovertible. Since Constantine the Great, however, lay participation in the election of bishops **increasingly** meant **imperial** involvement. The election of the Ecumenical Patriarch was virtually the Emperor's prerogative as the Byzantine Age moved on. For example, St. John Chrysostom was, by imperial decree, transferred from Antioch and enthroned as Patriarch in Constantinople (Emperor Arcadius). Emperors banished and replaced bishops at will, often over the protests of the Bishop of Rome. The struggle for control between emperors and the institutional church may have led to some of the restrictions on the role of the laity at large in the selection of bishops.

How Bishops are Elected Today in Greek Orthodox Archdiocese

Professor James Steve Counelis has written an excellent analysis of the four Constitutions of the Greek Orthodox Archdiocese of North and South America under which our Archdiocese has functioned since its establishment. The article appears in the 26th Biennial Clergy-Laity Congress Album, San Francisco, July, 1982. He concluded his analysis of the four constitutions with this personal observation:[2]

> *This writer believes that the development of an operative democratic church within the title of the Greek Orthodox Archdiocese of North and South America is inevitable, though he may not live to see it. Further, this democratization will occur only when the American Church takes seriously the theological anthropology of the Church and sees that that*

---

2. The full text of this article can be found in the PostScript beginning on page 297.

anthropology becomes the basis of a Christ-like church . . . a Christ-like ecclesiology in living practice. The true ecclesial independence of the American Orthodox Church rests in the achievement of a Christ-like ecclesiology, for creativity, wisdom and piety will be her gifts. The Church is one priesthood of believers, clergy, and lay, with one Head — the Christ.

If it is indeed inevitable that the Orthodox Church in America is going to develop into an "operative democratic church" as Dr. Counelis predicts, the recognition of the theological anthropology of the church must come from the entire church, not only from a few of its members. It will also be necessary for the church to confront, and reverse, the "Constitutional Regressions" noted by Dr. Counelis in his analysis of the four (1922, 1927, 1931 and 1977) Constitutions of the Archdiocese. As Dr. Counelis notes:

[A] document by document review of the four Constitutions reveals that two retrogressions have occurred . . . (1) the participation and approval of the archdiocesan constitution by laymen and lower clergy; (2) the method of selecting bishops.

"The Constitution of 1922 was developed and approved by the 2nd Clergy-Laity Congress in 1922 . . . . The 1927 revision . . . was approved at a general meeting in the then Cathedral of St. Basil in Chicago. As to the monarchical constitution of 1931, it is a well known fact that it was imposed by the Ecumenical Patriarchate and the Greek Government. And as for the 1977 Constitution, it was never presented at a referendum at any Clergy-Laity Congress, though a small committee of bishops, lower clergy and laymen participated in its construction. It appears that the Ecumenical Patriarchate was more Christian and more trusting in the past than in the present.

The method of selecting bishops has also retrogressed since the 1922 and 1927 Constitutions. In these two earlier constitutions, the Clergy-Laity Congress had the opportunity to *submit the names of three clergymen for transmission to the American Synod of Bishops. They, in turn, would nominate one of the three, sending that candidate's name on to Constantinople. The Synod of the Ecumenical Patriarchate would accept the decision of the American Synod and would elect that candidate to episcopal office. No such process is available in the 1977 constitution; and certainly nothing is said in the 1931 constitution. In the 1977 constitution there is a vaguely worded reference to the American Synod of Bishops consulting with the Archdiocesan Council, on which laymen and lower clergy are present. However, the Ecumenical Patriarchate reserves the right to name bishops to American dioceses. Obviously, the ancient tradition of the local diocese selecting its own bishop and proclaiming him "Axios," is dead. **There is no question that the 1922 and 1927 Constitutions were superior to the 1977 Constitution in both the constitutional procedures and the method of selecting bishops.*** [Emphasis Supplied]

Notwithstanding Professor Counelis's commentary, the evidence seems to indicate that this "right" of the Patriarchate exists in theory rather than in practice. The practice appears to be that the **Archbishop handpicks his bishops** and the Ecumenical Patriarch simply rubberstamps his choices and validates them for consecration. However, there is some anecdotal evidence that on one occasion in recent years, Constantinople withheld its approval for a candidate submitted by the Archbishop until he agreed to submit another candidate favored by Constantinople, whereupon both candidates were approved.

How Bishops are Elected in Other Orthodox Jurisdictions

In Russia, where the Church is only now emerging from seventy years of often brutal suppression, the Patriarch of Moscow was recently elected by 66 bishops, 66 priests and 66 laypersons representing each of the 66 Dioceses. The Commission has not been able to determine how the priests and laypersons were selected, but the ancient tradition of participation by priests and laity in the election was reaffirmed.

The Orthodox Church in America (OCA) and the Antiochan Archdiocese here in America, also maintain at least to some extent the tradition of lay participation in the election of its Bishops. However, the Commission has received anecdotal evidence that OCA Hierarchy has on at least one occasion reversed an election in which the laity had voted.

As this Report is discussed in the coming months, we hope to develop more information about both the theory and the practice of other Orthodox jurisdictions. We invite comments, articles and information from all of our readers, which we will share with the entire Church.

Suggested Proposals for Improvement — The Greek Orthodox Jurisdiction

There seems to be little dispute that the laity has had an inherent and historically confirmed right to participate in the process by which priests and bishops are selected. Professor Lewis J. Patsavos of the Holy Cross School of Theology has written:

> Then there is the very sensitive issue to consider of the election of the clergy by the laity. The prominent role given the laity in the election of Matthias to replace Judas is an indisputable fact. It set the pace for what was to follow in this regard during the next three centuries. Abuses, however, and the ever-increasing influence of secular rulers in the affairs of the Church had as their consequence the abolition of the **God-given right of the laity to elect its spiritual leaders.** Sufficient historical precedents do exist as a reminder of what was once an inherent right of the laity, even though the final act of laying on of hands was always the exclusive privilege of the episcopacy. [Emphasis Supplied]

All Orthodox are familiar with the now ritualistic shouts of "Axios" (he is Worthy) which the laity are called upon to proclaim at every ordination of a priest and elevation of a hierarch, which in Orthodox Churches must occur during a Liturgy. Although we have heard of no instance in the Greek Archdiocese in America, stories abound of instance where the laity in Greece have actually caused the proceedings to be halted by their shouts of Unworthy, which required the convening of an investigation into the reasons for rejection. Such occurrences are surely not to be encouraged, but they may disclose a weakness in the process which excludes the laity from any meaningful role in the process which permits only such a public last ditch venue for the expression of the laity's will. This right is still exercised, albeit in a sometimes purely symbolic manner, in some Orthodox Churches. In the Church of Cyprus, for example, the laity participate in the election of the Archbishop. Likewise, in Russia, a new Patriarch of Moscow was recently elected at a meeting called for that purpose which included bishops, clergy, and laity representing every Diocese. If the laity in Cyprus and Russia do not exclusively exercise their God-given right to select their spiritual leaders, they at least have the opportunity to participate in the process. Any effort to involve the laity in the selection process in any meaningful manner must take into account the cautionary admonition of Professor Patsavos that:

> *Only believing and worshipping laypersons should be allowed to assist in the governing of the Church; nominal Christians should at all costs be excluded.*

The issue should not be whether the laity should have a voice, rather the issue should be what that voice should be and how, and by whom should it be expressed? Regrettably, in the past, it can be argued that in some instances the least spiritually qualified were involved. Even today the risk persists. Historically, wealthy, secular-minded barons in the court of the Church could cast a decisive vote. In the recent past the wealthy merchant class of Phanariots in Constantinople were influential in elections of the Patriarch. In the Soviet Union, it is suspected that the KGB has played a role in the selection of Bishops. The restoration of lay participation as such is not necessarily a guarantee that the *laos*, or People of God, is participating. The baron-type of laity can turn into rubber-stamping the preference of some Church prelate or primate. We do not need that in the Church in America.

External Improper Influences

One objection that can be made to lay participation in the election of bishops is the possibility that secular influences will be introduced into the choice. However, it is likely that the current practice of the Greek Orthodox Church is far more vulnerable to such influences than is a system in which the laity exercise their appropriate role.

The "Church," which we define for our purposes here, as **all** of the Orthodox communicants who find themselves in America today, regardless of ethnic jurisdiction, enjoys total freedom from any influence from any secular leaders of the United States Government. The genius of the Founding Fathers of this Nation was in their understanding that Religion would **flourish** in an environment where it was not only **free**, but totally separate from, and **unsupported by** the Government. If there are any influences of secular rulers in the affairs of the Orthodox Church in America, they are the influences which the Turkish Government has over decisions of the Ecumenical Patriarchate located in Constantinople and which the Greek Government exercises over the Greek Archdiocese, directly through the Church of Greece, or indirectly through its influence over the Ecumenical Patriarchate. To a greater or lesser extent, other foreign governments, such as Russia, Bulgaria, Romania, Syria, etc. may exercise, or attempt to exercise, some influence through the Mother Churches of those jurisdictions over the affairs of their daughter Churches in America.

In order for the Orthodox Church in the United States to address the problem of the unwarranted and improper influences of secular rulers especially the Greek and Turkish Governments, the Church in America must define its existence in terms of its own needs, realities and self-governance, while at all times maintaining its ties with its historical past and roots. This discussion cannot avoid the question of the establishment of one Autocephalous Orthodox Church in America.[3]

Although this issue will be discussed by the Commission which is studying the issue of Orthodox Unity, it is one which has to be addressed as well in our discussion concerning the elimination of improper influences from the election of bishops. Clearly, the constitutional guarantees that have existed for more than two hundred years in this Country are so well-established that there is no question of U. S. governmental interference with the affairs of the Church in America. A single, united and autocephalous Orthodox Church in America would be able to elect its bishops and patriarch without interference from secular rulers. If the model we wish to establish for Church governance of an Orthodox Church in America is closer to that of the first three centuries of our Church, and further from the Byzantine "Emperor-Patriarch" or the subsequent "Sultan-Patriarch" models, there has never been a better time or a better place for the establishment or re-establishment of such a model. Christianity flourished during its first three centuries, in spite of persecution because of the spiritual fervor of its adherents. Although the Church achieved political recognition after its establishment by Emperor and later Saint Constantine, and material gains during the next several centuries, the decline in spiritual life led to the establishment of the Monastic Movement. Most will agree that the spiritual life of the faithful is damaged when the Church becomes established and intertwined with the affairs of State. This indeed is one of the central insights of the American Bill of Rights, that both the State and the Church function best when they are independent of one another.

---

3. For a brief discussion of Autocephaly versus Autonomy see Something is Stirring in World Orthodoxy, by Rev. Dr. Stanley Harakas, Light and Life Publishing Co. Minneapolis, MN, 1978. pages 23-31.

As we have seen, the involvement and participation of the laity in the election of the clergy of all ranks has roots in Christianity's earliest days. Another aspect of the clergy-laity relationship has a geographical dimension to it.

The episcopate is the essence of the church only because it belongs within the sacramental framework of the believing community. According to Orthodox teaching the bishop is the chief celebrant of all the sacraments, with the priests receiving their limited sacramental authority from the bishop. Thus, the bishop should be a local chief pastor. "Wherever the bishop appears, there let the people be," writes St. Ignatius of Antioch. This would be impossible and meaningless if the bishop is hundreds, or even thousands of miles away. "There is one altar as there is one bishop with the priests and deacons." (To the Phil. 3) A bishop could not be at the altar of all churches at the same time as would be expected in a jurisdiction the size that is under the supervision of the "Archbishop of North and South America and Exarch of the Atlantic and Pacific." The community/parish model was a limited number of faithful in a limited geographical area under one bishop. The whole church was the local church found most often within the bounds of a single city. For if the prayer of one or two has so much power, how much greater is that of the bishop and of the whole church? (To the Eph. 3) The bishop is viewed always in connection with the council of priests. The collegiality of the priests is directly related to the authority of the ruling bishop. This too is comprehensible only on a local level.

When St. Ignatius states: "You must continue to do nothing apart from the bishop," he is referring to a bishop who is physically accessible and not a remote ceremonial figurehead hundreds or thousands of miles away. Otherwise the life of the church would be paralyzed and remain at an impasse caused by inaction, indecision and anxiety arising from the remoteness of the bishop. It is, therefore, clear that St. Ignatius sees the bishop as a father of a small, tightly-knit spiritual family in which the lay members and the priests are in close proximity to the bishop. "Be obedient too to the priests as the Apostles of Jesus Christ our hope" demonstrates the authority of the collegiality of the priests within a given area who maintain a close proximity with the ruling bishop. The bishop is a *typos* or icon of Christ only in a local setting. The wisdom of the practices of the early church having localized bishops (in the fourth century, for example, four hundred bishops existed in Asia Minor) has relevance in our times as well. The human heart is lashed with the same kinds of failings throughout the ages and pride has never ceased to be among the most pernicious evils. Bishops are not immune from this sin. Indeed the early church recognized this and used the practice of limiting the geographic sway of bishoprics to reinforce the dictates of spiritual humility. Many lay members of the Greek Archdiocese of North and South America apparently view church governance in terms of the Roman Catholic rather than the Orthodox model. Generations of adherence to the principle of blind obedience coupled with little, if any, religious education have conditioned the laity into acceptance of a mind-set that varies between indifference or hopeless exasperation on the one hand, and blissful hero-worship bordering on cult-like adoration of visible "Ethno-Religious" leaders, on the other hand. Few among the appointed lay leaders in the American Church seem to be aware that "the Patriarch of Constantinople's role is essentially that of a convener rather than that of a chief executive of a closely organized corporation. Orthodoxy is governed, on the world scene, by a spirit of consensus, rather than by directives from above . . . . **For the Orthodox the head of the Church is Christ, both in spirit and in reality."** (Rev. Dr. Stanley Harakas.) We believe that a return to the democratically elected bishops and decentralized authority of the early Church represents a model for the modern Church in America.

More than twenty years ago, Archimandrite Eusebius Stephanou addressed the issue of laity involvement in church governance as follows:

> *The Church is the Body of Christ consisting of laity and clergy. It is the prerogative and obligation of Christ's followers to state their views after investigating the issues. So long as they sit back with indifference, the Church can never function as a living organism in which all its members and parts are organically related and alive.*

The "they-know-what-they're-doing attitude" toward our hierarchy can only injure the interests of the Church. It is time this mentality changed. It is said that people get the governments they deserve. This holds true especially when applied to the Church. We get Church leadership we deserve and the decisions we deserve. We cater also to the equally harmful "What-do-the-laity-know" attitude of the clergy.

Who can doubt that the Church in America has come of age? But the priests and laity must show their age and maturity by doing more thinking and talking on the issues confronting the Church . . . .

If the Orthodox Church is the best-kept secret in America, and if it represents a spiritual alternative for the ninety million un-churched Americans who are looking for the One, Holy, Catholic and Apostolic Church of our Lord and Savior Jesus Christ, it is because in its theology, beliefs, and liturgical practices it has remained true to the Church of the first three centuries. By ridding itself of the influences of the secular rulers of the Old World, the Church in America can turn its attention to Christ's Great Commission and to educating its laity in the Word of God, so that as believing and worshipping laypersons, they can assist in the governing of the Church, including the election of their spiritual leaders, without themselves being guilty of abuses in the exercise of their ministry.

Proposed Selection Procedures

We have seen that the early church has provided us with models which not only have relevance today, but which are uniquely appropriate for conditions in America. Two models that we believe must be adopted are: (a) lay participation in the election of their church leaders, and (b) a restricted geographic area over which church leaders have jurisdiction. Both models are consistent with Orthodox teachings and traditions, as is the tradition of married bishops. These are not revolutionary departures for the Orthodox Church.

The dramatic change advocated by OCL has already begun to take place. That change consists of generating the necessary study and dialogue that will engage the laity, priests and hierarchs in the search for approaches that will serve the Church in the way Christ would approve. This search must be conducted with prayer, mutual respect and love.

Some will propose that before the laity is included in the election of bishops, priests should first be given the right to elect their bishop. Only after the right of priests to elect their bishop has been established, should the laity be included, as a "natural next step." (See suggestions of Archimandrite Eusebius Stephanou under Concluding Thoughts.)

Others will propose systems intended to insure that "nominal and uninformed" laity are excluded from the process. Some will propose that candidates for bishop be nominated only by bishops, or only by bishops and priests with the final election to be made by representatives of bishops, priests and the laity. Others will propose that lots be drawn either for the selection of the lay or other representatives to the body that chooses the candidates or elects the bishop from among the candidates, or as the method for final selection from among the candidates. Changes in jurisdiction will follow as a natural consequence of Orthodox Unity and Autocephaly, but neither will happen if the entire Church in America does not discuss and reach a consensus on these two important issues. Priests and bishops who refuse to engage in dialogue with the laity about these and any other issues confronting the Church, do violence to the concept of conciliarity which is basic to the ecclesiology of the Orthodox Church. (Commission 34:3). The ordination of married priests as bishops may require action at the forthcoming Great and Holy Council of the Eastern Orthodox Church. Preliminary meetings to discuss the agenda have been held in 1961, 1962, 1963, 1968, 1971, 1972, 1973 and 1976. No date has been set as yet for the meeting itself but, once again, **the consensus of the Church cannot be arrived at if the matter is not discussed.**

Concluding Thoughts

Obviously, if the laity and the priests are to regain a voice in the selection of their bishops, archbishops and, yes, patriarchs — changes need to be made both in the Constitution of the Archdiocese, in the role that the laity and clergy exercise in the selection of representatives on the Archdiocesan Council, and in the planning and execution of the Clergy-Laity Congress. The time has come for the laity and the priests to recognize their responsibilities as members of the Body. Only when they do, can we hope to realize the goal of an operative democratic church in America.

In view of the current authoritarian control that the Archdiocese exercises over the agenda, planning and conduct of the Clergy-Laity Congress, the necessary changes can be made only by an outpouring of positive activity on the part of priests and laity. Generating that activity is obviously one of the major goals of the OCL ministry.

As long as priests view their attendance at Clergy-Laity Congresses as nothing more than an opportunity to have a reunion with their classmates from Holy Cross (usually subsidized in whole or in part by their parishes), as long as large numbers of parishes cannot afford the outrageous costs of attending Clergy-Laity Congresses, as long as parish council presidents, and other lay delegates view their attendance at Clergy-Laity Congresses as opportunities to attend gala banquets and luncheons featuring political speakers and secular dignitaries, as long as the majority of Archdiocesan Council members are appointed by the Archbishop, and all automatic delegates to the Clergy-Laity Congress, little progress will be made on the key issues facing the Church.

The issue of lay participation in the election of bishops is not a new issue. Twenty-two years ago, in the December, 1969 issue of The Logos, Archimandrite Eusebius Stephanou wrote:

> Lay participation in the election of the clergy, be they priests,
> bishops, or patriarchs, is normative in Orthodox practice and
> dates back to the earliest days of Christianity. Hence, the

established custom of wording the announcement of such elections at the hour of consecration with: By vote of both clergy and laity. In later times it was revised thus: By vote and approval of the God-loving Priests and Clergy of the City of . . . .

*This is the form used currently by the consecrating bishop who is about to lay hands with two other bishops upon the candidate. But ironically **not only the laity, but even the priests today in the jurisdiction of the Ecumenical Patriarchate are kept out of the elections of their bishops.** To take an example of close proximity, neither priests nor laity in the Greek Archdiocese of America are consulted in the election of auxiliary bishops, least of all, of the archbishop. **No practice in the Orthodox Church could be more untenable and harmful both canonically and historically.** Only proper enlightenment and religious maturity can displace the ignorance and religious infantilism that in this respect sustain the docility and inertia among the priests and laity in the Greek Archdiocese.* [Emphasis Supplied]

Father Stephanou has assisted this Commission as a consultant, and we asked him to share his current thoughts on this issue with us. He wrote to us the following:

I believe the issue of lay participation in the election of the Archbishop and Bishops is directly related to the mode of administration in the Greek Orthodox Archdiocese of North and South America.

It is generally recognized that the current mode of administration of the Church is extremely centralized: the entire Church on two continents of the whole western hemisphere comes under the authority of one prelate. His power is virtually absolute in terms of administering the internal affairs of this imperial-sized jurisdiction. In effect he is not answerable to anyone. He handpicks his bishops and prevails over the Ecumenical Patriarchate to endorse his choices. The priests are never consulted. The result is that they have shown an apathy in this regard, indifference and cynicism. The auxiliary bishops likewise have fallen into this mental state.

Our first concern should be the decentralization of the Administration of the Archdiocese. This should have first priority. It is an exercise in futility to strive for lay participation in the election of the episcopate within a framework of religious totalitarianism. Such a concern for decentralizing takes on a special urgency in view of subtle efforts already underway to abrogate the new synodical system and to restore the older system of one ruling Archbishop with several auxiliary bishops. Local diocesan authority is being eroded step by step, presumably because the synodical system has failed.

Not only should the synodical system be preserved at all costs, but it should be reinforced, improved and perfected. It is not the synodical system, as such, that is inadequate and defective, but possibly the men who are handpicked as diocesan bishops are inadequate and lacking in leadership ability and competence. It is not logical nor fair to discredit the synodical system, therefore, when we consider the fact that the ruling Archbishop selects men for the episcopate who are generally docile, subservient and harmless to his supreme authority.

There is more likelihood for success in the effort for lay participation in the election of the episcopate within the framework of a decentralized mode of administration. To decentralize the Church is to centralize Christ as the true head of the Church. Spiritual Renewal means to bring Christ out of obscurity and to allow Him to govern His Church which he purchased by His own Blood. Too long have men usurped the position of Christ!

But when God's people in collective disobedience and rebellion prefer idols in the place of the sovereignty of Christ, divine judgment falls upon them and He condemns them by giving them the idols they choose.

The Ecumenical Patriarchate has from the beginning cherished the prerogative to elect the ruling archbishop for the Greek Archdiocese in America. They will need a lot of convincing otherwise in order to change at this point and begin consulting the laity in this country, or for that matter, even the priests.

It is more logical and effective to strive first for the rights of priests in the election of bishops. *How can the laity expect to be consulted in this regard when the priests themselves are totally excluded from the process of election? The Orthodox Christian Laity will be more likely to succeed on this issue if it were to first champion the rights of the priests to be involved in the election process. Once the priests are consulted in such elections, it will be far easier for the laity to follow suit and claim their prerogatives.*

Priority, therefore, should be given to re-establishing the rights of the Presbyterate to participate in the election of the Episcopate. Normally a bishop is elected from within the ranks of the priests (or presbyters). If a bishop is truly ***"theobrobletos"*** *(singled out by God), as he is called liturgically in his pheme, then in what better manner can the divine choice be manifested than by the consensus of his fellow-presbyters?*

It should be pointed out, however, that in the Early Church the laity very often decided by public acclamation their choice for the position of the local bishop who was to shepherd them. It was not the presbyters. The reason for this was simply because in that early period of the Church the bishop usually exercised pastoral authority over one city. In one sense the chief parish priest of a mother parish church in our own day is *what the bishop was back then. City-bishops was the norm in the Early Church (kata polin episcopoi). Thus it was only fitting for the laity to decide who their spiritual shepherd was to be. He was a man whom they knew possibly from childhood and recognized him for his godliness and virtue. **He was not a stranger coming from a distant city or country.***

The vote of the laity must spring from the grass roots level of the Church, otherwise lay participation runs the danger of being no improvement over the current practice. If lay participation is defined as laity appointed by bishops, or even priests, or laity who are prominent only for their material wealth or social or professional standing with no thought to their spiritual standing and Christian character, it is doubtful that the results will be pleasing to God.

Whether, as Father Stephanou states, it will be easier or even more logical for the laity to regain the right to participate in the election of bishops by first championing the rights of priests to do so, is a question we do not answer here. It is sufficient to note that when OCL advocates the right of the laity to participate in the process, it does not mean to **exclude** the right of priests to also participate in the process. As we have noted elsewhere in this Report, the answer must come from the entire Church. We invite you to join in the deliberations. Every baptized, chrismated Orthodox Christian has received the gift of the Holy Spirit. To the extent that any of us remains indifferent and uninvolved we deprive the Church of the fullness it can only enjoy when we are all functioning, integral parts of the Body. Let us all join together and our efforts will surely be blessed.

ORTHODOX
CHRISTIAN
LAITY

CHURCH ADMINISTRATION AND ACCOUNTABILITY
Sotiri Tsoutsouras[1]

Introduction

Laity have the right to let their pastors know about their spiritual needs and how they can be fulfilled; to advise Church leaders about what is good for the Church; to form associations of like-minded persons; to hold meetings; to enjoy a good name and reputation; to enjoy academic freedom; to perform certain roles in the liturgy; to oversee Church finances; to receive protection from illegally imposed sanctions. (McManus)

It is an un-Christian and un-Orthodox idea that there can exist a division between the "material" and the "spiritual" in Church life, or a division in the powers and privileges in these two spheres between the Laity and the Clergy.

Today the truly Orthodox conciliar approach to the totality of Church life and activity, including everything from the collection and disbursing of funds to the celebration of the Sacraments, is increasingly understood as the concern of ALL God's People, both Clergy and Laity (Hopko).

One often hears the cry that the Church is becoming too secular, that its material preoccupations too often impinge or influence the spiritual; that the Laity is becoming more and more disenchanted by its exclusion from the governance of the Church by the Hierarchy.

But as our Christian brothers quoted above indicate, there is no real problem for the true followers of our Lord. There is no "split" in the Church between

---

1. Also assisting in this study were George Coupounas, Rev. Mark Arey, Stephen J. Sfekas, Van Livadas and Minerva Stergianopoulos.

the secular and the spiritual, but rather a cohesive bonding, or "Syndiakonia," that as the Body of Christ the Church is administered according to Christian principles, eschewing the techniques used by purely secular institutions for their funding goals.

It is the prayer of Orthodox Christian Laity (OCL) that the recommendations and ideas suggested in the following Commission treatise: Church Administration and Accountability will help open windows for more effective Church Governance.

Utilization of the substantial Laity resources of talent and professional skills and experience must be harnessed by the Archdiocese and Dioceses to help our Orthodox Church meet the challenges of the coming new century.

Purpose and Goals

It is the aim of this commission to study the strengths and weaknesses of the administration of our institutional church. If our Church on all its levels, Archdiocese, Diocese and Parish, were being managed efficiently and effectively, there would be no issues to discuss, no problems to solve, no need to conduct this study and prepare this paper. Therefore, let us state briefly the specific purposes and goals of our report:

- To review significant and relevant existing regulations, practices and procedures regarding administration and financial accountability;

- To identify, examine and define areas of special concern;

- To explore, describe and suggest ways and means to address the issues, and make recommendations for improving the administrative structure of our institutional church so that it may operate more efficiently and effectively.

Issues — Points of Conflict

We fully understand that our religious organization is firmly based on the doctrines and canons of our faith. This report is not dealing with that aspect of our church; we fully accept and understand that our religious dogma clearly prescribes matters of faith and spiritual practices. We are, however, concerned with those aspects of managing and administering the church institution so that the faithful can approach it for their spiritual needs without thoughts and feelings of distrust, or suspicion of administrative and financial irregularities. We believe our church administration suffers from careless or inept management, and violations of the trust of the communicants. Relative to mismanagement or careless administration, much of this is the result of inexperience, incompetence, and on occasion abuse of power.

Briefly, the issues revolve around such specific areas as:

1. The financial relationship between the parish and the archdiocese; the administrative authorities of the parish council and the parish priest, the diocese, or with the archdiocese;

2. The absence of cooperation between and among these levels of authority or persons of "power";

3. The need to know accurate data regarding financial matters on the three levels, parish, diocese, and archdiocese;

4. Who controls what within each level of church existence;

5. The need to know how money is spent and for what reason;

6. The contradictory practices that exist on each level; and

7. The reasons for some irregularities and damaging procedures that destroy parts of entire communities or individuals.

Very often questions have arisen by some individuals around the country as to whether or not our church institution(s) have developed around a "personality cult." The variety of issues we encountered only serve to damage the worth of a parish or diocese or archdiocese. Thus, we believe our problems cannot continue to be systematically ignored; they must be identified and addressed, and ultimately appropriate solutions sought.

Certainly, this report cannot and will not address ALL the issues or questions, but to some degree will attempt to analyze major problems and then offer suggestions for reconstruction.

The institutional church

Before we proceed, it is important that we explain HOW we are using the phrase "institutional church." First, we do not capitalize the word church — so that we can separate Church (capital **c**) meaning the theological or religious institution, that segment which concerns itself with doctrine, from the temporal or secular aspects.

We recognize that the term institution is used with different meanings by various people. We are using it to mean a system of human activity, having considerable and reasonable permanence, a legal entity organized for specific purpose(s), required to abide by some fundamental or specific rules and laws, in our case to serve and complement our beliefs in Orthodoxy and sustain the Church in this country.

Administration

We must also provide the reader with a basic explanation of how we are using the term administration. An institution must have direction, must be managed by persons who accept the responsibility for the proper, efficient and effective operation of that institution. To carry on the "business" for which the unit was organized requires order, goals, rules and regulations, in short, knowledge of management/administration. Those persons who conduct the work of the unit need to have the necessary knowledge, expertise, and skills to carry on the work in accordance with the goals, needs, and purposes of the unit. Administration includes the qualities of leadership.

Accountability

We use this term to refer to the responsibility a person "in office," or appointed to a specific function and role by a group or a representative of a group, or a person in a significant position while representing a group or organization, HAS for explaining actions that occurred while he or she is in that position of responsibility, especially as the actions, results, or reasons affect the institution.

Any person in any kind of leadership position, be it major or minor, or in a position of responsibility, especially if financial responsibility is involved, must account for his or her actions and outcomes. We especially emphasize financial accountability, for this is an area that has damaged many a church community. Accountability, as we use it, includes all levels of our church institution, parish, diocese, archdiocese. The institutional church is responsible to the people who belong to it; to the members who support it both physically, morally, and financially. We expect our leaders, church employees and volunteers to maintain ethical standards with respect to their work as clergy or laity serving the community (parish, diocese, archdiocese). Since they are the persons responsible for conducting the day-to-day affairs of our church institution, they are responsible for the efficient functioning of the church and are obligated to report to those of us who form the "body" of the church. It is essential that complete information about the operations of the church be reported regularly through the <u>Orthodox Observer</u>, the Clergy-Laity Congress, the Archdiocese's Council and other public bodies of the church.

Administrative Structure

Those of us who go to our church and offer our service certainly have to be confused by the way our church institution is structured administratively. As one of our bishops put it recently, "The church at the Archdiocese level is Papal, and on the parish level it is congregationalist" (a form of church

161

government in which each local religious unit is independent and self-governing).

We would like to examine and redefine the roles of the clergy and laity on the parish, diocesan, and archdiocesan levels.

The Parish Level

Because of the way the parishes were formed in the early years of our Church in America, the lay people who founded the parishes would seek out a priest and hire him, or even appoint someone with some theological background to act as their priest. Back in those days there was no formal institution, an archdiocese as we have today, that could administer the religious needs of a community and provide the priests to the parishes. Consequently, the parishes looked upon the priest as an employee to be hired and fired as they saw fit. Peter Kourides has described the early years in his booklet, The Evolution of the Greek Orthodox Church in America and its Present Problems. Those first years saw the priest's job as one of performing religious services, performing and keeping records of sacraments, perhaps even being responsible for the upkeep of the physical building housing the Church, and, if asked, to be the teacher of Greek lessons, and little else.

As our Church developed and expanded, this attitude and practice of the employer-employee relationship on the part of the lay leaders became, in some instances, a source of misunderstanding and dissension. This is one point of conflict that must be corrected. We are now an advanced religious and social institution in the Americas; we have established procedures and requirements which we must follow. The **religious life** and in many cases, the **social and cultural** lives of our communities are fully dependent upon the leadership and supervision of our priest and we must recognize this if we are to do the true work of our Lord Jesus Christ.

We are at a point in our institutional development where we must acknowledge our parish priest as the religious head of the parish, just as we acknowledge our Bishop as head of the Diocese, and the Archbishop as head

162

of the Archdiocese. We have, for the most part, well-educated and trained clergyman whose sole purpose is to lead the religious life of a parish. If we acknowledge and respect the roles of our clergy, we should not object to their authority in matters of **FAITH and THEOLOGY**. However, we also know that occasionally theological decisions are blended with the personal attitudes of either a bishop or a priest, and then a conflict probably arises. For instance, in one diocese a priest may permit the marriage of an interfaith couple to take place with the minister of the non-Orthodox party present; and in another diocese the priest will prohibit such a service. There are many other instances and examples of contradictory actions within the Greek Orthodox Church. Another example, the sponsor (Godparent) of a Greek Orthodox child would be a Roman Catholic person. These are only two examples; there are numerous examples when religious rules were "waived" or ignored for a variety of questionable reasons. Sometimes it appears that selective religious rules are adhered to or bent to fit the occasion.

By the same token, the clergy must recognize and accept the proper role that the laity must assume in the administration of the church parish. How, you may ask, can we accomplish this? Let's consider the following:

1. In theological matters, the clergy should be the final authority; but, when asked, should be able to give a verifiable explanation.

2. In the matters of administration the responsibility must be shared by both laity and clergy; and this is explicitly stated in ARTICLE V, PARISH ADMINISTRATION in the Regulations.

3. When it comes to the formation of a **Parish Council**, the election of laity to serve on that body must NOT be conducted as a popularity contest NOR as a political contest. This unit may well be the most significant body in the entire church organization — BECAUSE it is responsible for the well-being, growth, and cultivation of the **parish community**. Therefore, these parish leaders must be committed to the purpose of the Parish Council, must be dedicated to service to the

Church — and their selection and election to serve on the Parish Council should be based on their religious dedication, abilities and competence, past experience, service and participation in parish life. The Special Regulations and Uniform Parish Regulations very clearly spell-out in great detail the qualifications for members to serve on the Parish Council. (See Articles VIII through XVII of the Regulations.) All too often, we see groups with special interests — interests that have nothing to do with the spiritual life of the Church — campaign and gain control of the Parish Council just so their special interests will be met; thus they dominate the life of the parish, and in all probability suffocate and stunt the life of the community. And, sadly, we often see parishes divided and ruined by such thoughtless and damaging tactics.

Many years ago, as many people may remember, parishes became divided along political lines — not by American politics, but by the politics of Greece. What do Greek politics have to do with **our religious life** in America? This must not be construed to mean that we advocate denial of or indifference to our heritage and cultural background. But we believe our Church and institutional church must be concerned primarily with **our spiritual life**. There is no room nor is our parish community a place for political battles. It is our belief that the Church as a whole, from the parish to the Archdiocese, must avoid entering the political arenas of either the United States or Greece in the name of the Greek Orthodox Church. We believe that the Church should be extremely careful about including political figures, either Greek or American, at events of the Church. The pulse of the community should be taken before the church is unwisely used for political advancement of individuals. Further, we must certainly understand, and adhere to the laws of this country, especially as they pertain to the separation of Church and State. We owe our lives, achievements, and successes to what THIS country has offered us; so we are obliged to live by the laws of this country.

We who are of Greek birth or descent are fortunate to have many secular organizations, such as, AHEPA, AHI, and others which have faithfully and competently championed the cause of the Greek-American people. They are the ones who should be looked to and should be encouraged to assume the responsibility of our political, cultural, and linguistic needs.

4. A fourth aspect: In making the Parish Council truly representative of the community the Parish Bylaws should have a provision to include the President of the Philoptochos — perhaps the most vital laity group in implementing people-to-people missions.

5. Consider Standing Committees established in parishes to address all the needs of a particular community. The chairpersons of the Standing Committees should be selected by the combined judgment and efforts of the Parish Priest and the Parish Council. These Standing Committees should be involved in Parish Council business only when it is necessary for them to report on their activities or projects. The persons chosen to chair the Standing Committees should have some appropriate background, expertise or proven experience in the role to which they are assigned. For instance, some of the Standing Committees which could be considered are these: (in random order)

- Day Care Center for children — where needed and facilities exist.

- Adult Religious Education — Spiritual Renewal, Bible Study, Preparation for Interfaith Marriage and Chrismation.

- Orthodox Unity — Interaction with other Orthodox Churches in the area.

- Mission and Outreach — reach out to the unchurched/welcome converts and interfaith couples.

- Youth programs and Young Adult programs.

- Golden Age programs.

- Afternoon Greek Classes, Parochial School (where needed and if possible).

- Evening Greek or English Classes for adults.

- Soup Kitchen for the Homeless.

- Liaison to non-Orthodox religious civic or humanitarian groups.

- Counseling Services, Family and Personal (by qualified persons).

- Ways and Means — Fund-raising projects.

- A Talent Pool of Retirees or Available Parishioners. (There is a great deal of expertise available from this group that is seldom tapped and used in our parishes.)

- Study of liturgical music for Greek and English services.

And so many more possibilities that can be established according to the needs of and the availability of volunteers in a particular parish.

These are but a few ideas regarding the life of the parish community. Each parish has its own unique requirements and should, therefore, study its environment and profile carefully in order to decide how to approach the administration of the parish **most efficiently and effectively**.

We impress upon the reader that SERVICE TO THE CHURCH must be recognized by both clergy and laity as a **shared ministry**. We are a family of God, and we must respect each other's responsibilities and efforts. Thus, as we undertake our various roles in the parish, we must remember that we are serving HIM, together with our fellow parishioners; and we must not engage in egocentric maneuvers that will destroy the very institution we are all working to strengthen. Our Church must remember that its responsibility is to be INclusive and NOT EXclusive.

The Diocese Level

Clearly prescribed in the Special Regulations of the Archdiocese (ARTICLE III) are the formation and requirements of a Diocesan Clergy-Laity Assembly. Section 4 of the Article states: **The Diocesan Assembly shall be convened by the Bishop annually.** Yet, some Bishops **never** convene such an assembly, while others convene assemblies only biennially.

There is no doubt that the Diocesan Assembly can be a very helpful part of the governance structure. It is interesting to note that the same article cited above states that the Assembly should "discuss matters of common concern and . . . submit proposals and recommendations to the Archdiocese for submission to the next Clergy-Laity Congress." Too often the meeting is not held and/or proposals not submitted.

We believe the Diocesan Assembly must not be ignored or omitted from the life of the institutional church. For purposes of efficiency and effectiveness, each Diocese should have a standard date for its meeting to take place and, of course, announced by the bishop "no later than ninety days in advance" as the regulations stipulate. This way the parishes can plan, prepare, and propose topics they want to place on the agenda. This time-frame also affords the parishes the opportunity to elect and instruct their delegates on the topics. And, knowing in advance when the Diocese Assembly will take place will also afford sufficient time for the host parish to make preparations.

The Diocese Assembly should be a working conference with a minimum emphasis on social and ceremonial activities and a maximum emphasis on working committees, workshops and discussion groups. Every opportunity should be given to the delegates and guests to exchange ideas, evaluate programs, study common problems and concerns, and take the necessary steps to enhance their Diocese and meet the needs of their constituent parishes.

It is our belief that in order to conduct a free and open conference, in order to share ideas and problems and understand them, and in order to make wise decisions, the **conference officers** must be elected by the delegates. This is not to say that the Bishop of the Diocese is not the Head of the Diocese, for he is. But, if he is also the presiding officer of the annual assembly, it is obviously very difficult to have a free and open conference, and in the long run it puts him in a very difficult position. He is the **spiritual leader** and can rule speakers out of order. It is imperative that the Bishop should maintain his position as the **religious leader** and be the guiding light and adviser to the assembly. He should counsel and help direct; he should NOT control and make the decisions for the entire body. In a democratic society and organization, the member delegates have the right and privilege of electing the officers of a meeting. This is correct parliamentary procedure and will allow the delegates to challenge, if necessary, the rulings of the Chair without feeling intimidated by the authority of a Bishop, thus, avoiding a confrontation with a religious leader. In this manner, we could truly have a free and open conference, and the delegates would know that they DO have the right, responsibility and opportunity to express their views. In the long run, the results will be far more acceptable and understandable, and the delegates will not return to their parishes with complaints and negative impressions.

If the real purpose of these Diocese Assemblies is to establish and cultivate a shared ministry between the clergy and the laity, then the **right** must be given to each Diocese **to elect those persons — men and women — whom the delegates believe will best represent their work, hopes, dreams, aspirations, and goals for their Diocese.** We, therefore, advocate the free election of conference officers.

Elect a Diocesan Council

If the Diocesan meeting operates with democratic principles, then it will be easy to continue that spirit and form a DIOCESAN COUNCIL which will be workable and productive. We suggest that the Diocesan Council be formed in the following manner. At the Diocese Assembly, five clergy and five lay persons should be elected by the delegates; the Bishop will appoint five additional persons, either clergy or lay or a combination, **making a total of fifteen persons on the Diocesan Council.** At their first meeting, they should elect their chairperson and secretary; and, of course, should meet at least quarterly with the Bishop. Further, both men and women should be considered for these positions, and the best qualified should be chosen.

The elected body of Diocesan Council members would also assist the Bishop in carrying out the mandates and programs of the Diocese.

We, of the Orthodox Christian Laity ministry, firmly believe that this type of fair and equal representation is absolutely essential if we are to establish and develop a ministry of lay participation. No matter how honorable and well-meaning the present members of the Diocesan Council may be, **they are not elected representatives of the parishes and dioceses**; they are appointees of the Bishop and they serve the one who appointed them, and not necessarily the church-at-large. More often than not, this closed and exclusionary procedure is a roadblock to free and open discussion of the real problems and needs of our parishes.

This is NOT how we should operate. We should not penalize people who may have differing points of view or who present a responsible opinion, or express an opposing idea; we should listen and try to understand and then let the majority decide whether or not the idea has merit. Too often we hear that the Diocesan Councils are run in an authoritarian manner.

There is no doubt in our minds that a Diocesan and ultimately the Archdiocesan Council will best serve our interests **when they are truly elected bodies.** We allow for one-third of the Diocese Council to be appointed by the Bishop; but the Council must be elected. They MUST be the representatives of the church members, their parishes. When the decisions and programs of the Diocese Assembly are made and announced, they reflect the work of all the parishes together, by the representatives of those parishes. Thus, the results, decisions and mandates will be accepted with greater interest and understanding. The parish delegates will return to their parishes with greater enthusiasm and vigor to put the programs to work, and not simply ignore the outcomes of the Assembly. There WILL BE greater satisfaction in cooperative work when the input has come from all the delegates.

If our church leaders, our hierarchs, expect the full and total support of the laity, and they should, then they must realize that the elected laity along with the elected clergy have the clear right and responsibility to participate in the decision-making process. ONLY THEN WILL WE BE ABLE TO EXPECT THE FULL AND TOTAL SUPPORT OF OUR PEOPLE.

As to the composition of the Assembly program, we must reflect what the parishes need and what their activities are. We must have workshops in which we teach and prepare delegates and guests about the specifics of parish administration and programming. We do have the **responsibility of preparing our people for service**. If the Diocese ignores this aspect of its work, it stands to lose many willing and capable people, who simply need a little inspiration, confidence, and training.

We may be too idealistic. We think not. The educational level and experience of our laity and clergy has advanced tremendously these past few decades. It is time for us to understand the needs of our people, especially our young people, **as we prepare to enter the 21st century**. If we can institute some of the procedures described here, we could truly reflect a SHARED MINISTRY OF LAITY, CLERGY, AND HIERARCHS. **The Diocese level is the middle of our church structure. It must be structured with the same democratic pattern as the parish.**

The Archdiocesan Level –
The Clergy-Laity Congress

Those of us who have attended the Clergy-Laity Congresses during the past twenty years or more, are certainly aware that these biennial meetings have become largely social, ceremonial, and political in nature. If we are to do the work of the church properly on the national level, then all the social functions must be either removed or minimized drastically. There is no need for a continual series of formal breakfasts, luncheons and dinners, with a variety of receptions in between. At most, there should be ONE formal luncheon, and one banquet with a limited number of speakers, and with speakers who will reflect the religious theme and tone of the event they are attending. Otherwise, the attendees are victims of irrelevant subjects and embarrassing moments.

Those of us who have attended the Congresses have ALSO seen inordinate delays in starting meetings; in postponements and cancellations of committee meetings because a social event ran too long; or a social event has to begin; or delegates need time to dress for a formal event; and so forth.

As a result, important meetings have been compressed into an hour or two, leaving little or no time for thorough and honest examination of the issues before the delegates. At best, topics are considered in a superficial manner.

It is disturbing to see hundreds of delegates, both clergy and laity, milling around in a hotel lobby with nothing to do because of the delays or cancellations. This is hardly **productive time-use**, and is really very costly for our parishes and delegates.

The Archdiocese should also consider the wisdom of moving the Clergy-Laity Congress **out of the big cities** where there are too many distractions, the costs are too high, and the atmosphere is not conducive to the spiritual-religious-administrative nature of the Congress. There are many **very appropriate conference centers** throughout the country that would be ideal for our kind of meeting. These conference centers also have their own hotel facilities, and they are located in more tranquil and appropriate environments than big-city hotels. If the atmosphere is appropriate, delegates are more likely to be more productive in their mission; and the tone of the Clergy-Laity Congress will be dignified and appealing. It is essential that the parish delegates have opportunities to meet and discuss topics of mutual concern with each other, with clergy and with hierarchs. Most professional, civic and religious organizations have already learned to use the facilities of conference centers where they are able to concentrate on their work and where they stand a better chance of achieving their goals. It's time for us to do the same.

Another area of our Congress structure and planning that requires attention is the **educational and training areas**. It is vitally important that we establish and conduct workshops on topics of religion, interfaith marriages, liturgical music, social issues, senior citizens, missions, outreach, youth program, fund raising, funding of our institutions, and administration and management of a parish and its components, and so many more subjects that are crying for attention and direction **from the top**. We need to utilize our competent professionals IN and OUTSIDE the church who can help prepare, guide, and conduct the workshops and training sessions we need. We need workshops that will help our men and woman who serve on parish councils understand their functions and roles better. We need workshops that will inspire young people to understand and be willing to participate in church administration properly.

Unless we use the Clergy-Laity meeting that is held every two years for **improving** our church institution, and **training** our people to better administer, and **providing** our people with spiritual renewal, WHY go to the trouble of holding these congresses? The legislative assemblies can do their work better when they have experienced the real meaning of CHURCH LEADERSHIP and ADMINISTRATION. It is incumbent upon the Archdiocese to provide such opportunities for making our church and parish administration more effective and productive.

As we explained earlier, it is essential for the Clergy-Laity Congress officers **to be elected** in the same manner that they are elected for the Diocese Conference. No one doubts that His Eminence the Archbishop is the over-all CHAIRMAN of the Congress; but the officer who actually conducts and presides over the assembly should NOT be the Archbishop or a Bishop or lay person **appointed** by him. It behooves the Archbishop to remain outside the legislative debates and to be present only to offer information, opinion and advice. The Archbishop should maintain his position as the **religious leader** and not be involved in "personality debates" nor must he be put in the position of ruling speakers out of order; this only tends to damage his role as religious leader. We must maintain respect and love for the Archbishop. He should be the guiding light and adviser to the congress; he should counsel and inspire.

He should **NOT** control and make decisions for the entire body, overlooking and ignoring the responsibilities of the delegates. Therefore, the elected presiding officer should be an unbiased person, man or woman, who is competent and capable, and who will be able to hold the respect of the delegates and conduct the proceedings in a truly business-like and professional manner according to established rules of parliamentary procedure. Furthermore, the Congress Committees must also have **elected** chairpersons, for they, too, need to be independent and responsive to the delegates.

We strongly recommend that strict adherence to schedules and meeting times be an important element of Congress. The plenary session MUST BE run in an orderly manner and take place as scheduled. Too often the program and schedule of the Conferences have been badly ignored and abused.

As we all know, the agenda for the Clergy-Laity Congress is prepared in advance by the various departments of the Archdiocese. Before the agenda is finalized, the parishes have **the right** to submit to the Archdiocese any item or topics they deem important to be INCLUDED on the agenda. In accordance with the Regulations, the Archdiocese notifies and invites the parishes to forward their input. The staff of the Archdiocese has the responsibility and obligation to prepare the **final agenda,** and to include ALL THE INPUT from the parishes, and then distribute the final agenda to the parishes **three months in advance of the Congress.** Only if that procedure is followed can we accept Archdiocesan claims that the congress is being conducted in a fair and open manner. Only if that procedure is followed will it be possible for the parishes to study the topics and instruct their delegates

173

accordingly. But, this procedure, though stipulated in the Archdiocese bylaws, has NOT BEEN FOLLOWED in the recent past.

Finally, in keeping with what should be the primary focus on religious matters, we recommend that secular political figures and governmental figures, whether Greek or American not be invited to the Congress. We believe that there should be only two exceptions to this rule. The mayor or governor of the host city or state may be invited to give a **brief** "welcome" and public officials of the Orthodox faith can participate having the same status as any other Orthodox lay person.

Archdiocesan Council

Regarding the Archdiocesan Council, let us, once again, review the recommendation we made in this paper for the Diocese level. The Archdiocesan Council should be comprised of at least two elected laypersons and at least one elected clergyman from each Diocese. Then, we must ADD to that combined group all the Bishops of the church, the elected president of the Presbyters' Council, the elected president of the Retired Clergy, and ten more qualified individuals (either clergy or laity) appointed by the Archbishop. The numbers could easily be adjusted, if it is appropriate to do so; but, the end result must be a fair and equal representation so that they will share the responsibility of "interpreting and implementing the decisions of the Clergy-Laity Congresses." We believe that such a structure is truly more representative, more democratic, and is in a better position to represent the interests of the entire church because it is accountable to a cross-section of our entire church institution.

ARTICLE II, Sec. 5 of the Special Regulations spell out in detail the purpose and functions of the Archdiocesan Council. The Archbishop is given the authority to select and appoint from the Archdiocesan Council an "Executive Committee of nine which shall have in the interim between meetings of the Archdiocesan Council all of its authority, excluding legislative powers." However, in Sec. 6 of the same Article, it states: "In the event legislation is required between Clergy-Laity Congresses, the Archbishop shall convene the

Archdiocesan Council for the purpose of adopting legislation." In other words, the Archdiocesan Council can have the same powers as the Clergy-Laity Congresses.

On the other hand, several members of Archdiocesan Councils have admitted that **very little, if any** serious work is covered in Council meetings; that most of the real work is done by the Executive Committee — the "super nine." Thus, most of the significant decisions of our Archdiocesan administration are made by nine persons who serve at the Archbishop's beck and call and owe allegiance totally and completely to him. This centralization of real legislative authority in the Church is a significant factor for sapping the vitality of both the Clergy-Laity Congress and the Archdiocesan Council. The restoration of power, authority and information to the Clergy-Laity Congress and the Archdiocesan Council are essential steps to revitalizing these fundamental structures of the Church. Reducing the size of the Council and providing for the election of its clergy and lay members will do much to make the Council more effective.

Financial Management

Recently serious questions have been raised by OCL and by other concerned laypeople concerning the financial management of the Church. The Archdiocese has announced that it is suffering a significant deficit and that it has had to reduce its support of important ministries of the Church. Additionally, the Archdiocese has sold off substantial real properties it owns in New York, and very nearly gave a long term lease for much of the land of the Holy Cross Seminary to private developers.

These indications of financial stress raise grave concerns of several types for OCL.

First, are the funds and operations of the Archdiocese being managed in as efficient and cost effective a manner as possible? Proper financial management is essential not only to reduce costs, but also as part of an effective fundraising program.

Second, if Archdiocese properties are to be sold, are they being sold as a result of a rational business plan or are they being sold for ready cash?

Third, are church properties being sold in a commercially reasonable fashion or is the church being burdened with excessive commissions, fees and charges?

Fourth, a full accounting of the church's financial position performed by outside independent auditors should be published regularly in the Orthodox Observer.

OCL is not in a position to state conclusions as to the financial status of the Archdiocese, but we do recognize the legitimacy of the concerns for our church.

We strongly recommend that a thorough review of the Archdiocese's financial affairs be performed by a firm of independent financial consultants to study the financial management of the Archdiocese, to recommend improved practices, and to create a financial plan to eliminate the deficit and, if necessary, to guide the disposition of real property.

The Orthodox Observer

The Observer is not only the voice of the Archdiocese to the community, it is also the voice of the community to itself. The newspaper on the whole has not performed either task in a satisfactory manner. Although the Observer covers the Archbishop's schedule in meticulous detail, there is rarely an article on the condition of the Archdiocese or its major ministries. Significant stories involving Orthodoxy are written in such an unbalanced fashion that the reader often has to read between the lines to catch the meaning of an article. A person could regularly read the Observer and be totally unaware of the status of the Archdiocese.

Furthermore, the Observer, perhaps uniquely among bilingual publications, functions as two different documents. The Greek language portion of the paper is not a translation of the English, but is often a wholly different newspaper with different articles and a different focus. The <u>Observer</u> thus treats the Church community as two separate audiences with very little in common.

The <u>Observer</u> also fails as a voice of the community. It is a scandal that the editorial policy of the <u>Observer</u> forbids any mention of OCL or other groups in its pages even though OCL frequently has been covered by the Greek, religious and secular papers. The <u>Observer</u>'s editorial policy should include objective articles and commentary about all issues of concern to the Church. It requires a "Voice of the People" section on vital concerns of the community.

Discipline

One of the most embarrassing moments in the history of the Church in this nation occurred when a bishop of the Church was accused of sexual misconduct with the daughter of a parish priest by a national newsmagazine. OCL cannot comment on the guilt or innocence of the Bishop. However, the procedural course of this case raises many questions about the operations of the Church.

So far as is known, the accusations against the Bishop have never been fairly resolved in either a civil or ecclesiastical tribunal of any kind. A civil suit against the Archdiocese was dismissed because it was filed after the expiration of the statute of limitations. The "ecclesiastical" court that was purportedly convened did not hear the testimony of the alleged victim. Thus, he has never had an opportunity to clear his name; the accuser has never had an opportunity to present her case, and the faithful even now cannot say whether a Greek Orthodox Bishop has disgraced himself and the Church or whether he is the innocent victim of false accusations.

The Church must adopt clearly understood procedures by which to resolve cases like this in a fair, just and open fashion. The status of this case does no one justice.

Management of the Archdiocese –
Another Approach to the Problems
We believe this paper has certainly focused on some of the most glaring problems in the administration (or governance) of our institutional church. We also believe that some important recommendations and solutions have been considered and included. Yet, we recognize that there are more ways to view the problems and perhaps find inspiration and guidance from them. Thus, we add to our report the following ideas that are strongly based in theological reasons.

Is THE CHURCH an institution? Even if the Church uses **institutional forms**, yet She is clearly NOT an institution. (It would be wise to speak of the Church as a person, rather than a thing.) The Church is the Body of Christ, a mystical, somatic entity. A better foundation for any call for "inclusiveness" would be the words of St. Paul.

> *Now ye are the Body of Christ, and members in particular.*
> *And God hath set some in the Church, first Apostles,*
> *secondarily prophets, thirdly teachers, after that miracles, then*
> *gifts of healing, helps, governments [administration might be*
> *included here], diversities of tongues.*
>
> *I Corinthians 12:27,28*

Now there certainly is a need to discuss these roles which define leadership in the Church. A discussion of the Apostolic, Prophetic, and Didactic duties and responsibilities of both the clergy and the laity is long overdue in the Orthodox Church. And it is in the somatic model of the Church that we have our paradigm for inclusiveness.

> *For the Body is not one member, but many. If the foot shall*
> *say, Because I am not the hand, I am not of the Body; is it*
> *therefore not of the Body?*
>
> *I Corinthians 12:14,15*

This approach would serve not only to encourage the laity in the tremendous diversity which our Church **really does afford** them, but it would also challenge the clergy as to **their real** role in service to Christ in His Church. What has happened instead is that the clergy, bishops and presbyters alike, have adopted the institutional forms of the secular world. These forms are nothing more than luxurious apparel on the Body of Christ, weighing down and burdening the Faith.

But what of the pretentious and imperious damasks we clothe our behavior in? Thankfully, in Christ we have a solution to this divergence from the meaning of Orthodoxy:

> *Jesus knowing that the Father had given all things into His hands, and that He was come from God, and went to God; He riseth from Supper and took a towel, and girded Himself. After that He poureth water into a basin and began to wash the Disciples' feet and to wipe them with the towel wherewith He was girded . . . . So after He had washed their feet and had taken His garments, and was set down again, He said unto them, Know ye what I have done to you? Ye call me Master and Lord: and ye say well, for so I am. If I then, your Lord and Master, have washed your feet; Ye also ought to wash one another's feet. For I have given you an example that ye should do as I have done to you. Amen, amen, I say unto you. The servant is not greater than his Lord; neither he that is sent greater than he that sent him. If ye know these things, blessed are ye if ye do them.*
>
> *John 13:3-5,12-17*

This is an Orthodox model for administration! It's timely for our day.

It is important to show how the basic foundation of any theological argument influences the approaches to solutions. Philip Sherrard said it this way in <u>The Eclipse of Man and Nature</u> (45):

*It is useless for Christians to try to grapple with and find
solutions for contemporary problems if the only intellectual
weapons they have to hand are those which contributed to the
production of these problems in the first place.*

Concluding Thoughts

In this report we have tried to focus on the major problems that seem to
impede the work of the institutional church. We are fast approaching the
21st century; we are living in a world of great social and political intensity.
We will see changes around us that we cannot begin to imagine at this time.
Are we ready to face this world with personal peace and understanding? Will
our children move into that environment knowing they have a religious home
— a Church — that can give them inspiration, peace, and guidance?

We fear that our institutional church will be facing more problems as the
world makes more demands on our lives. Our Orthodox people will not be
able to find an understanding church, a church governance and administration
that has **looked ahead** to envision and prepare for their needs, not to
mention the needs of the Orthodox in the 1990s.

We want to be proud of our institutional church and the manner in which it
is administered and managed; we want it demonstrated that it is achieving its
goals, that it is truly serving the faithful. We want to see it fit into the
world effectively, not only as a beautiful religious faith, but also as an
institution that can and will serve her people in an exemplary manner.

ORTHODOX UNITY[1]

Andrew Kopan, Chairperson[2]

PREFACE

At the Third Annual Conference of the Orthodox Christian Laity held in Chicago in November, 1990, Project For Orthodox Renewal was launched. Seven commissions defined the project, and were appointed to study matters/issues/problems confronting and of concern to the Orthodox Christian faithful in America in the 1990's. The Commission Report on Orthodox Unity follows.

The Commission on Orthodox Unity was composed of lay persons from several Orthodox jurisdictions in the Metropolitan Chicago Area. It was further assisted by a national advisory group of concerned Orthodox, both clerical and lay. The Commission approached its work with missionary zeal and met diligently over a two and a half-year period. It deliberated the multifaceted problem of canonical Orthodox unity from many perspectives starting from Scriptural and Patristic texts, the nature of the Church and its unity, as well

---

1. This Commission Paper is written in Commemoration of Ecumenical Patriarch Athenagoras, 1886-1972 and dedicated to the memory of Rev. John Meyendorff, 1926-1992, priest, scholar and theologian, whose lifetime devotion to the cause of Orthodox Church unity in America was tireless.

2. This paper was authored by the Commission on Orthodox Unity which in addition to Dr. Kopan, consisted of the following members: Dr. Thomas E. Klocek, Vice Chairman, Peter N. Kent, Secretary, George D. Karcazes, James A. Koulogeorge, Leon C. Marinakos, John S. Vougis. Also offering assistance as consultants were: Clifford T. Argue, Rev. Dr. Anastasius C. Bandy, Rev. Dr. Demetrios J. Constantelos, Dr. James Steve Counelis, Rev. James L. Doyle, Rev. Vasile Hategan, Nick Mamalakis, George Matsoukas, Dr. John E. Rexine, Rev. George J. Scoulas, V. Rev. Eusebius A. Stephanou, H. Keith Sterzing, and Rev. Steven J. Vlahos.

as applicable canon law, and developed a historical profile of the present "disunited" Orthodox jurisdictions in America. Seriousness, respect and a sense of dedication fueled all aspects of the discussion and deliberations which were preceded by the invocation for guidance by the Holy Spirit.

From the outset, the Commission recognized its own fallible shortcomings and the always present pitfalls of arrogance. In embarking on its task, the point of departure was the existing situation which many feel must be either justified or changed. Since no adequate position on the perceived "problem of disunity" has been articulated and forthcoming from the hierarchy, the laity, in its role as the "royal priesthood" (I Peter 2:9), has exercised not only its right but its obligation, reminding the Church when it is remiss, for whatever reasons, in exercising spiritual leadership. If Truth is the pronouncement, promise and province of the Church, then its pursuit, perfection and promulgation is no less the responsibility of the laity who also comprise that Body.

Thus, this Report represents a consensus of the views of the members of the Commission and, in the search for that Truth, the Commission believes it reflects the thoughts and opinions of the general membership of the Orthodox Christian Laity. As such, it is a "grass roots" input to the unity question of concern to many.

The deliberations of the Commission on Unity arrived at three models for achieving jurisdictional/ administrative/organizational unity. They constitute the core of this Report. They are presented to all the Orthodox faithful — clergy and laity alike — with humility and no pretense for having exhausted all scenarios to achieve unity. It is prayerfully hoped that this Report will be received with the seriousness that permeated its creation and will become a springboard for discussion and, ultimately, for decision and a positive course of action on the part of all. This Report will be circulated broadly to hierarchy, clergy and lay leadership of the several Orthodox jurisdictions in America.

The Commission wishes to express its appreciation to the many individuals, clerical and lay, who have contributed to this Report and provided their valuable expertise to critique it. Any possible errors in the text are the responsibility of the Commission and not of these individuals. The Commission also expresses to the OCL Board of Directors its deep appreciation for its cooperation and support.

> *Behold how good and pleasant it is when brethren dwell together in unity.*
>
> *Psalms 133:1*

COMMISSION ON ORTHODOX UNITY
Feast of the Annunciation   March 25, 1993

183

**ORTHODOX
CHRISTIAN
LAITY**

ORTHODOXY IN AMERICA: THE UNITY WE SEEK

By one Spirit we were all baptized into one body — Jews and Greeks, slaves or free — and all were made to drink of one Spirit.

I Corinthians 12:15

INTRODUCTION

Charge to the Commission

When the Commission on Orthodox Unity was appointed in the Autumn of 1990, its members were all aware of their solemn responsibility before God and man. Indeed, of all the commissions appointed by OCL, this one is seriously charged with the difficult and even painful task of confronting the reality of Orthodoxy in America. Of course, the temptation to gloss over the unpleasant and nettlesome facts were great. However, all of the Commission members agreed that the ultimate commitment to Christ and His Church lay in affirming the truth precisely because, for Orthodox Christians, Truth itself is a Person, namely Jesus Christ. In this manner, the members have prayerfully sought the Lord, Himself.

I do not ask in behalf of these alone, but for those also who believe in Me through their word; that they may all be one; even as You, Father, are in Me and I in You, that they also may be in Us; that the world may believe that You have sent Me.

John 17:20-21

In Christ's High Priestly prayer before His life-giving Passion and Death on the Cross, He speaks again and again of the unity of His disciples. The prerequisite for true discipleship is unity with others in and through Christ. In fact, John 13's description of the betraying Judas is cast in terms of his separating from the other disciples. In short, true discipleship is defined by and demands unity with Christ and with one another.

185

As Orthodox Christians in America, we are sadly aware that the inner reality and the external manifestation of that reality are at variance. No one can seriously view Orthodoxy in this country and judge otherwise. Yet, for various complex and sundry reasons, the situation continues (and grows worse). Such a spiritual crisis deeply affects every Orthodox Christian. Accordingly, we have undertaken the task of both detailing the Church's past and present, especially as it exists in America, as well as attempting some tentative and provisional recommendations for the future. Obviously, some will view all this as audacious and ask, "Who gave you the authority?" The decision to offer this report flows from the OCL's concern for the future of the Church and from the Commission members' concrete and personal experience in the Church and their serious and prayerful reflecting on the Word of God. Further, the witness of the Holy Fathers is conclusive as to the absolute necessity for unity in the Church.

Finally, the most telling and condemnatory evidence lies in the misapplication of Orthodox ecclesiology here in America. As a result of skewing the facts, the results cannot be but warped. The truth is that no Orthodox Christian in America is living a "normal," canonically correct life. All experience the reality of our abnormal situation. This Report humbly and prayerfully attempts to address this very serious matter.

Rationale For Seeking Unity
This Report is specifically directed to the People of God, Orthodox believers in America. The question of unity affects their entire life in the Church on a number of levels. Primarily, the canonical union of the Orthodox jurisdictions here will bring the American Church in line with the richest possibilities of Orthodox life. Much of the Church's difficulty in witnessing in the United States lies in the dissonant, uncooperative nature of the present status of Orthodoxy in America. Consequently, we lose a unique opportunity given to us by historical and spiritual circumstances which is the mission to the West. "A universal missionary Orthodox Church simply cannot endure or survive for long within an American context without unity" (Papadakis 187).

A narrowly constructed, ethnically-centered Orthodoxy betrays an unfortunate sectarian tendency which renders other work ineffectual or meaningless. Scarce human and financial resources are divided into duplicative projects in Christian education, philanthropy and mission outreach. Orthodox jurisdictions "do things," but not the Orthodox as a whole. Particularly telling is Orthodoxy's lack of a moral-ethical voice in the American arena. Many perceive that Orthodoxy either has no moral positions or else that they are simply unknown. The net result is the same. Orthodoxy remains America's best-kept secret.

The present predicament is caused by human error and misperception. The solution can only come from us. Once we have prayerfully and sincerely determined who we are and what our mission is, the light will appear at the end of the tunnel. "Our destiny is to witness to Orthodoxy in the West. It is our duty, as informed churchmen and laity, to make the solidarity of our future a genuine reality now. To remind our hierarchy of this fact firmly, persistently, and politely is our prerogative as members of the Catholic Church of Christ" (Papadakis 188).

ORTHODOX ECCLESIOLOGY AND CHURCH UNITY
Introduction to Scriptural Texts
The following citations from the New Testament are striking exponents of the unity theme which course through the Gospel, Acts of the Apostles, as well as the Epistles. Of particular significance is the fact that all four Gospels record sayings and exhortations of Christ, Himself, on the subject, especially in the context, both of His forthcoming Passion and His last words to the apostles before His Ascension. In both cases, the Lord reminds His followers that unity is characteristic of the Church, an essential mark of its work and mission. These selections from the Acts and the Epistles are proof positive that, in the development of the early Church, the issue of unity was paramount. This concern is expressed in concrete terms in the communications which the Epistle writers addressed. The words of Christ and the expressions of the early Church community form an eloquent and convincing call for unity.

Scriptural References to Church Unity (RSV)
John 17:20-23

> I do not pray for these only, but also for those who are to believe in me through their word, that they may all be one; even as thou, Father, art in me, and I in thee, that they also may be in us, so that the world may believe that thou hast sent me. The Glory which thou hast given me I have given to them, that they may be one even as we are one, I in them and thou in me, that they may become perfectly one, so that the world may know that thou hast sent me and hast loved them even as thou has loved me.

Matthew 28:18-20

> And Jesus came and said to them, "All authority in heaven and on earth has been given to me. Go therefore and make disciples of all nations, baptizing them in the name of the Father and of the Son and of the Holy Spirit, teaching them to observe all that I have commanded you; and lo, I am with you always, to the close of the age."

Mark 16:15-16

> And he said to them, "Go into all the world and preach the gospel to the whole creation. He who believes and is baptized will be saved; but he who does not believe will be condemned."

Luke 24:45-47

> Then he opened their minds to understand the scriptures, and said to them, "Thus it is written, that the Christ should suffer and on the third day rise from the dead, and that repentance and forgiveness of sins should be preached in his name to all nations, beginning from Jerusalem.

John 7:33-38

> Jesus then said, "I shall be with you a little longer, and then I go to him who sent me; you will seek me and you will not find me; where I am you cannot come." The Jews said to one

another, "Where does this man intend to go that we shall not find him? Does he intend to go to the Dispersion among the Greeks and teach the Greeks? What does he mean by saying 'You will seek me and you will not find me,' and, 'Where I am you cannot come'?" On the last day of the feast, the great day, Jesus stood up and proclaimed, "If any one thirst, let him come to me and drink. He who believes in me, as the scripture has said, 'Out of his heart shall flow rivers of living water.'"

John 10:16

And I have other sheep, that are not of this fold; I must bring them also, and they will heed my voice. So there shall be one flock, one shepherd.

John 15:18-21

If the world hates you, know that it has hated me before it hated you. If you were of the world, the world would love its own; but because you are not of the world, but I chose you out of the world, therefore the world hates you. Remember the word that I said to you, "A servant is not greater than his master." If they persecuted me, they will persecute you; if they kept my word, they will keep yours also. But all this they will do to you on my account, because they do not know him who sent me.

Acts 10: 34-35

And Peter opened his mouth and said: "Truly I perceive that God shows no partiality, but in every nation any one who fears him and does what is right is acceptable to him."

I Corinthians 1: 22-24

For Jews demand signs and Greeks seek wisdom, but we preach Christ crucified, a stumbling-block to Jews and folly to Gentiles, but to those who are called, both Jews and Greeks, Christ the power of God and the wisdom of God.

I Corinthians 12:12-13

> *For just as the body is one and has many members, and all the members of the body, though many, are one body, so it is with Christ. For by one Spirit we were all baptized into one body — Jews or Greeks, slaves or free — and all were made to drink of one Spirit.*

I Corinthians 14:19

> *Nevertheless, in church I would rather speak five words with my mind, in order to instruct others, than the thousand words in a tongue.*

Galatians 3:27-28

> *For as many of you as were baptized into Christ have put on Christ. There is neither Jew nor Greek, there is neither slave nor free, there is neither male nor female; for you are all one in Christ Jesus.*

Ephesians 4:4-6

> *There is one body and one Spirit, just as you were called to the one hope that belongs to your call, one Lord, one faith, one baptism, one God and Father of us all, who is above all and through all and in all.*

Colossians 3:9-11

> *Do not lie to one another, seeing that you have put off the old nature with its practices and have put on the new nature, which is being renewed in knowledge after the image of its creator. Here there cannot be Greek and Jew, circumcised and uncircumcised, barbarian, Scythian, slave, free man, but Christ is all, and in all.*

Introduction to Patristic Texts

The following Patristic selections all center around the theme of unity. After Christ's Ascension and the coming of the Holy Spirit at Pentecost, the Church grew rapidly throughout the civilized world, spreading to the major cities of the Roman Empire. Certain Christian teachers and preachers became famous for their knowledge and defense of the Faith. In the changing circumstances and cultural tumult of those early centuries, these "Church Fathers" acquired a pre-eminence of authority and veracity precisely because they added to the essential Gospel message. Indeed, they formed the direct lineage from Apostolic times, since, taken as a whole, these authorities continued to witness to Christ in their own times, and, down to ours, in an infallible fashion. In every passage cited of the Fathers — Eastern and Western — the focus is the unity of the Church. These holy men knew, from direct and concrete experience, that all else in the life of the Church depended upon it, is nurtured by it. In short, for the Fathers, to be in Christ, to be Christian, is to be **one**. There could not be any substitution or obfuscation — One Faith, One Lord, One Baptism.

Patristic References to Church Unity (Jurgens)[3]
St. Ignatius of Antioch: <u>Letter to the Smyrnaeans</u> (1, 1)

> *I give glory to Jesus Christ, the God who has made you wise; for I have observed that you are set in faith unshakable, as if nailed to the cross of our Lord Jesus Christ in body and in soul; and that you are confirmed in love by the Blood of Christ, firmly believing in regard to our Lord that He is truly of the family of David according to the flesh (1), and God's Son by the will and power of God, truly born of a Virgin, baptized by John so that all justice might be fulfilled by Him (2), (2) in the time of Pontius Pilate and Herod the Tetrarch truly nailed in the flesh on our behalf, — and we are of the fruit of His divinely blessed passion, — so that by means of His resurrection He might raise aloft a banner (3) for His saints and believers in every age, whether among the Jews or among the gentiles, united in a single body in His Church (4).*

---

3. All numbered references are as organized by Jurgens.

Hermas: The Shepherd (Par. 9, 17, 4)
(The shepherd said:)   "All the nations which dwell under heaven, when they heard and believed, were called by the name of the Son of God. When, therefore, they received the seal, they had one understanding and one mind; and their faith became one, and one their love; and they carried the spirits of the virgins along with the name; and that is why the structure of the tower was in one splendid color like the sun (5)."

Hermas: Letter to Diognetus (6, 1)
To put it briefly, what the soul is in the body, that the Christians are in the world. (2) The soul is spread through all parts of the body, and Christians through all the cities of the world. (3) The soul dwells in the body, but it is not of the body; and Christians dwell in the world, though they are not of the world. (4) The soul is invisible, but it is sheathed in a visible body. Christians are seen, for they are in the world; but their religion remains invisible.

St. Justin the Martyr: Dialogue with Trypho the Jew (117)
(Justin)   "There is not one single race of men — whether barbarians or Greeks, or of whatever name they may be called, either wagon-dwellers or those who are called homeless or herds-men who dwell in tents — among whom prayers and thanksgivings are not offered to God the Creator of all things, in the name of the crucified Jesus."

St. Irenaeus: Against Heresies (1, 10, 2)
For, while the languages of the world are diverse, nevertheless, the authority of the tradition is one and the same.

Neither do the Churches among the Germans believe otherwise or have another tradition, nor do those among the Iberians, nor among the Celts, nor away in the East, nor in Egypt, nor in Libya, nor those which have been established in the central regions of the world. But just as the sun, that creature of

God, is one and the same throughout the whole world, so also the preaching of the truth shines everywhere and enlightens all men who desire to come to a knowledge of truth.

Nor will any of the rulers in the Churches, whatever his power of eloquence, teach otherwise, for no one is above the teacher (6); nor will he who is weak in speaking detract from the tradition. For the faith is one and the same, and cannot be amplified by one who is able to say much about it, nor can it be diminished by one who can say but little.

St. Irenaeus: <u>Against Heresies</u> (3, 4, 1)

If there should be a dispute over some kind of question, ought we not have recourse to the most ancient Churches in which the Apostles were familiar, and draw from them what is clear and certain in regard to that question? What if the Apostles had not in fact left writings to us? Would it not be necessary to follow the order of tradition, which was handed down to those to whom they entrusted the Churches?

Tertullian: <u>The Demurrer Against Heresies</u> (20, 7)

Any group of things must be classified according to its origin. Therefore, although the Churches are so many and so great, there is but the one primitive Church of the Apostles, from which all others are derived. (8) Thus, all are primitive, all are apostolic, because all are one. The communication of peace, the title of brotherhood, and the bond of hospitality prove her unity: (9) privileges which no other principle governs except the one tradition of the same sacrament (4).

Eusebius Pamphilus: <u>History of the Church</u> (3, 1, 1)

The holy Apostles and disciples of the Savior, however, were scattered throughout the whole world. Thomas, as tradition holds, received Parthia by lot; Andrew, Scythia; John, Asia, busying himself among the people there until he died at Ephesus. (2) Peter, however, seems to have preached to the

Jews in the diaspora in the Pontus and in Galatia, Bithynia, Cappadocia, and in Asia; and at last, having come to Rome, he was crucified head downwards, the manner in which he himself had thought it fitting to suffer. Is it needful to say anything of Paul, who fulfilled the gospel of Christ from Jerusalem to Illyricum, and afterwards in the time of Nero was martyred in Rome?

St. Cyril of Jerusalem: <u>Anti-Clerical Lectures</u> (18, 26)

And if ever you are visiting in cities, do not inquire simply where the House of the Lord is — for the others, sects of the impious, attempt to call their dens the Houses of the Lord — nor ask merely where the Church is, but where is the Catholic Church. For this is the name peculiar to this holy Church, the Mother of us all, which is the Spouse of our Lord Jesus Christ, the only-begotten Son of God.

Nationalism and Phyletism in the Church

Our Lord established one church, ". . . one Lord, one faith, one baptism," (Ephesians 4:5). From the very beginning, there were divisions, theological and doctrinal, most of which have been dealt with and resolved by the Ecumenical Councils of the first seven centuries. But some of these divisions have had a nationalistic or ethnic base. This was first manifested in Apostolic Times when early Jewish Christians conceived the new faith for those of the Jewish world only. The defiance of St. Paul, who became the "Apostle to the Gentiles," (Acts 15) and the decrees of the Apostolic Council of Jerusalem resolved that issue — that Christianity was indeed for all people: "There is neither Jew nor Greek, there is neither slave nor free, there is neither male nor female; for you are all one in Christ Jesus." (Galatians 3:27-28).

But notwithstanding this Biblical exhortation, nationalism or phyletism always reared its divisive head in both parts of the Universal Undivided Church of the first ten centuries as evident by the rise of "national" churches in Spain and France and in Egypt and other parts of the East. Yet by the time the Council of Chalcedon (451) and certainly by the two following Ecumenical Councils of

Constantinople II (553) and Constantinople III (680), the assembled bishops were seen as representing five patriarchates — Rome, Constantinople, Alexandria, Antioch, and Jerusalem.

Authentic ecumenicity required the participation of these five patriarchates, either in person, or by proxy, or, at least, as in the case of Pope Vigilius and the Council of 553, in the form of a *post factum* approval. This system of *pentarchy*, the governing of the Universal Church by five rulers, equal in dignity, but related to each other by a strict order (taxis) of precedence, was a Byzantine vision enshrined in the legislation of Emperor Justinian I (Meyendorff Imperial Unity 327). The only exception to this was the Church of Cyprus, a lonely survivor of the old provincial system which was declared autocephalous in 432 by the Third Ecumenical Council at Ephesus (Callinikos 57).

But the unity of the Church was not destined to last long. Already in the early centuries of the Church there were forces creating divisions. The rise of heresies such as Monophysitism and Monotheletism, among others, brought about a rupture in the unity of the Church resulting in the creation of schismatic churches (now called Non-Chalcedonian or Oriental Orthodox churches) during the 5th and 7th centuries.

The Great Schism of 1054 between East and West was, of course, a significant rupture which brought about the end of the Undivided Church of the first ten centuries resulting in the creation of two major rival churches — Greek Orthodoxy in the East and Roman Catholicism in the West. Later in the 15th century another rupture was caused in the Western Church by the Protestant Reformation.

Following the travails of the Byzantine Empire in its attempts to stave off its imminent collapse under the Ottoman Turks, the Church of Russia, which had always been administratively dependent on the Ecumenical Patriarchate at Constantinople and whose Metropolitan of Kiev and All Russia was generally a Greek, rebelled against the authority of Byzantium and in 1448 selected its own metropolitan to replace Isidore the Greek who had signed the Unionist Agreement with Rome at the Council of Florence. However, the new metropolitan, Jonas of Ryazan, was not acceptable to Constantinople and the rupture continued until 1587 when Patriarch Jeremiah II of Constantinople visited Russia and established the new "Patriarch of Moscow" to replace Rome which had fallen away because of the Great Schism and thus restoring the *pentarchy*. Thus, the Church of Russia became the first national church of Orthodoxy (Meyendorff Byzantine Tradition 45-60).

In 1830, following the successful Greek Revolution and the independence of Greece from Turkish domination, the religious authorities of the new nation, not wishing to be under the control of the Ecumenical Patriarchate, which was subject to Turkish suzerainty, declared the Church of Greece autocephalous, thus establishing the second "national church" of the modern era. This act was not recognized by the Ecumenical Patriarchate, and the Greek church remained in schism until 1850, when the Ecumenical Patriarchate recognized a *fait accompli* (Sherrard, 182-199).

This pattern was to recur over and over again as one by one the Balkan nations gained their independence from the Turks. Thus Serbia became formally autocephalous in 1879; Romania in 1885; Albania in 1937; and Bulgaria in 1945, after a long schism lasting from 1870. Georgia became autocephalous in 1917. This chain of events created the modern "national" autocephalous churches which today comprise the worldwide Orthodox Church (See Directory, Appendix I).

Synod of Constantinople (1872) and Condemnation of Phyletism

It was the Bulgarian Schism, however, which precipitated for the part of the Church as to the precise role of nationalism or ethnicity (then known as phyletism) in the life of the Church. The claim of the Bulgarians that on the basis of their ethnicity they were entitled to be an autocephalous church despite the fact that at that time it did not comprise a national state (still being part of the Ottoman Empire), unlike the newly independent Balkan states, provoked the Ecumenical Patriarchate to convene a Synod at

196

Constantinople in 1872 which was attended by the heads or representatives of all the autocephalous churches of Orthodoxy. Presided over by Patriarch Anthimus VI of Constantinople, the Synod condemned as heresy the acceptance of *phyletism* or ethnicity as being the decisive factor in church organization.

Conforming to that decision is a condition for Orthodox Christian unity in today's world, and remains the basic principle regarding church unity — that is, that the organization of the Church along ethnic lines in the same geographical area is a heresy (Meyendorff Vision 67 & 69). The ethnic divisions of Orthodoxy existing in America today, are thus clearly inconsistent with the decision of the 1872 Synod of Constantinople.

Relevant Canon Law on Unity in the Church (Schaff and Wace; Cummings; Mastrantonis)
As there are scriptural and patristic references to Church unity, likewise there are similar references to be found in canon law. Of particular importance to this theme are canons 8 and 15 of the 1st Ecumenical Council (Nicea, 325); canon 2 of the 2nd Ecumenical Council (Constantinople, 381); canon 5 of the 4th Ecumenical Council (Chalcedon, 451), and canons 14 and 15 of the Synod of the Holy Apostles (Jerusalem, 1st century).

Canon law, of course, is the product of the Ecumenical Synods or Councils which were convened in the first seven centuries of the early Undivided Church to combat the rising heresies that threatened the unity of the Church. According to the conciliar system that prevails in the Orthodox Church, the right of administration of the Church is given not only to clergymen, but even to the laymen, a system which has been preserved to this day. In the Orthodox Church, the laymen are not excluded from the administrative functions of the Church. They are especially prominent in the election of candidates for clergymen and in their indispensable cooperation in the formulation of the "Conscience of the Church," which is the unshakable basis of conciliarity and supreme authority in the Orthodox Catholic Church.

Thus, on the basis of the principle of the oneness of the Church, the highest administrative tribunal in the ecclesiastical hierarchy and government is the Ecumenical Synod, the General Assembly of the bishops of the entire Church. The decrees of such a Synod or Council, when definitely accepted by the "Conscience of the Church," constitutes the supreme authority in the Orthodox Church.

The decrees of the Ecumenical Synods are of two types: One refers to doctrinal subjects, usually in the form of statements of faith called *oroi*; the other refers to the administration or juridical subjects in decrees usually called *canons*. The *oroi* (for example, the Creed, the doctrine of the two natures in Christ), are unchangeable. The *canons* can be amended, but only by a decree of a new Ecumenical Synod. There are some *canons* with doctrinal content in their preamble or in their objective, although they are of a secondary value.

The canons relevant to Church unity are of this latter type. They were formulated in order to establish an order for discipline and administration, as well as for the regulation of some of the external functions of worship and devotion. While most of these relevant canons were formulated by the Seven Ecumenical Synods meeting from 325 to 787, some were decreed by earlier regional synods such as that of the Holy Apostles at Jerusalem in the 1st century and have equal validity as the canons of these earlier councils ratified by the Ecumenical Councils.

The relevant canons are as follows:

Canon 14 (Canons of the Holy Apostles)[*]

> *A bishop is not to be allowed to leave his own parish, and pass over into another, although he may be pressed by many to do so, unless there be some proper cause constraining him*

---

[*]   These canons were compiled during the Apostolic Era and were confirmed by the 1st Ecumenical Council in 325.

as if he can confer some greater benefit upon the persons of that place in the word of godliness. And this must be done not of his own accord, but by the judgment of many bishops, and at their earnest exhortation.

Canon 15 (Canons of the Holy Apostles)`

If any presbyter or deacon, or any other of the list of the clergy, shall leave his own parish, and go to another and having entirely forsaken his own, shall make his abode in the other parish without the permission of his own bishop, we ordain that he shall no longer perform divine services; more especially if his own bishop having exhorted him to return he has refused to do so, and persists in his disorderly conduct. But let him communicate there as a layman.

Canon 34 (Canons of the Holy Apostles)`

It is the duty of every nation to know the one among them who is the first, and to recognize him as their head, and to refrain from doing anything unnecessary without his advice and approval; instead, each of them should do only whatever is necessitated by his own district and by the territories under him. But let not even such a one do anything without the advice and consent and approval of all. For only thus will there be concord, and will God be glorified through the Lord in Holy Spirit, the Father, and the Son, and the Holy Spirit."

Canon 8 (1st Ecumenical Council, Nicaea, 325)

. . . For in one city there shall not be two bishops.

Canon 15 (1st Ecumenical Council, Nicaea, 325)

Neither bishop, presbyter, nor deacon shall pass from city to city. But they shall be sent back, should they attempt to do so, to the churches in which they were ordained.

Canon 2 (2nd Ecumenical Council, Constantinople, 381)

The bishops are not to go beyond their dioceses, nor bring confusion on the churches; but the Churches of God in heathen nations must be governed according to the custom which has prevailed from the time of the Fathers.

Canon 3 (2nd Ecumenical Council, Constantinople, 381)

The Bishop of Constantinople, however, shall have the prerogatives of honor after the Bishop of Rome; because Constantinople is New Rome.

Canon 23 (Synod of Carthage, 419)**

That any province on account of its distance can have its own primate.

Canon 8 (3rd Ecumenical Council, Ephesus, 431)

None of the God-beloved bishops shall assume control of any province which has not heretofore, from the very beginning, been under his own hand or that of his predecessors.

Canon 5 (4th Ecumenical Council, Chalcedon, 451)

Concerning bishops and clergymen who go about from city to city, it is decreed that the canons enacted by the Holy Fathers shall still retain their force.

Canon 18 (4th Ecumenical Council, Chalcedon, 451)

The crime of conspiracy or banding together is utterly prohibited even by the secular law, and much more ought it be forbidden in the Church of God. Therefore, if any, whether clergymen or monks, should be detected in conspiring or banding together or hatching plots against their bishop or fellow clergy, they shall by all means be deposed from their own rank.

** This is Canon 17 in the Latin version text.

Canon 9 (4th Ecumenical Council, Chalcedon, 451)

And if a bishop or clergyman should have a difference with the metropolitan of the province, let him have recourse to the Exarch of the Diocese, or to the throne of the Imperial City of Constantinople, and there let it be tried.

Canon 28 (4th Ecumenical Council, Chalcedon, 451)

For the Fathers rightly granted privileges to the throne of old Rome, because it was the royal city. And the 150 most religious Bishops actuated by the same consideration, gave equal privileges to the most holy throne of New Rome, justly judging that the city which is honored with the Sovereignty and the Senate, and enjoys equal privileges with the old imperial Rome, should in ecclesiastical matters also be magnified as she is, and ranks next after her; so that in the Pontic, the Asian and the Thracian dioceses, the metropolitans only and such bishops also of the Dioceses aforesaid as are among the barbarians, should be ordained by the aforesaid most holy throne of the most holy Church of Constantinople.

Canon 20 (6th Ecumenical Council, Constantinople, 680-681)

It shall not be lawful for a bishop to teach publicly in any city which does not belong to him. If any have been observed doing this, let him cease from his episcopate.

Canon 36 (Quinisext Council, Constantinople, 692)

Let the throne of Constantinople be next after Rome, and enjoying equal privileges. After it Alexandria, then Antioch, and then Jerusalem.

A cursory review of these canons indicate clearly the unity intended for the Church by the decrees of these synods. Indeed, there shall not be two bishops in one church (jurisdiction) nor shall bishops and priests go from one city or jurisdiction into another without approval. Nor shall clergymen (or laymen), bring confusion into the churches by ordaining priests or enthroning bishops and those who travel from place to place are subject to the canon law that governs administration and jurisdiction of those places. Furthermore, bishops are not allowed to leave their jurisdiction for another jurisdiction without official approval. If he or any clergyman does so, they are not permitted to perform their ecclesiastical functions but are to be returned to the ranks of the laity.

Added to this is the confusion in the interpretation of these canons. Canons 9 and 28 of Chalcedon and canon 36 of the Quinisext Council are indirectly related to the unity issue insofar as they ascribe to the See of Constantinople extraordinary privileges. By interpretation of some Byzantine canonists such as Balsamon and Blastiras, they make the bishop or patriarch of Constantinople the highest court of appeals for the clergy. Whether this refers only to the provinces under the direct jurisdiction of Constantinople, or even to those of the other great patriarchs properly so-called, has been debated for centuries (Schaff and Wace 272-76; Cummings 253-56; and Maximos 148ff). Similarly, canon 28 of Chalcedon and subsequent canons that reaffirmed it, such as canon 36 of the Quinisext Council, have frequently been cited by the Ecumenical Patriarchate for claiming jurisdiction over all churches in barbarian (read diaspora) lands, hence its claim over churches in the Western Hemisphere and elsewhere. "For this reason the metropolitans of Pontus, Asia and of Thrace, as well as the Barbarian bishops, shall be ordained by the bishop of Constantinople." (Ancient Epitome of Canon 28) (Schaff and Wace 287-90; Cummings 271-76; and Maximos 203ff). It was on the basis of this canon that the Ecumenical Patriarchate granted autocephalous status to the churches in the Balkan nations during the 19th Century (Bogolepov, 20). Some canonists have interpreted canon 28, not only as a mere ratification of canon 3 of Constantinople in 381, placing the bishop of that city second after the bishop of Rome, but indeed, as the "legal establishment of the Patriarchate of Constantinople; the precise legal recognition of its bishop as the first in the East and the second after Rome in the entire ecclesiastical hierarchy." (Maximos 231). According to this interpretation then, "all the areas lying outside the limits of any specific ecclesiastical jurisdiction are subject ecclesiastically to the Bishop of Constantinople" (Maximos 229). It is on this basis then, that the Ecumenical

Patriarchate claims jurisdiction over the churches in "barbarian" lands that is, the churches of the diaspora in Northern and Western Europe and the New World. In this respect, therefore, these canons and their interpretation have a direct bearing upon the issue of ecclesiastical unity in America.[1]

Such, however, is not the case in America! Indeed, each of the canons have been repeatedly violated by the Orthodox jurisdictions in the New World. Major American and Canadian cities (as well as some Western European cities) have two or even three bishops, and the ethnic divisions along which our jurisdictions are organized are a repudiation not only of canon law but also, as mentioned earlier, of the decree of the Synod of Constantinople in 1872 which prohibits the establishment of two competing churches or jurisdictions in the same territory along ethnic and linguistic lines — the new heresy of phyletism which has been formally defined as the establishment of particular churches accepting members of the same nationality and refusing the members of other nationalities, being administered by pastors of the same nationality," and as "a coexistence of nationally defined churches." Clearly, then, these multiple jurisdictions are uncanonical as defined by the church canons. That is precisely the status of the Church in America which this Commission is addressing.

In this respect, however, the existing multiplicity of jurisdictions and the uncanonical status of the Church in America, need not be a permanent situation. The early Church faced some of the problems we face today in realizing concretely the unity of the Christian community in each Place. This is evident by the fact that such canons were decreed by the synods. But we can learn much by considering the means which were used to overcome the temptation of divisiveness. Indeed, if we believe in Tradition — as we say we do — the experience of the apostles and the fathers is part of our inheritance. We simply have no right to reject it, although we can and we must see how the guidelines which they provided can and must be applicable to our conditions, in our time. Our link with Tradition, in this respect, is the canons.

Taken as a whole, the Orthodox canonical inheritance is not a "juridical system" or a code. It contains texts which today are inapplicable, or in contradiction with others. Those who attempt to use canons as Protestant fundamentalists use Scriptures, ignore how much they themselves are influenced by Western approaches which absolutize legalism and institutional structures. Canons need interpretation in the light of Tradition as a whole, and their interpreters must first of all acquire that mind of the Church, without which individual canonical texts are often meaningless.[2] It remains, however, that with regard to some basic theological, ecclesiological and moral principles there is clear canonical consensus, and it is possible to understand why this consensus exists. Such a consensus exists on two points which are of crucial importance for our problem: 1) the Church must be one in each place; 2) the office of the episcopate is particularly responsible for realizing and witnessing to the unity of the true Church locally, regionally and universally. Both of these points are obviously not only "canonical," but theological, ecclesiological and spiritual.

"Unity in each place" is, of course, a flexible concept. A "place" can be a house, a village, a city, an area or a country. With modern means of transportation and communication, with communities organized at workplaces, etc., there are various ways in which one can define a "place." What is involved here is the desire, the readiness and the ability of Orthodox Christians to share a common sacramental and community life with their neighbors on the basis of no other criterion and principle than a common faith, belonging to the same Church, hoping for the same salvation, sharing in the same anticipation of the Kingdom of God. This is, after all, exactly what St. Paul meant when he was wondering, in his writing to the Corinthians, whether "Christ was divided" in Corinth. If the readiness and desire to share one's faith exists, practical accommodations are always possible to meet difficulties, such as the absence of a common language. But the canons are unanimous in requiring local unity, and place particular responsibility on the bishops. In each place, the local church is headed by a bishop, **originally the only celebrant of the Eucharist**, image of Christ and center of unity. "There may not be two bishops in a city," proclaims the First Ecumenical Council of

Nicea (canon 8). And, quite logically, the bishops (who were **elected** for life by the **clergy and laity** of their particular church) "are not to go beyond their own diocese to churches lying outside of their bounds, nor bring confusion on the churches. . . . And let not bishops go beyond their diocese for ordinations and any other ecclesiastical ministrations, unless they be invited" (Second Ecumenical Council, canon 2).

But the "one bishop in each place" principle does not mean that each local church is isolated and self-sufficient. Canons require that bishops of each province meet in synod twice a year (First Ecumenical Council, canons 4 and 5). The regular meetings are necessary for solving common problems, but particularly to fill vacant sees; for no bishop can ordain another bishop alone, particularly not his own successor. Conciliarity is therefore a basic principle. Within each church, the bishop heads the community together with his presbyters (who are compared to the apostles by St. Ignatius of Antioch), and the affairs of the province are directed by the bishops together. Among the bishops of a province, one is a *primate*, often designated as *metropolitan*. His personal approval is necessary for the creation of all new bishops, and the bishops are forbidden to act without his knowledge, just as he, too, does not act without theirs (Apostolic canon 34). He, therefore, coordinates and sanctions episcopal conciliarity on the level of the province.

On the universal level, the emperor (at least in the early Byzantine period) acted as coordinator, not by himself, but together with five *patriarchs* (the so-called *pentarchy*). With the disappearance of the Western empire, the bishop of Rome, always recognized as the first among patriarchs, developed a self-sufficiency which would eventually lead to schism. The Ecumenical Patriarch of Constantinople, who had been granted "privileges of honor after the bishop of Rome" (Second Ecumenical Council, canon 3), became the recognized coordinator, as *first bishop* within Orthodoxy. His actual powers, however, varied from period to period. Before the fall of Byzantium (1453), he acted in close coordination with the emperor. Under the Turkish regime, he became the political head of the entire Christian millet of the Ottoman empire, which gave him a de facto control over the other Eastern patriarchs.

205

Russia developed quite independently, as did the independent kingdom of Georgia and its ancient patriarchate.

Responsible for unity locally, a bishop also shares in the universal episcopate; he is not bishop by himself, but only because he is in communion and conciliar cooperation with the world episcopate of the Church. All this is symbolized by the so-called *diptychs*. At the liturgy a local bishop mentions the head of the province or of the autocephalous church to which he belongs, while the head of the church mentions all the other heads by order of precedence.

Patriarchal Encyclicals on Church Unity

Contrary to what has sometimes been asserted, the Orthodox Church was involved in seeking Christian unity long before the founding of the World Council of Churches at the Amsterdam Assembly in 1948, and was ecumenical before the Ecumenical Movement. The Western churches may have become aware of the scandal of division in recent decades, but the Orthodox Church has been aware of the tragedy of division from the earliest times. In many instances when errors emerged in either the East or the West, pastoral letters or encyclicals were written and local synods or peace-making conferences took place with the goal of resolving disputes or of taking the appropriate steps to re-establish church discipline and order. Even the convening of the Ecumenical Councils in the first centuries prior to the Great Schism of 1054 were examples of such efforts. Additional examples are the Byzantine delegations at the Council of Lyons (1274) and at the Council of Florence (1438), not to mention the bilateral meetings with the Armenians and other Monophysite bodies, and even the Muslims. Eagerness and passion for the restoration of the broken unity can be found in the written records of these meetings. If the pace and rhythm of the movement for reconciliation later slowed down due to unfavorable historic conditions, it would be wrong to attribute this decline of unity efforts to a lack of concern or to isolation in a confessional ghetto. And while these efforts initially pertained to the ecclesiastical divisions in the Old World, they have relevance today to the fragmented Orthodox jurisdictions in the New World.

The attempts to bring about unity were generally in the form of encyclicals issued by the five ancient patriarchates — Rome, Constantinople, Alexandria, Antioch and Jerusalem. But since 1054, those of the See of Constantinople, as the ranking patriarchate of the East, have taken precedence. Some of the modern encyclicals on the theme of unity issued since 1848, have been as follows:

Patriarchal Encyclical of Anthimus IV (1848). This encyclical was issued in response to the encyclical of Pope Pius IX to the Greeks urging that they — the lost sheep of Christ "should return at last to the flock of Christ." The papal encyclical was issued at the time the Greeks were having difficulty with the Ecumenical Patriarchate regarding the autocephaly of the Greek Church which was unilaterally declared in 1830 but was not formally recognized by the Patriarchate until 1850. The patriarchal document which is entitled "An Encyclical Letter of the One, Holy, Catholic, and Apostolic Church to the Orthodox Everywhere," (Constantinople 1848), stressed the catholicity of the Orthodox Church as the Universal Church of Christ (Frazee 169-70).

Patriarchal and Synodal Encyclical of Anthimus VI (1872). This encyclical which resulted from the decision of the Synod of Constantinople in 1872 and which is signed by the patriarchs of Alexandria and Jerusalem as well, "censured and condemned phyletism (i.e., excessive nationalism and national dissensions, and disputes) in the Church of Christ as being opposed to the teaching of the Gospel and to the holy canons." The synod and its encyclical were engendered by the excessive nationalism exhibited by the Bulgarian Church which unilaterally declared itself autocephalous in 1870. The schism was not healed until 1945 (Karmiris 173).

Patriarchal Encyclical of Anthimus VII (1895). This epistle was the response of the Ecumenical See to the appeal of Pope Leo XIII in 1895 to all non-Roman Christians "to return to the fold." Written by His Holiness, Anthimus VII and signed by all the members of the Holy Synod and entitled "The Reply of the Orthodox Church to Roman Catholic Overtures on Reunion," the encyclical remains among the best and most comprehensive exigesis of the position of the Orthodox Church regarding church unity.[3]

Patriarchal Encyclical of Joachim III (1904). Addressed to the Orthodox churches by the great Patriarch Joachim III, the letter criticizes "ethnoracism" which "because of racial traditions and linguistic peculiarities, resulted in the rupture and dismemberment of the one, catholic Church of Christ into recognizable pieces and sections." Consequently, the encyclical goes on to state that the Church was compelled synodically to condemn this "strange and foreign spirit," capable of having a catastrophic effect on the unity and catholicity of the Orthodox Church. The encyclical goes on to decry the fact that certain local Orthodox churches have been induced into unadulterated nationalism and racism beyond all necessity to their own nations and states and which at times they have become involuntary instruments of the chauvinistic pursuits of their respective nations, that is, "the servants of worldly goals and political programs" (Karmiris 172-73).

Encyclical of the Ecumenical Patriarchate (1920). Issued at a time when the Ecumenical Throne was vacant and entitled "Unto All the Churches of Christ Wheresoever They Be," this encyclical urged closer cooperation between separated Christian bodies and suggested an alliance of Churches, parallel to the newly founded League of Nations. Many of the ideas in this letter anticipated later developments in the Ecumenical Movement and the encyclical itself is credited as leading to the establishment of the World Council of Churches at the Amsterdam Assembly in 1948 (Ware, Orthodox Church 331-32).

Patriarchal Encyclical of Meletius IV (1922). This encyclical revoked the Patriarchal Tome of 1908 which had temporarily placed the administration of the Greek Orthodox Church in the New World under the jurisdiction of the Church of Greece, returning it under the Ecumenical Patriarchate, and established the Greek Orthodox Archdiocese of North and South America. The letter calls for the unification of all Orthodox bodies in the New World under the Ecumenical Patriarchate (Efthimiou and Christopolous 15-16, and 99-101).

Patriarchal Encyclical of Athenagoras (1952). This encyclical of Athenagoras, perhaps the greatest post-Byzantine patriarch of the Ecumenical Throne, officially approved of Orthodox participation in the Ecumenical Movement and membership in the World Council of Churches, under certain conditions. The letter launched the involvement of the Orthodox Church in the search for Christian unity.

Message of Demetrius (1990). Message read by the late Patriarch Demetrius upon the occasion of his visit to the United States in 1990 and expanded from the episcopal throne of the Washington, D.C., St. Nicholas Cathedral of the Orthodox Church in America, in which he denounced the tragedy of Orthodox disunity in America as uncanonical and as a heresy and calling for an end to such disunity.

Definition of Diaspora[4]

The term *diaspora* has a rich history in the Old Testament generally referring to the Jews who were obligated, for one reason or another, to live among the Gentiles. This exile from the Promised Land was perceived as a just retribution from God for unfaithfulness to Him. Still, diaspora was a temporary situation, for the Jews always belonged to His people in Zion.

For the Christian, there is no true homeland except for the Kingdom of God. Spiritually speaking, all are in diaspora while living on earth. The essential difference between this New Testament viewpoint and the Old is that, for the Christian, the **only** return is to the Fatherland of the Kingdom. There is **no** earthly home. Thus, the Christian Church itself is in dispersion throughout the world until the fulfillment of all things in the Kingdom.

Applied narrowly, the term diaspora has come to mean the relationship of certain Orthodox bodies in the Western world with their "Mother Churches." This view of the Church is necessarily influenced by secular forces and even determined by them. It is to see the vibrant church life across many new lands as dependent upon churches in traditional Orthodox countries, and that is simply contrary to the empirical facts.

The reality of the Orthodox Church in the U.S.A. is a two-hundred year history, including churches and a whole host of religious and charitable institutions. Taken as a whole, the Church in America is mature and fully developed, already standing on its own in the country in which it gives full witness to the Truth. No longer need the Church make excuses for her presence here, since she has become an integral part of the American landscape. No longer a stepchild, she is perfectly capable of being the Church in the fullness of that term.

ORTHODOX JURISDICTIONS IN AMERICA[5]

Demographics

Informed estimates place the total number of Orthodox Christians in the United States at between 5 and 5.5 million (5.9 million for North America).[6] Organized jurisdictions (dioceses or archdioceses) exist for Albanians, Bulgarians, Byelorussians, Carpatho-Russians, Greeks, Macedonians, Romanians, Russians, Serbians, Syrians (Antiochians), and Ukrainians. There are, in addition, separate parishes without the rank of diocese for small groups of Estonians, Finns, and for political reasons, for particular groups of Byelorussians, Russians, and Ukrainians. The Greek Orthodox Archdiocese of North and South America and the Orthodox Church in America (formerly the Russian Orthodox Greek Catholic Metropolia in North America) account for probably three-fourths of the Orthodox Christians in the United States — between them approximately 3.5 million.

History (General)

Orthodoxy formally came to the United States in 1794 when a group of Russian monks began missionary work among the Aleuts, Eskimos, and Tlingit Indians in Alaska, establishing the first Orthodox Church at Kodiak Island in that year. Informally, however, in 1768, a colony of over 500 Greek laymen settling in New Smyrna, Florida, established a chapel for worship. In 1848, a Russian diocese was established in Alaska which was transferred to San Francisco in 1872 and later, in 1905, to New York City. Up to World War I, the Russian Orthodox diocese was the only one in America and serviced all Orthodox churches of various ethnic backgrounds. Following the political upheaval in Russia in 1917, the cessation of material support by the imperial Russian government and the interruption of normal canonical direction resulted in the formation of other U.S. dioceses, subject to Mother Churches abroad: Albanian (1918), Ukrainian (1919), Serbian (1921), Greek (1921), Romanian (1930), Antiochian (Syrian) (1936), Bulgarian (1938), Byelorussian (1951), and Macedonian (1960). Although this pattern of multiple episcopates with overlapping geographic areas of jurisdictions was alien to traditional Orthodox practice and contrary to canon law, by 1940 it had become an accepted fact of church life.

The Ethnic Dimension of the Church
Ethnicity is deeply rooted in church history because it is an inescapable component of human history. Every individual born into this world is a part of, or member of, an ethnic group. Each of these has its own particular and peculiar genius, system of values and focus. The very term *ethnic* comes from the Greek *to ethnos,* referring to tribe or clan. Undoubtedly, the word ethnic pre-dates many more modern conceptions of the nation — state. Clearly, it is basic and fundamental.

It is clear that the very Incarnation of Christ took place in a specific and ethnic context. The early church was comprised largely of Jewish disciples of an itinerant rabbi. The Gospel *kerygma* and the Great Commission of Matthew 28:18-20, though universal in scope, nevertheless have a local basis. The lifting of strictures from Gentile Christians in Acts 15 freed the Church from Mosaic law, but not from ethnic concerns.

In Acts 2, the Pentecost event is vividly described as an *ethnic* event, with the entire inhabited world being present in Jerusalem by way of tribal representation. At Pentecost, the Holy Spirit **transforms** ethnicity from its exclusivity and narrowness, making it into a vehicle for God's grace. The various ethnicities in Jerusalem for the feast form one People of God at that miraculous moment of Pentecost and is therefore, as St. Basil says, the undoing of Babel. The Old Testament story of Babel with its disunity and divisions, is reversed as ethnicity becomes a means to greater and more

211

intense unity in the Spirit. God Himself has taken the very human factor of ethnicity and rendered it a fit vessel for the divine.

This transformation of ethnicity is not automatic. In fact, ethnicity is really neutral; one's intentionality is the key to transforming it. For the Christian, the affirmation of one's own ethnicity simultaneously opens him to the affirmation of the same in others. Without this "openness to the Spirit," there would simply be no Christian Church; Jesus' message to the whole world would be a curious relic, an archaism found in a narrow Jewish sect.

Let us as Orthodox Christians be open and courageous enough to permit such growth here in America. Let us not permit our own particular "Laws of Moses" to prevent ourselves or others from entering the fullness of Truth that is Orthodoxy.

MAINTAINING THE STATUS QUO

It is the point of view of the Commission on Orthodox Unity that there is something missing in the earthly manifestation of the Orthodox Church. That something, absence of unity, in the institutional/organizational/administrative expressions of the various ethnic jurisdictions, especially in the Americas diminishes the Orthodox Christian witness and ministry. Subsequent parts of this report address the prospects for bringing about jurisdictional "unity" and possible models for achieving it. Before such thoughts are presented and explored, it is appropriate and good to examine the status quo in the light of the historical roots, assumptions and questions that perhaps are driving the "push" for unity. Thus, in this part of the report the argument is advanced that no attempt should be made to contrive a schema for Orthodox unity as it may disrupt an already fragile situation and bring about further disunity. Rather, it is best to let the natural progression of unity evolve in the fullness of time.

The Argument for Maintaining the Status Quo

The Premise for Orthodox Unity. This Commission Report is based on the premise that Orthodox Christians in the Americas are not united and that the time has come to bring them under one umbrella in a structure to be defined.

Several approaches are suggested for consideration, such as autocephaly, autonomy, or under some interim transitional structure that eventually will evolve into one or the other of the two other alternatives.

Underlying assumptions for this position are:

- That unity is always a desirable thing;

- That it provides the springboard for a coordinated projection of the Faith; and

- That in its absence, dissension not only can arise but can and often does lead to conflict.

Beyond the attraction that basic observation has, the unity or lack of it among Orthodox, especially among the faithful in the diaspora, is viewed somewhere between the extremes of the ineffective to the scandalous. It is this last appellation, cited elsewhere in this report, that the late Patriarch Demetrius used when he visited the United States in 1990.

The Roots of the Churches in the Diaspora. If there are many overlapping Orthodox jurisdictions in the Americas with more than one bishop in a given city or area, this is so not because of some deliberate plan, but it is from the natural flow of immigrants from various Orthodox lands in Europe. People coming to these shores brought their Faith with them, a Faith at its core Orthodox, but also colored by the ethnic and cultural particularities of their origins.

A Scandalous Situation? It is hard to understand why this situation is labeled as scandalous. It is an expression of Orthodoxy in a multifaceted way, colored by customs and traditions that are testimony not to a rigidity of expression, but to a flexibility that underscores the universality of the accommodations that can exist under the Orthodox umbrella. Further, the various ethnic Orthodox groups in this country, unlike sometimes the situation among their countries of origin, co-exist quite peacefully and share in expressions proclaiming the unity of the Faith, such as Pan-Orthodox vespers.

What About Canon Law? It is difficult to understand why the existing situation of the Orthodox in the Americas is labeled as uncanonical. True, canon law says that there should be one bishop in a given city or region. However, this law was proclaimed hundreds of years ago when the cities/ locales were small to modest in size, unlike today, and the Christians in them were limited in number. Also, the human compositions of these locales were often culturally consistent if not to say, for all practical purposes, homogeneous. In other words, they were ethnically and culturally the same.

Thus, one bishop for one area seems like a reasonable administrative set-up. The application of an ancient canon law to an obviously changed social environment can be called into question.

Chauvinism and Cultural Realities. It's true that quite often the Orthodox church communities in this country have been affected by the spillover of politics from the homeland. Upheavals of a "political" nature, with passions and factions, are not unknown in all manner of church communities of whatever persuasion. In addition, quite often ethnic chauvinism takes precedence over Christian charity and projects an unhealthy image to the unbelievers of a community supposedly reflecting the spirit of Christ. Obviously, this not only should not be tolerated, but should be condemned.

Beyond that, however, the various Orthodox churches have a rich cultural component that is deeply ingrained in their life, is of inestimable value to their faithful and should not be a candidate for arbitrary change since it is not a

214

fundamental detriment to the Faith. Such diversity is a manifestation of the creativity that the Holy Spirit can work in the hearts of the faithful and has nothing to do with ethnic chauvinism.

Many are too willing, because of their ignorance and lack of appreciation, to turn their back on their roots. An example of this is in some Greek parishes where many want to eliminate as irrelevant the Greek language from the Divine Liturgy. They view it as an insurmountable barrier to the appeal of the Faith to young people. This, while at the same time more and more Protestant preachers, in the confusion spawned by all sorts of translations, constantly refer to the original Greek word or phrase for precision in meaning.

Unity Versus Unified. There seems to be some confusion between the notions of unity and unified. The implication suggested in the present situation of the Orthodox in the Americas is that because we are not structurally unified we are not united, and this is a detriment to the Faith.

If anything, the opposite is true. In matters of faith, most of the Orthodox are united. Thus, unity is manifested primarily in the universality of the Eucharist as the centrality of worship of all the Orthodox and acceptance of all the Sacraments as the bedrock of their faith. This should be a powerful testimony to those who think different ethnicities implies that either people cannot pull together on crucial matters or are in quarrelsome disagreement. If anything, it strongly suggests an affirmation of the compatible existence of cultural antecedents not that different from what a culturally pluralistic America is all about.

Why a Unified Orthodox Church?

For Reasons of Identity? There is hardly any need for this since we all know who we are and presumably know what our Faith is. Are non-Orthodox confused? If so, let us consider the large number of Protestant churches whose tenets of faith are all over the map; from who Christ is, to what is sexually moral. There certainly is no unity in the Protestant world, yet no one has difficulty identifying all those divisive and conflicting beliefs as Protestant. So why are we concerned with the various Orthodox churches where there is a unity of faith?

For Reasons of Protection? This is probably the reason that has caused many to be concerned with unification. As Orthodox Christians, our concern should not be ego-projecting motivations, such as numbers of faithful to impress. If there is something of inestimable value and meaning in our Faith, the question should be to what degree this Faith is part and parcel of our being and how do we live and radiate its richness and meaning and Truth.

For Reasons of Power? It has been said there is strength in unity — yes, that old trap — power. But what has power in the secular sense — political, financial, organizational — got to do with the Christian Faith? In terms of the Faith's essence, absolutely nothing. The power the Christian has is in the realm of the spirit, the power of conviction about the truth that is Christ, the power to stand firmly and uncompromisingly with the strength to do so even at the cost of sacrifice.

So that the Orthodox Church will be "American?" When it comes to the Faith, what does that mean? Language? We already have English where the pastoral decision is to have it. Does being "American" imply that we can enforce the use of a particular language on parishes that are already comfortable with another? On the part of some, does not that represent the height of arrogance, unrealism and lack of Christian spirit?

So that the Orthodox can Elect Their own Hierarchs? If what goes on in many parishes is any indication of the insensitivity of the members to the principles of the Faith, then there is much to be concerned about. But with prayer and the guidance of the Holy Spirit, some process can be formulated whereby the American faithful of the various jurisdictions can participate in electing their church leaders as they did in the Church of the first centuries.

One Voice to Speak for the Faith? This refers to one bishop in one locale which seems to serve the perceived need that there be one spokesman for the Faith. The wisdom of Orthodoxy is that there is a reservation as to how much power should rest in one person. The behavior and actions of some hierarchs, and indeed some priests, bears this out. In matters of faith and action beyond the ordinary routine prescribed matters, there can be a synodical jurisdiction in a particular area which can meet to chart its course of action and representation in gatherings with other religious leaders.

A Concluding Thought

From what has been said, it would seem that on the part of some, there is no real need for a unification of the various Orthodox jurisdictions other than for reasons of power. Also, there seems to be an attitude of disdain by some for their ethnic and cultural roots. This, in turn, is fueled by a sense of inferiority by those who feel the use of a foreign language in the Divine Liturgy is not in tune with American realities. They say, "Make the language English and the youth will rush to the churches. If you don't we've lost them." Other faiths have had English for centuries and how are they faring? An observation! One of the busiest nights of the year is Good Friday when young college students home for Easter break, instead of attending church services, seek secular pursuits elsewhere.

As important as process and structure are, they are not the main problems the Christian churches face. The Church's problem is not communicating the Light of Christ, either as a message or as an example that inspires. Quite often the message is nothing more than insipid proclamations. Christianity's message is unequivocally demanding, with an uncompromising commitment to Christ and His Truth. That is the message that is not being preached because people do not want to hear it, and those that do preach it are often pilloried.

So what do we do? We dash off in other directions like pursuits for unification which, to many, is a betrayal of their heritage and culture. These are pursuits that will sap attention and energies for decades while the focus on Jesus Christ goes wanting. Other than addressing how better to meet the need for better communications among the Orthodox jurisdictions, and establish on a local basis better mechanisms for more coordinated efforts on issues affecting society at large, the Orthodox jurisdiction status quo should not be tampered with at this time. It should be maintained. **Despite the diversity of languages in the Liturgy, customs and expressions, the Orthodox have one theology, one doctrine, one manner of worship and the same Sacraments.** In other words, where it matters the Orthodox are united.

PROSPECTS OF UNITY IN AMERICA
Expressions and Attempts at Unity
The idea of Orthodox unity is not of recent emergence in the consciousness of a few. Its origins in America can be traced to activities as early as the last century. A detailed listing of those efforts are included in Appendix III.

Present Status
A total of 76 "Orthodox" jurisdictions are listed in current encyclopedia as existing in North America comprised of genuine Orthodox churches, schismatic groups, Old Catholic jurisdictions, and indigenous American sects. The vast majority uncanonical according to Orthodox ecclesiology (Merton Encyclopedia).[7] Including:

- Seventeen jurisdictions which are recognized as Orthodox bodies.

- Only nine are recognized as fully canonical churches (members of SCOBA), together with the Western Rite Vicariate and the Evangelical Orthodox Mission.[8]

- Non-Chalcedonian or Oriental Orthodox churches, such as the Armenian Orthodox, Coptic Orthodox, Ethiopian Orthodox, and others that believe only in the one nature of the Divinity.[9]

218

- Numerous bodies of Byzantine Catholic and Uniates who are "Orthodox" in theology and practice but are under the jurisdiction of Rome.

- Old Calendar bodies of various ethnic groups, some of which are scattered throughout the Orthodox world.

The above illustrates the enormity of task in bringing about Orthodox unity.

Recommended Procedures for Achieving Unity

Study of applicable canon law and practice with reference to ecclesiastical jurisdiction of Church in "Diaspora." As it has been seen there is much disagreement and confusion about the interpretation of canon law, especially those dealing with jurisdictional authority. The Orthodox Church, even today, has no exhaustive canon law comparable with the Corpus iuris canonici of the Roman Church. The councils have never claimed to compose any document of this kind and the Nomocanon itself, (a Byzantine collection of canonical and legislative texts concerning ecclesiastical life), merely summarized the few rules which had almost all been enacted by Church authority in order to settle certain definite cases.[10] It is, therefore, not surprising that there should be disagreement about the canon law in the Orthodox Church right up to the present time and that these old laws should be interpreted in different ways. This is, therefore, part of the reason for the disunity that exists as to the governance of the Orthodox Church in the "Diaspora." Failing any consensus reached by the different jurisdictions, any study of applicable canon law must await the convening of the forthcoming Great and Holy Council of the entire Orthodox Church, which has been in the planning stage for several years and will mark the first "ecumenical" meeting of Orthodox hierarchs in over a thousand years, since the 7th Ecumenical Council at Nicaea in 787. This long-overdue meeting recently received some impetus when newly-installed Ecumenical Patriarch Bartholomew hosted in Constantinople in March of 1992, a synaxis, a gathering of leaders of the autocephalous Orthodox churches — the first such event in a thousand years.[11]

Study of historical precedents in establishment of autocephalous churches in Europe. Any attempt to plan for church unity in America must first review the advent of autocephalous churches in the Old World. Jesus Christ founded One Church, but from the very beginning different manifestations of the One Church began to appear in terms of regional rites (such as the Byzantine and Roman, among many).

But this did not compromise the unity of the Church. Later during these Apostolic Times, the Church evolved into five areas of governance, ranked by the Ecumenical Councils, centered in the five great cities of the Roman Empire. These became the famous patriarchates of Rome, Constantinople, Alexandria, Antioch and Jerusalem. But even among these, several independent or autonomous churches began to evolve also (with ecclesial sanction), such as those that survive to this day; the churches of Cyprus and Mt. Sinai. Following the Great Schism of 1054, which divided the Undivided Church of the First Millennium into two antagonistic factions, East and West, the Church, for the first time lost its unity. The West went on to evolve into the monarchical Roman or Catholic Church until it was sundered again by the Protestant Reformation of the 16th Century resulting in the rampant denominationalism that exists today in the West. The East went on to evolve into the Greek or Orthodox Church under the aegis of the Ecumenical Patriarchate. In time, and because of the inroads of the Muslims and other demographic changes which seriously eroded the efficacy of the venerable patriarchates of Alexandria, Antioch, and Jerusalem, the Patriarchate of Constantinople, by virtue of its history and prerogatives, emerged as the leading governing authority in the East, administering and assisting its sister churches in a conciliar fashion and always on the basis of canon law.[12] (See Figure 1 on p. 226).

The first great change in the structural unity of the Orthodox Church occurred with the rise of Russian nationalism. The relations of Russia with the Mother Church at Constantinople were severed in the 14th Century when a Russian was elected as Metropolitan of Kiev who heretofore had always been a Greek appointed by Constantinople. This *fait accompli* was finally resolved in 1589 when Patriarch Jeremiah II of Constantinople journeyed there and installed a Russian, Job, as Patriarch of Moscow who later, by counciliar action, was admitted to the fifth place (after Constantinople, Alexandria, Antioch, and Jerusalem).

The second change in the structural unity of the Church began to take place in the 19th Century with the progressive liberation of the Balkan peninsula from Turkish domination and the appearance of a number of new, independent states. The first of these was Greece which, after gaining its independence, declared its church autocephalous in 1830, not wishing to be under the tutelage of Constantinople which was subject to Turkish suzerainty. Twenty years later in 1850, the Ecumenical Patriarchate recognized the autocephaly of the Church of Greece by a synodal tomos (decree).

At the beginning of the 19th Century there were seven autocephalous or autonomous churches in the Balkans: Four of the Serbian language (Montenegro, the Patriarchate of Carlovitz, the Archbishopric of Belgrade and the autonomous Church of Bosnia-Herzegovina), two Romanian speaking (Romania and Transylvania), and one Romano-Serbian (Rucovina). Their boundaries corresponded with the administrative districts of Austria-Hungary and the Turkish Empire. With the liberation of Serbia from the Turkish yoke and the recognition of its church as autocephalous by the Ecumenical Patriarchate in 1879, the four Serbian-speaking churches were placed under the Archbishop of Belgrade, who was raised to the rank of patriarch in 1925. Also in 1925, the Romanian churches were united under the Patriarch of Bucharest which had been granted autocephalous status in 1885.

The case of the Bulgarian Church caused a series of troubles. The negotiations between the Bulgarian representative and the Ecumenical

Patriarchate were obstructed by the existence of a large Bulgarian population in Constantinople itself. The Bulgarians claimed that these people were also subject to the authority of the new Bulgarian "autocephaly" as far as ecclesiastical affairs were concerned. A system of this kind would have been an official admission of the existence of two parallel church hierarchies on the same territory (the problem that plagues the Church in America today). It was impossible to avoid a rupture and in 1872 the Council of Constantinople officially condemned the primacy of racialism or nationalism in church affairs. It is interesting to note that the Orthodox Church officially condemned this psychological malady just at the dawn of an epoch in which Orthodoxy all over the world was to suffer as a result of ecclesiastical nationalism. The "Bulgarian Schism" was settled in 1945; Bulgarian autocephaly was then established and recognized without any infringement of the territorial principle.

Other Orthodox churches which were recognized as autonomous or autocephalous by the Ecumenical Patriarchate in the 20th Century are: Georgia in 1917 (and again in 1990); Czechoslovakia in 1923 (and since the separation of that country in 1993 into two nations, into two autonomous provinces, that of the Czech Republic and that of Slovakia); Finland, also in 1923; Poland in 1924; and Albania in 1937 (reconstituted again in 1992 after the collapse of Communism there). Today the Orthodox Church world-wide is made up of 15 autocephalous "branches" united doctrinally and in full communion with one another, unlike the situation which prevailed in the Western Church as a result of the Protestant Reformation. But while they are united in faith, they remain administratively divided. These churches, ranked in order of their precedence, are as follows:

> Ecumenical Patriarchate of Constantinople
> Patriarchate of Alexandria and all Africa
> Patriarchate of Antioch and all the East
> Patriarchate of Jerusalem and New Zion
> Church of Russia
> Church of Serbia
> Church of Romania
> Church of Bulgaria
> Church of Cyprus
> Church of Greece
> Church of Georgia
> Church of Czechoslovakia
> Church of Finland
> Church of Poland
> Church of Albania
> Orthodox Church in America[13]

For a more complete description of these churches see Appendix I, "A Simplified Directory of Autocephalous Churches" (p. 264).

It must be remembered that autocephaly, in the strictly canonical sense, remained a simple right for a province to elect its own bishop and to be self-governing. In the 19th Century, however, it acquired a new sense; it identified itself, at least as far as the Balkans were concerned, with the absolute independence of the new national churches. This psychological evolution was clearly linked up with the appearance of a modern form of nationalism, unknown in the Middle Ages, which always remained true to the ideal of a universal Christian theocracy. The idealogists of the new "autocephalies" were not solely responsible for this; their action was often provoked by confusion between the interests of Orthodoxy and those of modern Hellenism, as sometimes reflected in the activities of the Ecumenical

Patriarchate. Nonetheless, the emergence of these autocephalous churches was the realization of the adoption since the Council of Nicaea by the Orthodox Church, of dividing its dioceses so that their frontiers coincided with the political frontiers of the provinces or states.[14]

It is a regrettable fact, however, that after 1920 the "nationalization" of the Orthodox autocephalies, dispersed in different countries, gave rise to violations of the territorial principle, especially in America, where every national or ethnic group established its own jurisdiction dependent on the mother country. This violation of the territorial principle did considerable harm to the Orthodox message in the world. The unity of the Church, which is one of the essential elements of its nature, requires that Orthodox Christians, living in the same place, should form a single community and be under the authority of a single bishop. As seen earlier, the defense of this principle was the cause of the "Bulgarian Schism" of 1872. But do not the Orthodox "dispersed" in America or Europe, make a point today of being "non-canonical" and of systematically infringing this principle without any justification? It is this problem that we all are called to correct and is the very essence of this Report.

Resolution of the ethnic factor in American Orthodoxy. A review of Appendix II (p. 269) lists (perhaps for the first time in one place) a chronological outline of the history of the various Orthodox ethnic groups that settled in America. Among those listed are: Greek, Russian, Syrian-Lebanese, Ukrainian, Serbian, Romanian, Carpatho-Russian, Bulgarian, Albanian, Byelorussian, and "Macedonian." It is the history of a proud people who came to the New World with extremely limited economic resources but the carriers of an ancient faith. It is the story of our forebears who against all odds prospered and founded their homes and families here and established their pristine faith reflected in the numerous churches that were erected to the glory of God. It is also the story of ethnic achievement, of ethnic pride and of ethnic identity which nurtured them in the new land. But it is also a story of ethnic division and isolation which has impeded the development of a unified Orthodox Church in the land. The ethnic factor is one of the major problems that needs to be resolved if such a church is to evolve here.

224

Ethnicity, however, is natural and is part of every human being's cultural ethos for the Church itself lives in a cultural milieu, hence the rise of the "modern" autocephalous national churches. The problem is, therefore, how to overcome the excessiveness of ethnicity or nationalism to make possible a united Church without denigrating the positive aspects of ethnicity; indeed, how to cultivate and preserve its nobler dimensions and preserve them as part of the cultural heritage of the Church in America. This is the task that confronts us today.

Similarly, a review of Appendix III (p. 281) reflects the various attempts that have been made in the past to bring about Orthodox unity in America. From the prophetic visions of Archbishop Tikhon on church unity along ethnic lines in 1904 and those of Archbishop Meletius in 1921, along with the pioneer work of Archbishop Fan Noli in the 1930's, and the exhortations of Archbishop Athenagoras during his long tenure in America from 1931 to 1948, and the gentle urgings of the saintly Bishop Nicholas Velimirovich in the 1950's from his residence at St. Sava Serbian Monastery in Illinois, to the concrete establishment of the Federation of Orthodox Greek Catholic Churches in America, the Council of Eastern Orthodox Youth Leaders (CEOYLA), and the Standing Conference of Canonical Orthodox Bishops in the Americas (SCOBA), and finally the proclamation of the autocephaly of the Russian Orthodox Metropolia as the Orthodox Church in America in 1970, all were to lead hopefully to a unified Church. Despite these efforts along with efforts of Archbishop Iakovos as the permanent chairman of SCOBA, and the establishment of a Bilateral Commission to study organic unity between OCA and the Antiochian Archdiocese inaugurated by Metropolitan Theodosius and Archbishop Philip in the 1980's, real unity has not taken place.

FIGURE 1

MILEPOSTS ON TIME LINE OF CHURCH HISTORY

ONE HOLY CATHOLIC AND APOSTOLIC CHURCH						THE ORTHODOX
33	37	63	325	787	958	1204
36	49	66	451	880	1054	

33	Pentecost: Birthday of Church
36	St. Andrew founds Church of Byzantium (Constantinople)
37	St. Peter establishes See of Antioch
49	Apostolic Council of Jerusalem St. James presides as bishop
63	St. Mark establishes See of Alexandria
66	SS. Peter and Paul put to death in Rome
325	First Ecumenical Council and Nicene Creed
451	Fourth Ecumenical Council at Chalcedon makes Constantinople equal to Rome
787	Seventh Ecumenical Council restores icons for veneration
880	Photian Schism — first major rupture between East and West
988	Baptism of St. Vladimir, Conversion of Russia begins
1054	Great Schism, final break between Rome & Constantinople
1204	Sack of Constantinople by Fourth Crusade
1274	Council of Lyon — attempt to heal schism between East and West

226

WITH SPECIAL REFERENCE TO AMERICA

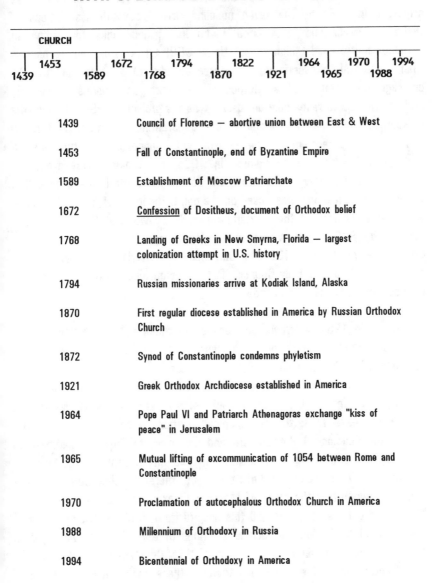

CHURCH

1439 | 1453 | 1589 | 1672 | 1768 | 1794 | 1822 | 1870 | 1921 | 1964 | 1965 | 1970 | 1988 | 1994

1439	Council of Florence — abortive union between East & West
1453	Fall of Constantinople, end of Byzantine Empire
1589	Establishment of Moscow Patriarchate
1672	<u>Confession</u> of Dositheus, document of Orthodox belief
1768	Landing of Greeks in New Smyrna, Florida — largest colonization attempt in U.S. history
1794	Russian missionaries arrive at Kodiak Island, Alaska
1870	First regular diocese established in America by Russian Orthodox Church
1872	Synod of Constantinople condemns phyletism
1921	Greek Orthodox Archdiocese established in America
1964	Pope Paul VI and Patriarch Athenagoras exchange "kiss of peace" in Jerusalem
1965	Mutual lifting of excommunication of 1054 between Rome and Constantinople
1970	Proclamation of autocephalous Orthodox Church in America
1988	Millennium of Orthodoxy in Russia
1994	Bicentennial of Orthodoxy in America

The greatest disappointment has been the failure of SCOBA.[15] Established in 1960 primarily because of pressure from the rank and file of the Church in America as reflected through the efforts of CEOYLA which itself was organized in 1954 by the seven mainline Orthodox youth associations of Orthodox jurisdictions in America[16] who had joined ranks for promoting Orthodox unity, amidst high expectations, SCOBA has turned out to be less than successful. Never in its over three decades of existence did SCOBA envisage the creation of an autocephalous church in America. The only project which was repeatedly discussed was the project of a Synod under the jurisdiction of the Patriarchate of Constantinople, realized through pan-Orthodox agreement. The project was supported by the Russian Metropolia in this country, which in 1924 had broken away from the jurisdiction of Moscow in order to avoid Communist control, in the hope that the American question, once raised on the pan-Orthodox level, would be solved with the agreement of the Patriarchate of Moscow. But the project was rejected by SCOBA. It was then decided to appeal to the Pan-Orthodox Conference meeting in 1965 in Chambesy, Switzerland to plan for the forthcoming Great and Holy Council. But the Ecumenical Patriarchate refused to place the issue on the agenda.

Meanwhile in 1967, Metropolitan Irenaeus of the Metropolia wrote a letter to all Orthodox patriarchs on the necessity of unity and later solicited an audience with the Ecumenical Patriarch himself. His request, which was supported by Archbishop Iakovos, was turned down in the summer of 1967 by telegram. Unofficially, Constantinople let it be known that the Metropolia first would have to settle its canonical relations with Moscow. A little earlier, the Ecumenical Patriarchate had dissolved its Russian Exarchate in Western Europe, advising its bishops, clergy and laity to return to the Moscow jurisdiction. There seems to be little doubt, therefore, that Constantinople was fully supporting the claim of Moscow to exercise jurisdiction of all the "Russians" outside of Russia and this despite its own claim that by virtue of Canon 28 of Chalcedon, all such jurisdictions of the "diaspora" belonged to the Ecumenical Patriarchate. It seems that Constantinople always and consistently pushed the Metropolia towards these negotiations and opposed

228

with equal consistency, both American autocephaly and American Orthodox unity, even under itself, because unity would, in fact, have implied a loosening of its administrative relationship with the Greek American community. SCOBA's failure, therefore, was based on the fact that it faced a stalemate because neither Constantinople nor the other "Mother Churches" were desiring Orthodox unity in America.[17]

The fact was, however, that the Metropolia did not want to go under the Communist-controlled Moscow patriarchate, nor did it want to become a "Russian" Church. Its experience since 1924 in dealing with the Communist exigency in the Russian homeland had given the Metropolia patience and maturity which finally led to direct negotiations with the Patriarchate of Moscow. These efforts bore fruit on April 13, 1970, when the patriarch and the entire episcopate of the Russian Church signed the *tomos* or document granting *autocephaly* to the Metropolia, henceforth to be known as the Orthodox Church in America. This bilateral action between Moscow and the Metropolia, instead of helping to solve the issue of canonical unity in America, further compounded it. The fact that the Church of Russia, which was the first to establish a canonical diocese in America in 1870, was giving up its canonical rights and recognized OCA as its sister church, was a fact of tremendous importance. But the Ecumenical Patriarchate, calling attention to its ancient and historical prerogatives refused to recognize the act, claiming that under canon law no Church had the right unilaterally to grant autocephaly, but only by the Ecumenical Councils and in the absence of such councils by the Ecumenical Patriarchate with the consensus of all autocephalous churches. Constantinople was joined in this position by the ancient patriarchates and most of the autocephalous churches so that to date, only four churches beside Russia — Georgia, Bulgaria, Poland and Czechoslovakia — recognize the legality of OCA's canonicity.[18] And there the issue stands.

Resolution of a broad range of issues affecting the local and international Church. What must be done? If the issue of canonical ecclesiastical unity is to be resolved, much needs to be done at both the local, national and international levels. The task is almost insurmountable but unity is essential if the Church in America is to reach its full potential. Such a unity will make the Orthodox Faith accessible to all Americans, not as a foreign import — a "Russian," a "Greek," or a "Serbian," ethnic church — but as the truly Catholic and Apostolic faith, offering a canonical framework for Orthodox unity, without suppressing the wealth of legitimate pluralism of liturgical languages, traditions and customs which reflect the reality of Orthodoxy in America today. But Orthodox unity simply cannot be realized unless all the parties concerned recognize their past limitations and mistakes, and resolutely begin to build the future together. Such unity presents no threat to ethnic cultures, provided **Orthodoxy comes first**. There is simply no other way in which Orthodoxy can survive, and prosper, and develop, and pursue its missionary expansion, unless it is united in one Church where no nationality or group has any particular privilege. Other commission reports in this Project on Orthodox Renewal have already indicated the direct consequences awaiting the Church if it fails to unite in America.

It is, therefore, incumbent upon the Orthodox faithful to take stock of the worsening situation for Orthodoxy in America and apply pressure, lovingly but firmly and resolutely, upon our leaders, both clerical and lay, at the local parish, diocesan, national and international levels, to compel them to address this crucial issue realistically. This can be done by following the sage advice of the late Fr. Alexander Schmemann in his insightful little booklet, Mission of Orthodoxy, that we should organize movements within the Church to attend to these concerns and to provide for spiritual awakening, perhaps not unlike the ZOE and similar lay movements in Greece.[19] Such movements already have been organized, such as the Orthodox Christian Laity (OCL), Orthodox People Together (OPT), Orthodox Synergy and similar action-oriented groups who, along with concerned individuals, can suggest means by which realistic unity might be achieved and to convince our "Mother Churches" abroad of the lateness of the hour.[20]

In addition, it will be necessary to address the broad range of pressing issues that presently confront the Church, issues such as spiritual renewal, moral concerns, outreach, missions, religious education, liturgical reform, fasting, calendar, language, finance, women's role in the Church, and many others; issues related to the unity problem, many of which have been repeatedly discussed and reported in a number of excellent documents and reports to our hierarchs and churches and which have gone ignored and unresolved for much too long.[21] Only then will we take the first step toward that much-desired unity.

What follows in the Report are three models for canonical ecclesiastical unity in America which the Commission has carefully discussed and reviewed and presents as options for achieving such unity in America.

POSSIBLE MODELS FOR ACHIEVING UNITY

The Commission, sensitive to its charge and aware of its significance, has received and deliberated upon a broad spectrum of opinions, aspects, and prospects on the idea for Orthodox unity. In its discussions and deliberations, it has examined and considered ecclesiastical history, Scriptural, and Patristic texts on the nature of the Church and its unity. After consulting applicable canon law and other pertinent information regarding ecclesiastical unity, the Commission has arrived at three possible models for achieving canonical unity, which are developed and presented below. All models consider or imply arrangements for accommodating cultural identities relevant to the nature and practices of territorial churches.[22]

MODEL A (AUTONOMOUS)

Unification of all canonical jurisdictions into an autonomous (semi-independent) Church under the tutelage of the Ecumenical Patriarchate of Constantinople without particular reference to ethnic identities.

Support for Model A

Upheld by canon law (3rd canon of 1st Constantinople and canon 28 of Chalcedon).

The Ecumenical Patriarchate is recognized by all Orthodox churches as *primus inter pares* (first among equals) and final court of appeal for all Orthodox churches (Maximos).

Despite restraints imposed by Turkish authorities, the Ecumenical Patriarchate is recognized by international law (Giannakakis and Agnnides).

The Ecumenical Patriarchate has a worldwide multinational jurisdiction in Europe, Asia, North and South America, Australia, and New Zealand and, despite its "Greekness," is the only supranational Church stemming from antiquity.

The concept of "first bishop," a prerogative of the Ecumenical Throne, is a vital and necessary principle for the preservation and stability of the worldwide Church and for the fulfillment of its mission (Meyendorff, Catholicity).

Despite its harassments by Turkish authorities in Istanbul, the Ecumenical Patriarchate has indeed been able to administer and service its universal jurisdiction by virtue of its Orthodox Center of the Ecumenical Patriarchate at Chambesy (Geneva), Switzerland.

The weight of nearly 2,000 years of tradition and history of the Ecumenical Patriarchate necessitates its survival as the premier Church of Orthodoxy.

The Argument for Model A: An Autonomous American Orthodox Church Background. The need for, indeed the imperative of, a unified Orthodox Christian Church in the Americas has been presented in the introductory section of this report. From statements made by the late Patriarch Demetrius, to the realization that unification is desirable from many quarters in the laity, it is apparent that achieving unification is at least an issue for discussion, if not an objective whose time has come. The canonical order delineating church structure has not been followed in recent centuries. This structure was set forth by the one undivided Christian Church of the first centuries. Specifically, canon 2 of the 2nd Ecumenical Council of Constantinople requires one bishop in one city. Since the Great Schism of 1054, there can be and often are more than one bishop in a city adhering to the tradition of the Eastern Orthodox Christian Church and the Western Roman Catholic Church, not to mention a plethora of "bishops" without apostolic succession in the numerous Protestant churches. Beyond that there can be and are more than one bishop of the Orthodox Church from various ethnic backgrounds. These have emerged in the diaspora because of the transplant of Orthodox faithful from their Orthodox homelands.

The questions of canonical unity of the Eastern Orthodox Christian Church in the diaspora has not escaped the attention of the Ecumenical Patriarchate and other Patriarchates and autocephalous churches. These churches are engaged in preparing for the Great and Holy Council of Orthodox Christianity through the work of the Pre-Conciliar Pan Orthodox Conference. Ten topics are being explored by the Inter-Orthodox Preparatory Commission, one of which focuses on the *Orthodox Diaspora*. The Commission has issued a report on organizational principles which are cited elsewhere. The five principles reflecting canonical tradition and ecclesiological practices of the Church refer to the existing situation and cite transitional steps that can be taken in the march towards unification. Issues and problems that would have to be addressed to effect unification include:

- One bishop for all Orthodox in each city or region.
- The cultural, linguistic, national needs of the parishioners.
- The structuring of the institutional church.
- Training of Clergy — the existing seminaries.
- Finances.

The above, along with others, presents a formidable array of issues that the Inter-Orthodox Commission will explore.

It is not our intent to duplicate that work which is being carried out by the knowledgeable and capable Commission members. The intent here is to provide a basic view and comment on one of the alternative courses the churches of the diaspora can take in their restructuring effort.

The Case for Autonomy

Setting aside the multitude of issues and problems that would have to be consensually agreed to or resolved by the majority of the conferees, there is one fundamental question that this Report will concentrate on and that has to do with what the ultimate unified Orthodox Church will be. This section argues the case for an Autonomous American Orthodox Church.

In such a Church, the various currently overlapping (because of ethnic origins), jurisdictions would be unified into an autonomous or semi-independent Church under the Ecumenical Patriarchate. This means that, structurally speaking, there would be a line relationship between the Ecumenical Patriarchate and each newly autonomous Orthodox Christian Church. Thus, it becomes necessary to explore the status and importance of the Ecumenical Patriarchate as a necessary prerequisite for an autonomous relationship.

The Importance of the Patriarchate

The Canonical Decree. The 4th Ecumenical Council of Chalcedon held in 451 A.D., decided in canon 28 that the Ecumenical Patriarchate will appoint the bishop of the Diaspora. This canon is the basis for a line relationship between the Patriarchate and the Church in America which, at the moment, is thwarted by the ethnic paths the Orthodox jurisdictions followed in making their presence in the New World.

The Jurisdiction of the Ecumenical Patriarchate. The Ecumenical Patriarchate has a worldwide multinational jurisdiction in Europe, Asia, Australia, New Zealand, and North and South America. It is the only supranational Church stemming from antiquity.

234

The Ranking of the Ecumenical Patriarchate. All Orthodox Churches recognize the Ecumenical Patriarchate as *primus inter Pares* (first among equals) and the final court of appeal for all Orthodox Churches. This historical status of "first bishop," a prerogative of the Ecumenical Throne, is a vital and necessary principle for the preservation and stability of the worldwide Church and for the fulfillment of its mission.[23]

The Status of the Ecumenical Patriarchate. The Treaty of Lausanne (1923) guarantees the existence of the Ecumenical Patriarchate of Constantinople. This recognition has not prevented the Turkish authorities from restraining the operation of the Patriarchate. Harassment, especially during the last four decades, has decimated the Greek Orthodox population of Istanbul and has put in question the continued viability and effectiveness of the Patriarchate. However, along with its Orthodox Center at Chambesy (Geneva), Switzerland, it has been able to administer and service its universal jurisdiction.

The Roots of the Ecumenical Patriarchate and Tradition. The Ecumenical Patriarchate has history and tradition of 2,000 years rooted in Apostolic times. It has survived unprecedented assaults and vicissitudes and one must respect the human courage and resilience that have brought about that survival, inspired and nurtured, no doubt, by the Holy Spirit.

Much has been touted in recent years about roots and their importance in the self-awareness of identity and meaning on a personal as well as a group or social level. The importance of roots in the Faith is paramount, since everything, the Eucharist and the other Sacraments, is central to it, and go back to the very beginning: Christ and the Apostles.

The life of the Ecumenical Patriarchate which is the Eastern Orthodox Tradition, has a continuity that goes back to Andrew the Apostle. This tradition, these roots, cannot and should not be easily discarded. There are those who may be intimidated and frustrated by the harassments, the humiliations, the sacrifices that the Patriarchate has been subjected to and suffered over the recent centuries.[24]   But no one who understands what Christianity is all about is under the illusion that it is an ineffectual faith. Thus the conclusion must be that under no circumstances should any Orthodox Christian espouse the idea that the Ecumenical Patriarchate abandon its historical right guaranteed by treaty to be where it is. But what has all this to do with the unity of the Orthodox in the Americas and how this unity will be structured?

Autonomy Under the Ecumenical Patriarchate.
All of the above make a strong case for the united Orthodox expression in the New World to be an autonomous relationship with the Ecumenical Patriarchate. The reasons are compelling:

Autonomy — A Bond That Transcends Borders. Autonomy should not be viewed as diminishing the independence of the American Church nor does it imply foreign domination. Rather, the picture would be of a bond of continuity that transcends borders, is worldwide, and has solid roots in unshakable history and tradition that is still viable and goes back to the very beginnings of the Christian Faith.

Autonomy — A Bond of Mutual Support and Strength. In the circumstances of its location and existence in a hostile environment, an autonomous bond with the Church in the land that is the unquestionable leader of the free world would greatly strengthen the Patriarchate's position.   Any attempts to further undermine its claim for a continued presence where it now exists would create unwelcome worldwide publicity and outrage. Moves to persecute, no matter how subtle, would run the risk of open and worldwide public awareness and condemnation. As for the Church in America, an autonomous bond with the Patriarchate would give it the kind of prestige the Roman Catholics enjoy with the Vatican.   The Orthodox Church would be viewed, not as just one more independent Christian sect among hundreds, but a body of Christians of major significance on the stage of world Christianity.

236

Autonomy and the Patriarchate's "Greekness." It may be argued that unifying the many Orthodox ethnic churches in the Americas would find a stumbling block in the "Greekness" of the Ecumenical Patriarchate. Here a distinction must be made between "ethnic Greekness" and "cultural Greekness." The former has the notion of bonding with the Greek state, and certainly that is not the case with the Ecumenical Patriarchate. That it has strong Greek roots cannot be disputed. Its Greekness is more cultural; that is, it reflects the currents of thought and expression that charted its course. Secure in the knowledge of the universal appeal and power of its Greekness, it did not feel constrained or reluctant to carry the Truth of the Gospel to other lands, especially to the Slavs, and to create the linguistic presuppositions in the native idioms so that the Truth of the Gospel would be comprehended and disseminated without those kinds of impediments. Thus, the Russian Orthodox, Romanian Orthodox, and Bulgarian Orthodox, are no less daughter churches of the Ecumenical Patriarchate than the Greek Orthodox. So, the creation of a unified Orthodox Church in America under the Ecumenical Patriarchate would not be the result of an artificial bonding, but one that is rooted in a very real historical tradition, thus making it stronger than what it otherwise would be.

An additional note on Greekness having to do with the Greek language: Let not a sense of inadequacy or inferiority stemming from the lack of knowledge of the Greek, coupled by some notion of xenophobia propel the American Church to shove aside the importance of Greek and the knowledge of it. It would be a calamity of colossal proportion if this were to happen for it goes way beyond any sense of pride by Greek ethnics. Greek is the language of the New Testament, the Fathers of the Church, and the Ecumenical Councils. With a plethora of Bible translations entering the market in recent decades, the meaning of the original is often completely distorted. Thus more and more, we hear Protestant preachers in their sermons going back to the original Greek words for the precise meaning. How much more sensitive should all the

Orthodox be about the importance of Greek, since it is the heritage of all of them, and indeed of all Christians.

Autonomy and Independent Hierarchial Choices. Autonomy is understood to be a semi-independent relationship; that is, the Patriarchate would have the prerogative to appoint the Orthodox prelates in the American Church, while the latter administers its own affairs through its own synod. This is the present ecclesiastical status of the Greek Orthodox Archdiocese of North and South America since its founding in 1922, except for the period between 1930 and 1977 when it did not have its own synod.[25] However, the appointment of hierarchs in the American Church need not be devoid of input from the American flock. For example, an accommodation can be worked out between the Patriarchate and the "royal priesthood" on the American scene, whereby following the very ancient practice of the Church, the ecclesia of the faithful would make their recommendations and preferences known of several choices for hierarch from whom the Patriarchate would make the final selection.[26]

Indeed, such was the practice at Constantinople prior to 1925 when the Ecumenical Patriarch was elected by a Mixed Council which was comprised of four metropolitans from the Holy Synod and **eight laymen** providing a strong lay element in the selection of hierarchs. Only recently, with the election of Patriarch Alexius of Moscow, 66 bishops and 66 priests **along with 66 laymen** representing the 66 dioceses of the Church of Russia, participated in the electoral process. Even today in the Church of Cyprus laymen participate in the election of bishops.[27]

Conclusion
A consideration of all the above factors suggests that a unified American Orthodox Church in an autonomous relationship with the Ecumenical Patriarchate is desirable and practical for a number of reasons:

1. It would provide a unified voice for Orthodoxy in America and worldwide.

2. It will strengthen the status of the Ecumenical Patriarchate which exists in a hostile environment.

3. It will enhance the status and provide cognizant visibility and projection and weight of the American Church as a Christian body, with continuity and roots in Apostolic times.

4. It will express an appreciation for the profound riches in the teachings and traditions of the Orthodox which transcend time and space.

5. It will not trample or undermine the ethnic particularities of the parishes as they now exist.

6. It will proclaim the universality of the Orthodox Faith while at the same time recognizing that there can be a rich cultural diversity under the oneness and centrality of Christ.

MODEL B (AUTOCEPHALOUS)
Unification of all canonical jurisdictions into an autocephalous (self-governing) Church with its own elected primate and independent of all other world Orthodox jurisdictions without particular reference to ethnic identities.

Support for Model B
1. Canon law provides for it (23rd canon of Carthage).

2. Part of natural process of evolving Church as reflected in the establishment of modern Orthodox autocephalous churches of Europe.

3. Need for indigenous American Church to reach out to unchurched Americans as in the Great Commission of Pentecost.

4. Need to remove foreign aura of Church in America by adopting English language as vernacular of the Church to reach its youth and the great numbers who have fallen away.

5. The Ecumenical Patriarchate is a captive institution in a hostile environment subject to continuous constraints of the Turkish Government; as such, it is not an independent agency and cannot perform its religious obligations as the Great Church of Christ — center and font of world Orthodoxy (Runciman).

6. The Ecumenical Patriarchate is no longer located in a Christian environment but in a nation that is overwhelmingly Muslim, whose immediate flock has been reduced to less than 5,000 souls; as such, Constantinople has ceased to be a major metropolitan see, unworthy of being a center for world Orthodoxy.

7. It is for these reasons that the modern autocephalic churches evolved, not wishing to be subject to a patriarch under Turkish suzerainty; namely, Greece in 1830, and later Serbia, Romania and Bulgaria.

8. America is not a diaspora; it is home to millions of Orthodox Christians, more so than in the ancient patriarchates of Alexandria, Antioch, or Jerusalem; hence, there is a need to form an independent Church.

The Argument for Model B: An Autocephalous American Orthodox Church
Background. The solemn signing of the Tomos of Autocephaly in Moscow (April, 1970) between representatives of the old Russian Orthodox Metropolia in North America and Alexius I, Patriarch of Moscow and All Russia, marked

the culmination of a complex historical and spiritual process which began in Alaska in 1794.[28] In that year, the first missionaries were sent to that northern land by the then-Synodal Church in Imperial Russia. The mission gradually spread southward, with special concentration in northern California. Thus, the original evangelical work of Orthodoxy proceeded from west to east, a somewhat unusual phenomenon. Later waves of immigrants from Eastern Europe necessitated the founding of parishes throughout the Eastern seaboard, as well as the Midwest. The continuity of mission in America is something that the old Russian mission has always emphasized in its bold but humble claim to be the Orthodox Church in America. In fact, a careful study of Orthodox Church history and the establishment of other autocephalous churches bears this out.

Of course, the establishment of the Orthodox Church in America (OCA) caused some misunderstanding and even vituperation, but neither is exactly unknown to observers of the Orthodox scene in other circumstances as well. For the past twenty years, the OCA has been actively working for the unity of the Church in this country. As an ecclesiastical fact of life, the OCA stands as a witness to that unity as well as a genuine commitment to the American people on behalf of Orthodoxy. Her slow but steady growth is empirical proof that, for America, Orthodoxy is an idea whose time has come.

Proposed Development in Detail. The Model B plan for Orthodox unity in this country centers around the already existing autocephalous church, the Orthodox Church in America. The step-by-step program given below will explain in detail how such a plan might be implemented. (The following section will portray schematically the steps developed below.)

Step 1.   The OCA, created in 1970, already makes the claim to be the Orthodox Church in America. The Church of Russia recognized this autocephaly and granted recognition to the OCA as self-governing. Various ethnic dioceses have joined (Romanian, Bulgarian, Albanian), without diminution of their ethnic heritages. Formal recognition has been limited, but *de facto* sacramental participation with canonical

241

churches is all but universal. Sadly, the goal of unity among the Orthodox has not yet been realized, but the OCA, as a living organism, is a fact which must be accounted for in any quest for unity.

Step 2. The OCA would invite all Orthodox Churches in the United States to a meeting on Church Life and Unity. The focus is that we have a theological, a spiritual problem in phyletism, the existence of a multiplicity of jurisdictions in America, which erodes and undermines normal ecclesiastical life as well as the daily spiritual life of the Orthodox people. The OCA would act as convener.

Step 3. All participants above are to report to their respective Mother Churches the results of the meetings. Obviously, since the direct but often unstated interests of these mother churches will be different from those of their children, opposition is to be expected. Long experience here has demonstrated incontrovertibly that persistence is the key.

Step 4. With the OCA as presider, the various jurisdictions are to apply for "associate membership" in an umbrella-like organization attached to each other and to the OCA. Local bishops would be free to participate in this process, but the hierarchical structure of the OCA would remain necessarily intact. The various jurisdictions would retain control of their flocks.

Step 5. All participants are to report to their Mother Churches the fact of such proceedings. Opposition from some quarters is to be expected.

Step 6. Local jurisdictions are to apply for membership in an Orthodox Church in America. Within this larger and more comprehensive body, provision would need to be made for an association of bishops, a temporary measure until a full hierarchy could be functioning as the Orthodox Church in America. One possible avenue is for a rotation of bishops in sees which have experienced multiplicity, with an agreement as to lengths of terms in the various capacities.

Step 7. The proclamation of a true, canonically correct Orthodox Church in America, with participants from all jurisdictions. The settlement of diocesan questions, succession, and unified mission could be worked out once the structure is functioning.

Further consideration on Model B
Strengths (Positives) of Conceptual Framework
1. Allows for existing structures.

2. Allows "face saving" by all.

    a. The issue of power, prestige are laid aside in favor of <u>unity</u>.
    b. OCA and the Greek Orthodox Archdiocese are NOT perceived in adversarial terms.
    c. No canons need be cited nor disputed.
    d. The integrity of Orthodox Church bodies is preserved.

Weaknesses (Negatives) of Conceptual Framework
The following to be expected as the norm.

1. Head of *diasporal* churches may balk.

2. Some jurisdictions may go this route, others may not.

3. Not all jurisdictions would agree to accept because of "canonical irregularities" concerning the granting of autocephaly to the former Russian Metropolia.

FIGURE 2   MODEL B - GRAPHIC SCHEMA OF THE SEVEN STEPS

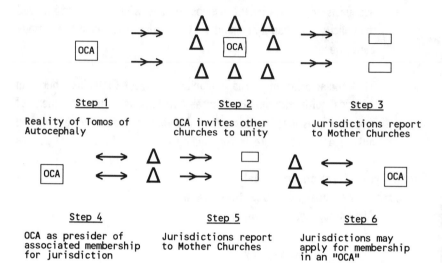

Step 1

Reality of Tomos of
Autocephaly

Step 2

OCA invites other
churches to unity

Step 3

Jurisdictions report
to Mother Churches

Step 4

OCA as presider of
associated membership
for jurisdiction

Step 5

Jurisdictions report
to Mother Churches

Step 6

Jurisdictions may
apply for membership
in an "OCA"

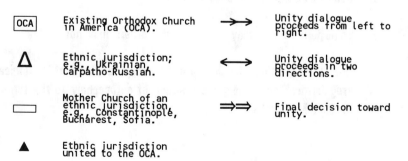

Step 7

The future of the OCA is realized:

a. Majority of Orthodox in U.S.A. as
    <u>members</u>.
b. Some in a temporary, associational
    status.

LEGEND

| OCA | Existing Orthodox Church in America (OCA). | → | Unity dialogue proceeds from left to right. |

| △ | Ethnic jurisdiction; e.g. Ukrainian, Carpatho-Russian. | ↔ | Unity dialogue proceeds in two directions. |

| ▭ | Mother Church of an ethnic jurisdiction, e.g. Constantinople, Bucharest, Sofia. | ⇒ | Final decision toward unity. |

| ▲ | Ethnic jurisdiction united to the OCA. | | |

244

Opposition to Autocephaly: The OCA Experience

It is fair to state that despite the reality of the OCA in America, its acceptance by most worldwide Orthodox churches is yet forthcoming. While the churches of Russia (which granted autocephaly), Czechoslovakia and Poland have recognized the OCA as autocephalous, most have not. Indeed, the canonical status of the OCA, even when it was the former "Metropolia," has been in dispute since 1924 when it declared itself "temporarily autonomous" of the Church of Russia. The granting of permanent autocephaly to OCA by the Church of Russia in 1970, continues the dispute. The Ecumenical Patriarch has only a tacit recognition of the OCA (as do most other autocephalous churches), until the matter can be settled by the forthcoming Great and Holy Council of the Orthodox Church.[29]

The granting of autocephaly to the Russian jurisdiction in America in 1970, elicited numerous formal responses from the ancient patriarchates of Constantinople, Alexandria, Antioch and Jerusalem, as well as from the Church of Greece, among others. In encyclicals written to Patriarch Athenagoras of Constantinople and Patriarch Alexius I of Moscow, in brotherly but unmistakable terms, the venerable heads of these sees objected on canonical grounds and on the basis of historical practice the unilateral action of the Patriarch of Moscow.[30]

In addition, a number of renowned Orthodox theologians, along with several laymen, have written extensively, citing canon law and historical precedents, which in their opinions, would invalidate the granting of autocephaly to the OCA (Trempelas and Kopan). Furthermore, these theologians have pointed out that there seem to be several conditions under canon law which would specifically rule out such an act. No less an authority than Bogolepov maintains that the opinion that the Mother Church alone (in this case Moscow) is entitled to grant autocephalous status, not only has no basis in canon law, but is also inconsistent with the principles of Orthodox Canon Law. Rather, for autocephaly to become an accomplished fact it is necessary for all existing autocephalous Orthodox churches to agree to it and to accept it. In other words, one member of the Community of Orthodox churches cannot by itself introduce a new church into the community without the consent of all the other members, who are equal in status. The Ecumenical Patriarchate, just as every other autocephalous church, has the right to withhold recognition of the autocephalous status of a new church, as granted by the Mother Church. In refusing to recognize the new status of the Metropolia, the Ecumenical Patriarch exercised the basic right of every autocephalous church, especially of the first among them (Bogolepov). Perhaps the most serious obstacle to the validity of autocephaly cited by many theologians is the fact that such a status cannot be granted to a given territory unless in that territory all Orthodox churches are united into one body. The late Fr. Schmemann, among others, has pointed out that this is the *sine qua non* for autocephaly in a given political territory such as the United States. This is obviously not the case in America where even the Russians had been divided into three jurisdictions (Schmemann, Primacy 49-75). This was the reason why the Synod of Constantinople in 1872 refused to grant autocephaly to Bulgaria as it lacked such unity as well as a clearly defined political territory.[31]

Thus, according to most Orthodox churches, what happened in the case of the Russian Metropolia (OCA) is clearly a canonical irregularity and constitutes a patent contradiction between what is the established law of the whole Orthodox Church and what has been or is done by a given local Orthodox church. It is precisely for correcting situations in which such painful irregularities have occurred that the future Great and Holy Council included in its agenda consideration of the following relevant subjects:

- The proclamation of autocephaly
- Who grants autocephaly
- Conditions and presuppositions for autocephaly
- Procedure for granting autocephaly
- Which churches today are recognized as autocephalous (Russian Autocephaly p.71).

A further point stressed by the Ecumenical Patriarchate is that on many occasions, in its great desire to maintain unity among all the sister Orthodox churches, it has exercised its privileges and prerogatives with great flexibility, and with an economy and charity dictated by love, instead of by a rigid and legalistic adherence to the letter of church law. On occasions, when the Patriarchate of Constantinople has been faced with *de facto*, arbitrary, or unilateral anti-canonical action, it has sought at all costs to maintain inter-Orthodox unity and to avoid division between the sister Orthodox churches by adopting an attitude of charity and understanding (as in the tacit recognition of OCA). But it has maintained that the adoption of such an attitude should not be construed to the belief that the disregarding of canonically established law should be allowed to become a regular and permanent practice (Russian Autocephaly p.71).

It thus seems that a resolution of the OCA issue must take place before canonical unity in America can begin to emerge. This will probably be effected by a renewed effort of all jurisdictions in America to bring about true canonical unity with the cooperation and blessings of the mother churches abroad, especially as reflected in the planned Pan-Orthodox synod.

Model B - Recommendations and Conclusions

Evidence from Scripture and Canon Law. It is evident even to the casual observer that ecclesiastical life is based upon the threefold basis of Holy Scriptures, canon law, and history. These form a sacred unity whereby the Church's mission in and to this world is revealed and its very character made manifest. With reference to the particularities of Model B, several important points need to be elucidated. First among these is the character of the church as one, its unity a cause of concern for Christ Himself even as he voluntarily went to His life-giving death. In John 17, the Savior gives a summary of His wish for His disciples in the High Priestly Prayer, a call that they be one precisely because such unity reflects the Godhead. Second, an examination of canon law reveals a certain variety of opinion as to the authority for granting self-government to a local church, and it is not the intention of this model to choose sides. It is in the third point, the history of Orthodoxy on this continent, that the strongest and most telling argument can he made for the growth and development that led to the recognition of the Orthodox Church in America in 1970.

Evidence from History. From the time of the first missionaries in Alaska in 1794, through the settlements in California and then in the rest of the United States, the impetus for an autocephalous church has been present. Significant efforts among the native people of Alaska led to the creation of a new diocese located at New Archangelsk (Sitka). From St. Herman through St. Innocent, first bishop, the seeds of an independent church were sown.[32] The focus on this vision culminated in the person of Bishop (later saint) Tikhon (Patriarch of Moscow), who ordained various ethnic hierarchs to serve **both** locally and ethnically. Bishop Tikhon's words concerning the mission to America were clear and resounding; in deeds he confirmed beyond any doubt his intentions to create a structure which would become autocephalous.

The tragic events of the revolution in Russia undermined, at least, temporarily, these plans. Communication between the local Church in America and the Russian Church became increasingly difficult. New waves of immigrants arrived in the United States just as the local church's efforts at unity were thrown into a chaotic state. Bolshevik attempts to divide the Church had a profound effect on the local administration, and, with no other real choices open to her, the temporary self-governance of the "American Metropolia" became a fact. Clearly, the canonical and spiritual situation was vague and unclear.

The Tomos of Autocephaly. It was precisely this vague and unclear status that hampered the local church in her missionary efforts for several generations. Finally, through an almost miraculous confluence of persons and events, the American Metropolia and the Russian Orthodox Church signed the TOMOS OF AUTOCEPHALY in April, 1970. The goal of this concordat was to regularize and normalize the canonical situation of the local church, and thus, Orthodoxy on this continent. The signing of the TOMOS continues and validates the vision of St. Tikhon and the early missionaries; the original ideal

248

of one church in America was truly "an idea whose time had come." The Russian Church correctly surmised that one canonically organized church would then be able to reach out to other Orthodox groups and jurisdictions while simultaneously pursuing serious missionary efforts among the various and varied peoples in America. In this schema, ethnicity is not denigrated but rather properly affirmed, given perspective from a spiritual point of view.

Accordingly, the OCA's goal has always been one Orthodox Church in America, with all the richness and diversity which that may entail. Indeed, the very name Orthodox Church in America is extremely important for understanding that mission correctly. The church is not to be understood narrowly and uncritically as wed to American culture and values; the church, as a pilgrim in this world, is always **IN** and **NOT OF** a particular place and culture. The Gospel's values and norms will always place them at variance with, and in contradiction to, the "established" thinking. Orthodoxy in America must witness to a set of criteria, sometimes radically outside the prevailing cultural values.

There is, then, one, unbroken mission to America, through the Russian Church's mission, and then eventually in the OCA. Unfortunately, some other Orthodox jurisdictions in America have been very slow to recognize the reality of the OCA, and others have ranged from indifferent to positively hostile. Many (although not all) other Orthodox use terms familiar to them, terms which allow them to continue "business as usual"; Russian Church, Russian Metropolia, Russian Orthodox Church, are some terms used in place of the proper OCA. From the material presented above, it should be clear that these older terms are totally inadequate to describe the spiritual and canonical reality that is the OCA.

MODEL C (TRANSITIONAL)

An "Assembly of Bishops" to be established in yet to be defined dioceses in the "diaspora" initially based upon ethnic identities and which will determine the primatial See whose bishops would preside at all common meetings and report to the Ecumenical Patriarch until such time as the convening of the

Great and Holy Council which would then approve of the multi-ethnic restructuring of these dioceses by the "Assembly of Bishops" into full-fledged canonical autocephalous Orthodox jurisdictions.

The Argument for Model C
Transitional (Inter-Orthodox Preparatory Commission)

Background. The Inter-Orthodox Preparatory Commission for the Great and Holy Council, at a meeting on November 10-17, 1990, at the Patriarchal Center in Chambesy, Switzerland, discussed the topic of the "Orthodox diaspora" and prepared a preliminary report that has been commended to the Churches for study. The Commission brought together the official representatives of the twelve autocephalous and two autonomous churches under the presidency of Metropolitan Bartholomew of Chalcedon (now the Ecumenical Patriarch of Constantinople) to discuss canonical unity in the diaspora.

The then Metropolitan Bartholomew, in his opening address to the delegates, affirmed that the time had come for the Churches to find a canonical solution to the organization of the *Orthodox diaspora*. He reminded the delegates of the remarks of the late Patriarch Demetrius, who said during his 1990 visit to America:

> *It is truly a scandal for the unity of the Church to maintain more than one bishop in any given city; it contravenes the sacred canons and Orthodox ecclesiology. It is a scandal that this is exacerbated whenever phyletistic motives play a part, a practice soundly condemned by the Orthodox Church in the last century.*

We may also add here the similar remarks made by Patriarch Alexius II of Moscow during his recent visit to the United States, who expressed the hope that "a single multi-national Orthodox Church" evolve in America (New York Times, Nov. 22, 1991, A8).

250

The first Pan-Orthodox Pre-Conciliar Conference called by the Ecumenical Patriarch to prepare for the convening of a Great Council, was held in 1976. This Conference established a list of ten topics which would be examined by the Church prior to the convening of the Great and Holy Council. The work of the Inter-Orthodox Commission is to study systematically these topics and prepare position papers. Thus, the work of this Conference led to the convening of the Second Pre-Conciliar Pan-Orthodox Conference in 1982, and to the Third in 1986.

Among the topics discussed at the Third Conference was the question of the "Orthodox Diaspora" which was assigned to several Churches for their deliberation. At the November, 1990 meeting of the Commission the reports of the "Orthodox Diaspora" produced by the Churches of Constantinople, Alexandria, Antioch, Russia, Romania, Greece and Poland were reviewed. A detailed analysis of these reports was provided by Metropolitan Damaskinos of Switzerland, Secretary for the Preparation of the Great and Holy Synod (See Appendix V, p. 288).

Following much discussion, the Commission unanimously adopted a number of recommendations that have been submitted to the Churches. Certain themes remain to be discussed by the Inter-Orthodox Commission. Among these is the recommendation with regard to the various regions where an "Assembly of Bishops" should be established. Moreover, the Commission must also review the organizational principles that can guide the proper development of the Church in the new lands. The report takes note of five principles that reflect the canonical tradition and ecclesiological practices of the Church. They are as follows:

1. The organization of the parishes in each diocese should be open to the possibility of the existence of parishes that serve the particular cultural, linguistic, national needs of their parishioners. These parishes will be under the jurisdiction of the local diocesan bishop.

251

2. There shall exist only one bishop in each city or in a clearly defined region.

3. The boundaries of dioceses shall be clearly established.

4. In each region where there is an "Assembly of Bishops," it will be necessary to determine the regional dioceses and the primatial See, whose bishop will preside at all common meetings. Until such time that the region becomes autocephalous, the presiding hierarch will commemorate the Patriarch of Constantinople.

5. The project of canonical restructuring shall be accomplished by the "Assembly of Bishops" in each place prior to the convocation of the Great and Holy Council and in accordance with established canonical procedures.

The preliminary report concludes by affirming that the Orthodox Churches are committed not to do anything which would hinder the process of the canonical organization of the various regions of the *Diaspora*. This would preclude the establishment of the new dioceses in addition to those in existence. Furthermore, the report calls upon the Mother Churches to do everything possible to bring about the normalization of canonical order on the basis of the principles noted above.

Discussion. It is obvious from the Inter-Orthodox Pre-Conciliar Preparatory Commission's Text on the Orthodox Diaspora that was adopted at Chambesy on November 10-17, 1990, that serious consideration is being given by the Orthodox Churches to the resolution of the problem of Orthodox churches in the diaspora, especially in the light of the forthcoming Great and Holy Council. The development of this transitional plan for achieving canonical unity in the diaspora, which will be presented for adoption at the Fourth Pre-Conciliar Conference which is scheduled to meet in the near future, provides for an alternative plan which has the backing of the entire Orthodox Church and therefore has a greater degree of successful promulgation. Furthermore, this model is in keeping with Orthodox canonical tradition and ecclesiological practice and will thus pre-empt any charges of schism or anti-canonical conduct as was the case with the establishment of the Orthodox Church in America (OCA) in 1970.

The establishment of an "Assembly of Bishops" in North America (certainly to be one of the regions to be designated for such an assemblage), draws attention to the very important role of bishops in fostering unity and underscores the need for continuing study of the role of the episcopate in the Church. Nonetheless, such a body will provide the necessary leadership for achieving canonical unity in America given the fact that (unlike SCOBA), it will have multi-jurisdictional sanction and support from the entire Orthodox world.

The implementation of this model will cause fewer divisions and dissension in the Orthodox jurisdictions in North America and will be a better guarantee of success provided it is activated with no inordinate delays and procrastinations (which have marked current attempts for unity), given the snail-pace that describes the preparation and convening of the Great and Holy Council.

Efforts to achieve unity of Orthodoxy in the diaspora, as the Commission realizes, is not only a practical matter of structural adaptation but also implies a theological vision. Discussion of ecclesiology and Church structures cannot be separated from discussion of the Church's mission and witness. In this respect, it is important to investigate in greater detail the particularities of the Orthodox situation in the United States and Canada, for as the Commission also realized, the situation of the Orthodox in the diaspora varies considerably from region to region. Certainly in North America there are a number of cultural and even legal circumstances that have impeded Orthodox unity and cooperation. At the same time there have been a number of significant developments, both on local and national levels, which have served to foster unity.

A CONCLUDING THOUGHT AND PRAYER

Any view of the Church in America cannot escape the reality that it is fragmented and broken, without the inner spirit and moral resources to proclaim the Gospel entrusted to Her by the Lord. Up to now, a plethora of jurisdictions in America has made any thought of unity strictly theoretical. In fact, one must be an accomplished Church historian merely to assimilate the details of Orthodoxy's history in America. The passage of time has seen, not unity, but a growth of factionalism and rank un-Christian behavior. The story of Orthodoxy in America is often one of unfortunate occurrences, everything but unity. When one confronts the state of Orthodoxy in America, it is obvious much work needs to be done. The disunity has created a situation that is apparent to the most casual observer, at cross-purposes to the truth of the Gospel as given over and over in Christ's call to unity. Orthodoxy's shortcomings in terms of mission, education, and morality can all be explained in these terms. Simply put, if we choose a path other than the Lord's, we shall surely suffer. And, to some degree, we have.

The work of this Commission on Unity is central, and in one sense, prior to all other work. The very life of the Christian community depends upon unity; without it, there is not very much to say (and little we can do). A critical test of this lies in the fact that many, perhaps even some in our own ranks, do not comprehend the reality of Orthodoxy on these shores. Soon we shall celebrate 200 years of the Faith on this continent. Would that the work of this Commission will begin a dialogue within the Church by her members, hierarchs, clergy and people. We have faced the past and the present; let us look now to a real future.

The Commission members brought to this discussion many points of view which are reflected in this report. The Commission also feels that it should not recommend a specific course of action. Rather, its work has provided a unique overview of historical and contemporary Orthodoxy, coupled with some very well-developed models for unity. However, this work does not in any way preclude other creative approaches to the problem.

The Commission presents this report in the hope and the expectation that it will stimulate a healthy discussion among all spectra of the faithful on this most important issue. All should be mindful of one caveat — not to fall into the trap that believes the Church's ills can be rectified by structure and process only. Ultimately, the issue of unity is a manifestation of spiritual fullness. With humility that banishes egos and self-centered interests, and with prayer on bended knee, opening hearts to the guidance of the Holy Spirit, the Orthodox *pleroma* will see its way to implement the will of God on this all-important issue of Orthodox unity. Amen.

NOTES

1. For an in-depth treatment on the Council of 381 and the primacy of Constantinople, see John Meyendorff, Catholicity and the Church (Crestwood, NY: St. Vladimir's Seminary Press, 1983) pp. 121-142.

2. For an insightful look into the complexity of this problem see John Meyendorff, "Contemporary Problems of Orthodox Canon Law," The Greek Orthodox Theological Review, Vol. XXII, No. 2, (Summer, 1977), pp. 41-50.

3. The encyclical was republished in 1950 upon the occasion of the opening of the Holy Year at Rome when Pope Pius XII once again issued a call for all non-Roman Christians to "return to the fold." An English translation of the entire epistle appears in The Reply of the Orthodox Church to Roman Catholic Overtures on Reunion: Being the Answer of the Great Church of Christ to a Papal Encyclical on Reunion (New York: Brotherhood Zealots of Orthodoxy, 1950). A later translation with additional comments appears in Orthodox and Catholic Union (Seattle, WA: St. Nectarios Press, 1985).

4. For a fuller development of this term see John Meyendorff, The Vision of Unity, (Crestwood, NY: St. Vladimir's Seminary Press, 1987), pp. 139-144. For a different view see Demetrios J. Constantelos, "The Orthodox Diaspora: Canonical and Ecclesiological Perspective," The Greek Orthodox Theological Review, Vol. XXIV, Nos. 2 and 3, (Summer/Fall 1979), pp. 200-211.

5. Information on the Orthodox jurisdictions in America has been extrapolated from the following: Leonid Soroka & Stan W. Carlson, Faith of Our Fathers: The Eastern Orthodox Religion (Minneapolis: Olympic Press, 1954), pp. 15-31; Stephan Themstrom, ed., Harvard Encyclopedia of American Ethnic Groups (Cambridge: Harvard University Press, 1980), passim.; and Charles H. Lippy and Peter W. Williams, eds., Encyclopedia

of the American Religious Experience, Vol. I, (New York: Charles Scribner's Sons, 1989), pp. 325-344.

6. According to Professor Charles Moskos, the exact number of Greek Orthodox Christians in America is more likely to be in the area of 900,000 to 1,100,000. See the OCL Commission Report on Faith, Language and Culture beginning on P. 17 of this volume.

7. Membership statistics and other information about American Orthodox groups have been extrapolated from the following: Statistical Abstract of the United States 1990 (Washington, DC: U.S. Department of Commerce Bureau of the Census, 1990), pp. 56-57; World Almanac Book of Facts 1991 (New York: 1991), pp. 609-610; and The Universal Almanac 1990 (Kansas City, 1990); J. Gordon Melton, The Encyclopedia of American Religions 3rd ed. (Detroit: Gale Research, Inc. 1989).

8. Both of these are in the Antiochian Archdiocese. For the conversion of the Evangelical to Orthodoxy, see Peter E. Gillquist, Becoming Orthodox: A Journey to the Ancient Christian Faith (Brentwood, TN: Wolgemuth & Hyatt, Publishers, 1989).

9. A series of conferences held between mainline Orthodox and the Oriental Churches is reportedly resolving the issue of Monophysitism between the two bodies of churches. See Thomas FitzGerald, "Toward the Reestablishment of Full Communion. The Orthodox-Orthodox Oriental Dialogue," The Greek Orthodox Theological Review, Vol. XXXVI No. 2, (Summer 1991), pp. 169-188.

10. For a synoptical overview of the canonical sources of Orthodox theology, see John Meyendorff, Byzantine Theology: Historical Trends and Doctrinal Themes, (New York: Fordham University Press, 1979), pp. 79-90.

11. Initial descriptions of the proposed Council can be found in Towards the Great Council: Introductory Reports of the Interorthodox Commission in Preparation for the Next Great and Holy Council of the Orthodox Church (London: S.P.C.K., 1972) and in Stanley Harakas, Something is Stirring in World Orthodoxy (New York: The Orthodox Observer Press, 1972). For more recent developments see: John Panagopoulos, "The Orthodox Church Prepares for the Council," One in Christ, Vol. XIII, (1977), pp. 229-237; and Ion Bria, "L'espoir du Grande Synode Orthodoxe," Revue theologique du Louvain, Vol. VIII (1977), pp. 51-54.

12. Appreciation is acknowledged to Peter E. Gillquist for the general format of "A Time Line of Church History." The content, however, has been revised by the Commission. See also his Becoming Orthodox: A Journey to the Ancient Christian Faith, (Brentwood, TN: Wolgemuth & Hyatt, 1989), pp. 52-533

13. Autocephalous status not fully recognized.

14. For the full ramifications of the issue of autocephaly see: Alexander Schmemann, The Historical Road of Eastern Orthodoxy, (New York: Holt, Rinehart and Winston, 1963), passim; Meyendorff, Orthodoxy and Catholicity, esp. pp. 17-48 and pp. 107-118; and Bogolepov, passim.

15. On the development of SCOBA and the structural organization of the various Orthodox jurisdictions in America see Arthur Carl Piepkorn, Profiles in Belief: The Religious Bodies of the United States and Canada, Vol. 1: Roman Catholic, Old Catholic, Eastern Orthodox (New York, 1977) pp. 61-116.

16. For the record, these groups were: American Carpatho-Russian Youth (ACRY); American Romanian Orthodox Youth (AROY); Federated Russian Orthodox Clubs (FROC); Greek Orthodox Youth of America (GOYA); Serbian Singing Federation of America (SSFA); Syrian Orthodox Youth Organization (SOYO); and Ukrainian Orthodox League of the United States (UOL).

17. For a fuller picture of these events from one person's perspective see Meyendorff, The Vision of Unity, pp. 15-110.

18. For the full text of the position of the Ecumenical Patriarchate to Moscow's unilateral action, see: Russian Autocephaly and Orthodoxy in America (New York: The Orthodox Observer Press, 1972); Panagiotis N. Trempelas, The Autocephaly of the Metropolia in America, translated and edited by George S. Bebis, Robert G. Stephanopoulos and N. M. Vaporis (Brookline, MA: Holy Cross School of Theology Press, 1973); and Andrew T. Kopan, "The Autocephaly of the Russian Metropolia," The Orthodox Observer Quarterly, Vol. XXXVI, No. 608 (November, 1970), pp. 7-8. For a rebuttal to Kopan see Meyendorff, Vision of Unity pp. 50-53.

19. For an excellent account of the ZOE movement see Demetrios J. Constantelos "The Zoe Movement in Greece," St. Vladimir's Orthodox Theological Quarterly, Vol. 3, No. 2 (Spring, 1959), pp. 11-25.

20. Interestingly enough, the publication of Fr. Vasile Hategan's (Romanian Orthodox), monumental newspaper, Orthodox Unity, Vol. 1, No. 1 (July, 1990), published upon the occasion of the Ecumenical Patriarch's visit to the United States; and Katherine Valone's (Greek Orthodox), article "An American Orthodox Church: Its Time Has Come," in the August 18, 1991 edition of the Greek Press of Chicago, offers some suggestions. See also James Steve Counelis "Polis and Ecclesia: Toward and American Orthodox Church," Diakonia, Vol. 7 No. 4 (1972), p. 310-325.

21. See Leonidass C. Contos, 2001: The Church in Crisis (Brookline, MA: Holy Cross Orthodox Press, 1981); "Report to His Eminence Archbishop Iakovos," in The Greek Orthodox Theological Review, Vol. XXXIV, No. 3 (Fall, 1989), pp. 283-306; Alexander Schmemann, "The Problems of Orthodoxy in America," St. Vladimir's Seminary Quarterly: "The Canonical Problem," Vol. VIII, No. 2 (1964), pp. 67-85; "The Liturgical Problem," Vol. VIII, No. 4 (1964), pp. 164-185; and "The Spiritual Problem," Vol. IX, No. 4 (1965), pp. 171-193; and Demetrios J. Constantelos,

"Religio-Philosophical Issues and Interreligious Dialogues in Eastern Orthodox Christianity Since World War II," in Religious Issues and Interreligious Dialogues, Charles Wei-hsun Fu and Gerhard E. Spiegler, eds., (Westport, CT: Greenwood Press, 1989), pp. 369-411, among others.

22. An excellent account of such accommodations was presented by Rev. Demetrios J. Constantelos in a presentation entitled "Ethnic Particularities & the Catholicity of the Church," at the Third Annual Meeting of the Orthodox Christian Laity, Nov. 11, 1990, in Chicago, to be published in The Greek Orthodox Theological Review (forthcoming). See also his Understanding the Greek Orthodox Church (Brookline, MA: Hellenic College Press, 1990); also his "The Greek Missionary Background of the Christianization of Russia and the Respect for its Cultural Identity," in Theologia (Athens, 1989).

23. For an excellent treatment of this historical fact see Constantelos, "The Orthodox Diaspora," The Greek Orthodox Theological Review, pp. 206-209, op. cit.

24. For an excellent account of this difficult period of the Ecumenical Patriarchate see G. Georgiades, "The Greek Church of Constantinople and the Ottoman Empire," Journal of Modern History. Vol. XXIV (March-December, 1952), pp. 235-250.

25. The Archdiocesan constitutions of 1922, 1927 and 1977 provided for a canonical synod. The constitution of 1930 did not. The synodical system was abolished then in order to heal the wounds inflicted upon the Church by the Venizelist/Royalist feud which had divided the community. The Ecumenical Patriarchate dispatched Archbishop Athenagoras to America with strong centralized powers to end the divisions. The synodical system was restored in 1977. See James Steve Counelis "Historical Reflections on the Constitutions of the Greek Orthodox Archdiocese of North and South America, 1922-1982," Album

of the 24th Clergy-Laity Congress (San Francisco: 1982), pp. 36-43. For a notable history on the development of the Greek Orthodox Church in America see George Papaioannou, From Mars Hill to Manhattan: The Greek Orthodox in America Under Athenagoras I (Minneapolis, Light and Life Publishing Company, 1976), *passim*.

26. For a good account of the role of the "royal priesthood" in the governance of the Church see Alexander Schmemann, Clergy and Laity in the Orthodox Church (Crestwood, NY: St. Vladimir's Seminary Press, n.d.). For a more formal account-see Jerome I. Cotsonis, The Place of the Laity Within the Ecclesial Organism According to the Canon Law of the Eastern Orthodox Church (Greek text; Athens, 1956), pp. 15-17. See also, Athenagoras Kokkinakis, Parents and Priests as Servants of Redemption (New York: Morehouse-Gorham Company, 1958) Chs. XXI-XXII.

27. On the election of the Ecumenical Patriarch see: "Orthodox Eastern Church," Encyclopedia Britannica 1911 ed., Vol. XV, p. 33y; for the election of bishops in Cyprus see: Mario Rinvolucri, Anatomy of a Church: Greek Orthodoxy Today (London: Burns & Oates, 1966), p. 119.

28. St. Vladimir's Theological Quarterly, Vol. XV, Nos. 1, 2 (1971), devoted its entire double issue to the history and reason for the Russian Orthodox Church in America's application for autocephalous status from the Moscow patriarchate. In that issue see especially the contribution of senior Orthodox theologian, Alexander Schmemann, "A Meaningful Storm: Some Reflections on Autocephaly, Tradition and Ecclesiology," St. Vladimir's Theological Quarterly, Vol. XV, (1971), pp. 3-27.

29. The Illuminator (Greek Orthodox Diocese of Pittsburgh), May-June, 1991. Also see The Orthodox Church, Fall, 1992.

30. For the full text of these encyclicals see: "The Four Ancient Patriarchates Condemn Russian Autocephaly in America," The Orthodox Observer Quarterly, Vol. XXXVII, Nos. 619, 620, & 621 (Oct., Nov.,

Dec., 1971), pp. 1-28; later published as Russian Autocephaly and Orthodoxy in America (New York: The Orthodox Observer Press, 1972).

31. The fact is that, historically speaking, the Ecumenical Patriarch has never granted autocephaly to any local church; in various circumstances, each of these merely declared autocephaly, and the fact was later recognized by the Ecumenical Patriarchs. Such was the case with the Churches of Russia, Serbia, Bulgaria, and even Greece. Therefore, the OCA is within an historical process of considerable antiquity and awaits the validation of this as did those venerable Churches preceding it.

32. This was indeed reflected by St. Innocent's advice for American Orthodoxy when as missionary bishop in Alaska and Siberia from 1841 to 1868, he admonished the faithful on December 5, 1867: "Appoint a new bishop from among those who know the English language. . . ordain to the priesthood for our Churches converts to Orthodoxy from among American citizens who accept all its institutions and customs. Allow the vicar bishop and all the clergy of the Orthodox Church in America to celebrate the Liturgy and other services in English. . . . To use English rather than Russian (which must sooner or later be replaced by English) in all instruction in the schools to be established in San Francisco and elsewhere to prepare people for ordination and missionary work." See Paul D. Garrett, St. Innocent: Apostle to America (Crestwood, NY: St. Vladimir's Theological Press, 1979), pp. 276-277. See also Again Magazine, Vol. XIV No. 4, (December 1992), p. 30.

APPENDICES
TO
ORTHODOX UNITY

LAMENT

We bear the guilt for the scandal of the lack of communication and lack of community of spirit among the orthodox Churches. Today when all men are nothing, we do not unite. We who are the universal Church do not live this reality and do not witness to it. . . . There is no worse scandal than that of divided Orthodoxy. Let us understand this clearly and repent. It is never too late. Let us humbly take our part in the great work of inter-Orthodox rapprochement in a spirit of faith, hope and love. Let us play our part in knocking down the walls of chauvinism, ethnicism, isolationism and autocephalism. Let us become aware of and declare the fact that we are not alone and that we cannot live alone. . . .

ZOE Brotherhood (Greece
<u>Atkines Magazine</u> (1964)

APPENDIX I

A SIMPLIFIED DIRECTORY

CHURCH	JURISDICTION	TRADITIONAL FOUNDER & DATE
Ecumenical Patriarchate of Constantinople	Turkey. Parts of Greece, Mt. Athos, Northern and Western Europe, No. and So. America, Australia and New Zealand	St. Andrew the Apostle 36 A.D.
Patriarchate of Alexandria	All of Africa	St. Mark the Evangelist 62 A.D.
Patriarchate of Antioch	Syria, Lebanon, Iraq, Iran	St. Peter the Apostle 37 A.D.
Patriarchate of Jerusalem	Palestine (Israel) Jordan, Arabia and Mt. Sinai	St. James the Lesser 55 A.D.
Church of Russia	Russia	St. Andrew the Apostle. Conversion and baptism of Prince Vladimir of Kiev and Russian people 988 A.D.
Church of Serbia	Yugoslavia	SS. Cyril and Methodius 867-886 A.D.
Church of Romania	Romania	Orthodoxy introduced in 1st Christian centuries by missionaries to roman seaport colonies on the Black Sea
Church of Bulgaria	Bulgaria	Baptism of Tsar Boris by Patriarch Photius, 864 A.D. Also SS. Cyril and Methodius, 867-886 A.D.

OF AUTOCEPHALOUS CHURCHES[1]

CANONICAL STATUS	PRESENT HEAD & TITLE	EPISCOPAL SEAT
451: Patriarchate	Ecumenical Patriarch Bartholomew, Archbishop Constantinople and New Rome	Istanbul, Turkey
325: Patriarchate	Patriarch Parthenius III Pope of Alexandria	Alexandria, Egypt
325: Patriarchate	Patriarch Ignatius IV of Antioch and the East	Demascus, Syria
451 Patriarchate	Patriarch Diodorus of Jerusalem and Holy Zion	Jerusalem, Israel
1037: Under Constantinople 1448: Autocephalous 1589: Patriarchate	Patriarch Alexius II Moscow and All Russia	Moscow, Russia
1219: Autonomous (St. Savas) 1346: Patriarchate (of Pec) 1766: Under Constantinople 1832: Autonomous 1879: Autocephalous 1920: Patriarchate of Serbia	Patriarch Paul of the Servs, Archbishop of Pec and Metropolitan of Belgrade and Carlovitz	Belgrade, Yugoslavia
1359: Under Constantinople 1885: Autocephalous 1925: Patriarchate	Patriarch Theocristus of Romania, Archbishop of Bucharest and Metropolitan of Ungro-Vlachia	Bucharest, Romania
917: Patriarchate (Tsar Simon) 1018: Under Constantinople 1235: 2nd Patriarchate 1767: Under Constantinople 1872: Schismatic (until 1945) 1945: Autocephalous 1961: 3rd Patriarchate	Patriarch Maximum of Bulgaria	Sofia, Bulgaria

CHURCH	JURISDICTION	TRADITIONAL FOUNDER & DATE
Church of Cyprus	Cyprus	St. Barnabas the Apostle 46 A.D.
Church of Greece	Greece	St. Paul the Apostle 51 A.D.
Church of Georgia	Southern Russia (Iberia)	St. Andrew the Apostle 44 A.D.
Church of Czechoslovakia	Czechoslovakia	SS. Cyril and Methodius 867-886 A.D.
Church of Finland	Finland	Orthodox Monks 1100-1300 A.D.
Church of Poland	Poland	Orthodoxy introduced by missionaries from Russia during Middle Ages
Church of Albania[2]	Albania	SS. Cyril and Methodius 867-886 A.D. Also dates back to Apostolic Times (See Rom. 15-19)
"Orthodox Church in America"[3]	United States and Canada	St. Herman of Alaska, 1794 (Archimandrite Joseph Bolotov)

CANONICAL STATUS	PRESENT HEAD & TITLE	EPISCOPAL SEAT
325: Under Jerusalem 413: Autocephalous	Archbishop Chrysostom of New Justinia and Cyprus	Nicosia, Cyprus
451: Under Constantinople 1850: Autocephalous	Archbishop Seraphim of Athens and All Greece	Athens, Greece
325: Under Antioch 451: Under Constantinople 1089: Autocephalous 1811: Under Moscow 1917: Autocephalous-Catholicate	Catholicos-Patriarch Elias II of Georgia and Metropolitan of Tiflis	Tiflis, Georgia
1346: Under Serbia (Pec) 1766: Under Constantinople 1923: Autonomous	Archbishop Dorotheus of Prague and All Czechoslovakia	Prague, Czechoslovakia
1809: Under Moscow 1918: Independent from Russia 1923: Autonomous	Archbishop John of Kalelia and All Finland	Koupio, Finland
1593: Under Moscow 1917: Under Constantinople 1924: Autocephalous	Metropolitan Basil of Warsaw and All Poland	Warsaw, Poland
1346: Under Servia (Pec) 1766: Under Constantinople 1937: Autocephalous	Archbishop Anastasium of Tirana and All Albania	Tirana, Albania
1794: Under Moscow 1924: Temporarily Autonomous 1970: Autocephalous	Metropolitan Theodosius of all America and Canada	Washington, D.C., USA

NOTES TO APPENDIX I

1. This Simplified Directory was compiled by Andrew T. Kopan and was originally published in The Goyan Magazine, Vol. IX, No. 1 (Winter, 1962), pp. 18-19ff. Thereafter, an updated version has appeared annually in the Yearbook of the Greek Orthodox Archdiocese of North and South America.

2. The See has been vacant since the advent of the Communist regime in Albania. With the demise of Communism there, the Ecumenical Patriarchate has appointed Bishop Anastasius of Greece as Patriarchal Vicar and Exarch to visit Albania for the restoration of the autocephalous Albanian Orthodox Church. The Illuminator (Greek Orthodox Diocese of Pittsburgh), May-June, 1991. In August of 1992, Anastasius was enthroned as Archbishop of Tirana and All Albania.

3. The Canonical status of the "Orthodox Church in America," the former "Metropolia," has been in dispute since 1924 when it declared itself "temporarily autonomous" of the Church in Russia. The granting of permanent autocephaly to OCA by the church of Russia in 1970 continues the dispute. The Ecumenical Patriarchate has only a tacit recognition of OCA (as do most other autocephalous churches), until the matter can be settled by the forthcoming Great and Holy Council of the Orthodox Church. The Illuminator (Greek Orthodox Diocese of Pittsburgh), May-June 1991. Only the churches of Russia, Czechoslovakia and Poland recognize OCA.

APPENDIX II
HISTORIES OF ORTHODOX
ETHNIC GROUPS IN AMERICA

Greek Orthodox

1528	-	First Greek explorers arrive in the service of Spain.
1767	-	Greek colonists settle in New Smyrna, Florida.
1864	-	First Greek Orthodox church in New Orleans.
1892	-	Second and third churches in Chicago and New York.
1893	-	Bishop Dionysius, first Greek hierarch comes to America.
1921	-	Archbishop Meletius (later Ecumenical Patriarch) visits U.S.A.
1922	-	Greek Orthodox Archdiocese established, Archbishop Alexander.
1922	-	St. Athanasius Seminary established, Astoria, N.Y.
1923	-	Dioceses established in Chicago and Boston; San Francisco in 1927.
1930	-	Archbishop Athenagoras succeeds Alexander.
1937	-	Holy Cross Theological School established.
1948	-	Archbishop Athenagoras elected Ecumenical Patriarch.
1949	-	Archbishop Michael enthroned.
1959	-	Archbishop Iakovos enthroned.
1978	-	Archdiocese reorganized into synodical system: 10 dioceses.
1990	-	Ecumenical Patriarch Demetrius visits U.S.A.
	-	Population: Original immigrants = 600,000; present = 2.3 million.[1]
	-	Greek Orthodox today organized into one main jurisdiction: Greek Orthodox Archdiocese of North & South America,

---

1. According to Professor Charles Moskos, the exact number of Orthodox Christians in America is more likely to be in the area of 900,000 to 1,100,000. See the OCL Commission Report on Faith, Language and Culture beginning on page 17.

with a membership of approximately 2,000,000 in 579 parishes; some insignificant break-away groups and a splintered Old Calendar jurisdiction also exist.

Russian Orthodox

1741 - Vitus Jonassen Bering explores North Pacific in the service of Russia.

1783 - First Russian colonization in Alaska.

1794 - First Russian Orthodox church established in Kodiak Island, Alaska.

1812 - Russian settlers, Ft. Ross, California.

1815 - St. Michael Church, Sitka, Alaska, established.

1848 - First diocese (of New Archangel) established at Sitka; Innocent first bishop.

1870 - Independent Diocese of Alaska and Aleutian Islands created.

1872 - Diocese transferred to San Francisco by Bishop John.

1879 - Bishop Nestor head of Diocese.

1888 - Bishop Vladimir.

1905 - Diocese relocated to New York by Archbishop Tikhon (later Patriarch of Moscow); Archbishop Eudokim follows Tikhon in 1914.

1908 - Seminary established by Bishop Tikhon at Minneapolis.

1919 - First Sobor held at Pittsburgh; Bishop Alexander heads Diocese.

1921 - Bishop Platon, reigning bishop.

1924 - Second Sobor in Detroit: Diocese proclaims itself independent of Moscow; Metropolitan Platon chosen ruling bishop.

1934 - Bishop Theophilus succeeds Metropolitan Platon; FROC established.

1938 - St. Vladimir Seminary established in New York.

1950 - Metropolitan Leontius heads Church.

1970 - Church declares itself autocephalous: OCA established.

1976	-	Metropolitan Theodosius elected head of OCA.
	-	Population: Less than 50% of 1.5 million Russian immigrants to U.S.A. were ethnic Russians, hence Orthodox Christians; Population today - 1 million plus.
	-	Russians split today into three factions:

1. Orthodox Church in America: 1,000,000; 440 parishes.
2. Russian Orthodox Church Outside Russia: 100,000; 197 parishes.
3. Patriarchal Church: 10,000; 38 parishes.

Syrian-Lebanese (Antiochian)

	-	Part of Arab migration to U.S.A., 90% Christian, 10% Muslim.
1878	-	First Syrian family arrives in U.S.A.
1890	-	Accelerated immigration from Syria and Lebanon.
1892	-	Syrian Mission of Russian Orthodox Church founded.
1895	-	Rev. Raphael Hawaweeny brought from Russia to supervise Syrian Church.
1901	-	Rev. Hawaweeny consecrated first Orthodox bishop in America.
1914	-	Metropolitan Germanus of Lebanon sent to U.S.A. by Patriarch of Antioch.
1917	-	Bishop Aftimius of Brooklyn succeeds Bishop Raphael.
1924	-	Bishop Victor, first Archbishop of Syrian Orthodox Archdiocese.
1924	-	Bishop Emmanuel succeeds Bishop Aftimius on other side.
1936	-	Bishop Anthony Bashir consecrated in New York.
1936	-	Bishop Samuel David, his rival, consecrated in Toledo.
1958	-	Michael Shaheen succeeds Bishop Samuel David in Toledo.
1966	-	Archbishop Philip Saliba succeeds Archbishop Anthony.
1975	-	Two Syrian factions united under Archbishop Philip, one of the most consistent and insistent spokesmen for a united American Orthodoxy.

1977	-	Patriarch Elias IV of Antioch visits U.S.A.
	-	Estimated population of Antiochian Orthodox = 280,000 in 125 parishes; Melkites = 25,000 in 28 parishes; and Maronite = 30,000 in 50 parishes, both united with Rome.
1985	-	Patriarch Ignatius IX of Antioch in America: meets with Evangelical Orthodox.
1987	-	Evangelical Orthodox accepted into Church.

Ukrainian Orthodox

Two waves of migration: 1870-1914 and 1945-1951 of approximately 500,000, most members of Slavic Uniate group in communion with Rome (Byzantine Catholic).

1918	-	Mass defection from Uniate Church due to pioneer work of Fr. Alexis Toth (1853-1909) of Minneapolis, leads to establishment of Independent Ukrainian Church under Russian Mission.
1924	-	Bolshevik Revolution leads to splintering groups; Bishop John Teodorovich from Kiev proclaimed bishop (self-consecrated), leads to more splintering, especially between American and Canadian branches.
1931	-	Further defection from Uniates brings about establishment of the Ukrainian Orthodox Church of America under Ecumenical Patriarchate with Joseph Zuk as first bishop, elected at first convention.
1937	-	Bishop Bohdan succeeds Bishop Joseph under Ecumenical Patriarchate.
1949	-	Archbishop John Teodorovich and Archbishop Mstyslaw unite their two factions to form the Ukrainian Orthodox Church of the United States and Canada under independent jurisdiction.
1950	-	Ukrainian emigres form Ukrainian Autocephalic Church under Archbishop Gregory.

1954	-	Ukrainian Orthodox Church in Exile under Metropolitan Polycarp.
1955	-	St. Andrew Theological College established in Winnipeg, Canada.
1966	-	Bishop Andrew succeeds Bishop Bohdan under Ecumenical Patriarchate.
1987	-	Bishop Vsevolod succeeds Bishop Andrew under Ecumenical Patriarchate.
	-	Today Ukrainian Orthodox are divided into three jurisdictions:

1. Ukrainian Greek Orthodox Church of Canada; 140,000; 250 parishes.
2. Ukrainian Orthodox Church of U.S.A.: 85,000; 92 parishes.
3. Ukrainian Orthodox Church in America (Ecumenical Patriarchate), 30,000; 28 parishes (balance of Ukrainians are Byzantine Catholics).

Serbian Orthodox

Early Serbian migration to New Orleans and southern coast, and to San Francisco in mid 19th Century; an estimated 175,000 Serbs emigrated to America.

1894	-	First church established in Jackson, CA; later in Chicago and in Pennsylvania.
1921	-	Charter to organize diocese given by Patriarch of Serbia.
1923	-	St. Sava Monastery in Libertyville, Ill., established; became diocese headquarters.
1926	-	Bishop Mardary consecrated first hierarch of Serbian Orthodox diocese.
1940	-	Bishop Dionysius arrives in U.S.A. to assume leadership of Church.
1943	-	Arranges for mass immigration of refugees fleeing persecution in Yugoslavia; among them, the pious Bishop

Nicholas Velimirovic who had served as administrator of Serbian churches in the 1920s.

1963 - Schism in the Church due to politics in Yugoslavia; two jurisdictions evolve in U.S.A.; one under Patriarchate of Serbia (under control of Communist regime; other independent of Patriarchate under Bishop Dionysius.

1964 - Bishops Fimilian, Stefan and Gregory assume control of Patriarchal Church.

1976 - Lawsuits decided in favor of Patriarchal (canonical) Church.

1977 - Bishop Dionysius moves headquarters to Grayslake, Ill., builds new Gracanica Monastery.

1978 - Bishop Christopher (native of Texas), bishop in Patriarchal Church.

1984 - Bishop Irenaeus succeeds Bishop Dionysius as head of "free" Church.

1991 - Schism healed with two parallel jurisdictions merging eventually into one.

1992 - Serbian Orthodox Patriarch Paul visits U.S.A. to confirm healing of schism. Today Serbian Church exists in two parallel jurisdictions:
  1. Serbian Eastern Orthodox Church for the U.S.A. and Canada: 100,000; 80 parishes.
  2. Metropolitanate of New Gracanica for U.S.A. and Canada: 30,000; 55 parishes.

Romanian Orthodox

- Romanians appeared sporadically in U.S.A. before 1870s; some were in California gold rush of 1849; some served in Civil War; between 1870 and 1900, about 18,000 immigrants arrived, mostly from Moldavia and Transylvania; by 1920 an estimated 85,000 had arrived.

1890s - First two Romanian churches in Canada.

1904 - First church established in America at Cleveland, Ohio.

1918	-	Abortive attempt to unite Romanian churches into episcopate.
1923	-	Youngstown, Ohio meeting established episcopate; remained inactive.
1930	-	Forty parishes chartered under Patriarchate of Romania.
1935	-	Bishop Polycarp Monusca consecrated for American diocese.
1937	-	Vatra Romaneasca established in Grass Lake, MI; diocese center.
1939	-	Bishop Polycarp returns to Romania and is marooned by outbreak of war; Romanian Orthodox bishopless until 1950 as a result.
1950	-	Romanian Diocese declared "autonomous" at Detroit convention.
1952	-	Layman Valerian Trifa elected bishop; consecrated by uncanonical Teodorovich Ukrainian faction.
1950	-	Remnant Romanians accept Bishop Andrew Moldovan from Romania.
1966	-	Bishop Victorin Ursache succeeds Bishop Andrew.
1985	-	Archbishop Valerian deported from U.S.A., succeeded by Bishop Nathaniel Popp, first American-born hierarch.
	-	Currently, two Romanian jurisdictions:

1. Romanian Orthodox Episcopate of America (OCA): 55,000; 83 parishes.
2. Romanian Orthodox Missionary Archdiocese: 15,000; 14 parishes.

Carpatho-Russian Orthodox

Migrations from the eastern provinces of the old Austro-Hungarian Empire, namely Moravia, Slovakia and Ruthenia (now Czechoslovakia), and from Galicia in the western Ukraine and the Carpathian Mountains in present-day Romania make up this jurisdiction; between 1880-1914 some 140,000 emigrated to America; today number over 600,000; by 1920, 78% lived in urban areas of Middle Atlantic States.

1891 - Beginning of defections from Uniate (Catholic) Church to which their ancestors were forced to belong by Treaty of Brest-Litovsk (1596).

1916 - Carpatho-Russian eparchy established within Russian Mission.

1936 - American Carpatho-Russian Diocese established under Ecumenical Patriarchate; Bishop Orestes consecrated at Constantinople (1937).

1951 - Christ the Savior Seminary founded at Johnstown, PA, diocese center.

1966 - Bishop Orestes elevated to rank of Metropolitan.

1986 - Bishop Nicholas succeeds Metropolitan Orestes.

- Today, Carpatho-Russians are divided among four jurisdictions:

    1. American Carpatho-Russian Orthodox Greek Catholic Church (under Ecumenical Patriarchate): 115,000; 70 parishes.
    2. In the Orthodox Church in America: 200,000.
    3. In the Patriarchal Russian Church: 18,000
    4. Balance of 225,000 are Byzantine Rite Catholics.

Bulgarian Orthodox

- Bulgarian immigration to America initially from Macedonia and later from Kingdom of Bulgaria: 50,000 came between 1900-1910; 70,000-100,000 today.

1907 - First church established in Granite City (Madison), IL.

1922 - Bulgarian Orthodox Mission established by Holy Synod in Bulgaria.

1938 - Mission raised to Diocese with Bishop Andrew as head in New York.

1947	-	Diocese elevated into Archdiocese for U.S.A., Canada and Australia.
1963	-	Dissension in Archdiocese over ties with Communist homeland.
1964	-	Faction breaks away and establishes diocese under Russian Church Outside Russia.
1972	-	Archbishop Andrew dies; Bishop Joseph succeeds him.
1976	-	Breakaway faction under Bishop Cyril joins OCA.
	-	Bulgarian Orthodox divided today among three jurisdictions:

1. Bulgarian Eastern Orthodox Church (canonical): 120,000; 21 parishes.

2. Bulgarian Eastern Orthodox Church (noncanonical): 105,000; 18 parishes.

3. In the Orthodox Church in America.

Albanian Orthodox

	-	Albanians first came to the U.S.A. at beginning of 20th century; today an estimated 70,000 Albanian Americans in U.S.A.; almost all Orthodox Christians.
1908	-	First Albanian Orthodox Church established in Boston under Ecumenical Patriarchate.
1908	-	Ordination of Fan S. Noli, Harvard educated Albanian immigrant into priesthood by Russian Orthodox Bishop Platon; later elected Bishop.
1932	-	Returning from Albania where he served as Prime Minister, Bishop Fan Noli organizes independent Albanian Orthodox Archdiocese, serving as its head until his death in 1965.
1950	-	Bishop Mark reorganizes Albanians into independent diocese under the Ecumenical Patriarchate.
1971	-	Fan Noli group joins OCA as ethnic diocese.
	-	Albanian Orthodox divided into two jurisdictions today:

1. Albanian Orthodox Archdiocese in America (OCA): 45,000; 16 parishes.
2. Albanian Orthodox Diocese in America (Ecumenical Patriarchate): 7,000; 10 parishes.

Byelorussian Orthodox

- A Slavic people from western Russia who migrated to America between 1880 and 1914; numbers today between 175,000 to 200,000; most absorbed into the Russian Orthodox Church of North America (now OCA).

1949 - Post-World War II immigrants establish independent ethnic jurisdictions; autocephalous diocese established in Cleveland, Ohio.

- Today, Byelorussians are divided into two groups:
  1. Byelorussian Autocephalic Orthodox Church in U.S.A. (Archbishop Mikalay).
  2. Byelorussian Orthodox Church under jurisdictions of the Ecumenical Patriarchate of Constantinople.

"Macedonian" Orthodox[2]

- Macedonian Americans, relatively small group emigrating from southern Yugoslavia in early 20th Century but identified themselves as Bulgarian Orthodox: some 50,000 in U.S.A.

1959 - Patriarch of Serbia forced by Communist Government to recognize schismatic Macedonian Orthodox Church for Republic of Macedonia in Yugoslavia.

1962 - First Macedonian Orthodox Church organized in Gary, Ind.

1963 - Archbishop Dositheus emigrates from Yugoslavia to lead mission.

---

2. The term *Macedonian* is a disputable term.

| 1967 | Dositheus named Metropolitan of Macedonian Church under jurisdiction of Holy Synod of Republic of Macedonia in Yugoslavia. |
| | Today, there are 11 active parishes under Bishop Cyril in Skoplje, Yugoslavia and known as the Macedonian Orthodox Church. |

Miscellaneous Orthodox

A number of other ethnic Orthodox churches in the U.S.A., too small to be organized into a diocese and consisting of only a few parishes each. Among them are:

1. Estonian Orthodox Church in Exile.
2. Finnish Orthodox Church.
3. Slavonic Orthodox Church in Exile.
4. "Turkish" Orthodox Church.[3]

RECAPITULATION

Of several jurisdictions listed above, two are multi-ethnic.

Under Ecumenical Patriarchate of Constantinople:

1. Greek Orthodox Archdiocese of North and South America.
2. American Carpatho-Russian Orthodox Greek Catholic Diocese U.S.A.
3. Ukrainian Orthodox Church in America and Canada.
4. Albanian Orthodox Diocese of America.
5. Byelorussian Orthodox Church.

---

3. An aborted attempt of Turkish nationalists to pre-empt the Ecumenical Patriarchate.

Under Orthodox Church in America:
1. Romanian Orthodox Episcopate of America.
2. Bulgarian Eastern Orthodox Church.
3. Albanian Orthodox Archdiocese.
4. Exarchate of Mexico.

APPENDIX III

ATTEMPTS AT ORTHODOX UNITY IN AMERICA

1. Pioneer work of itinerant priests Agapius Hocharenko (Ukrainian) and Ambrose Vrettos (Greek-Russian) and others in serving early ethnic parishes in 19th Century America.

2. Effort of Archbishop Tikhon in 1904-1906 to establish a multinational church jurisdiction in America with ethnic dioceses, under the Metropolitanate of Moscow (Meyendorff Vision 15-16).

3. Vision of Archbishop Meletius of Athens of a united Orthodoxy under the Ecumenical Patriarchate of Constantinople during his first American visit in 1918. Later as Ecumenical Patriarch in 1921, he expressed hope for a united "American Orthodox Church" (Barringer 13).

4. Synodical degree of Ecumenical Patriarch-elect Meletius IV in 1922 reassigning churches in the "Diaspora" to the jurisdiction of the Ecumenical Patriarchate.

5. Instructions of Patriarch Sergius of Moscow in 1925 to Russians in heterodox lands to ally themselves with Orthodox of other ethnic backgrounds in times of trouble.

6. Pioneer work of Albanian Archbishop Fan Noli for Pan- Orthodox unity in the 1930s.

7. Call for unity by Greek Archbishop Athenagoras during his American tenure, 1931-1948.

8. Establishment of "Federation of Orthodox Greek Catholic Churches in America" by Greek, Russian, Antiochian and Lebanese jurisdictions, which provided a semblance of unity, 1943-1960 (Surrency).

9. Establishment of SYNDESMOS in Paris in 1953 as an international youth movement for the purpose of encouraging Church unity and cooperation worldwide.

10. Founding of the Council of Eastern Orthodox Youth Leaders of the Americas (CEOYLA), in New York in 1954 by seven mainline Orthodox youth organizations for the purpose of promoting Church unity in the Americas.

11. Statement by famed theologian Hamilcar Alivizatos at 2nd Assembly of World Council of Churches in Evanston, IL, calling for a united Orthodox Church in America in 1954.

12. Establishment of the Standing Conference of Canonical Orthodox Bishops in the Americas (SCOBA) at New York in 1960, at the prompting of CEOYLA, to work for church unity at the highest levels.

13. Ecumenical Patriarchate begins series of Pan-Orthodox conferences in Rhodes, Greece in 1961 and again in 1963, 1964 and 1968, in preparation for convening a major Pan-Orthodox Council to address pressing theological issues; subsequent conferences held in Athens and Geneva, Switzerland; most Orthodox churches in attendance.[1]

14. Staging of largest ever Pan-Orthodox Vespers and Unity Festival with the participation of all American hierarchs at Pittsburgh Stadium in 1963 under CEOYLA auspices.

15. Request of SCOBA to place issue of ecclesiastical unity in America on agenda of a Pan-Orthodox meeting in Geneva, rebuffed by Ecumenical Patriarchate in 1965.

16. Christmas 1966 letter from Metropolitan Irenaeus of Russian Metropolia to all heads of autocephalous churches on church unity in America.

17. Establishment of autocephalous Orthodox Church in America in 1970 and its consequences:

    a. Refusal of Ecumenical Patriarchate to recognize autocephaly of OCA.[2]

    b. Church of Russia calls upon Ecumenical Patriarchate to grant autocephaly to Greek Orthodox Archdiocese in U.S.A. to work out accord of unity with OCA.

    c. Patriarchate of Alexandria advocates theory that all ethnic Orthodox Christians in America accept jurisdiction of Ecumenical Patriarchate as per canon law (Meyendorff Unity 100-102).

    d. Patriarchate of Antioch supports theory of autocephalous churches in America in that administrative independence is the road to unity.

    e. Church of Romania supports notion of ethnic ties with mother churches.

18. Ecumenical Patriarchate places issue of unity of Orthodox churches in "Diaspora" on agenda of forthcoming "Great and Holy Council" at Inter-Orthodox meeting Geneva, Switzerland in 1976.

19. Conference of American Orthodox hierarchs at Johnstown, PA on Orthodox unity, 1978, under the chairmanship of Archbishop Iakovos.

20. Evangelical Orthodox received into Antiochian jurisdiction by Metropolitan Philip in 1987.

21. Establishment of Bilateral Commission to study organic unity between OCA and Antiochian Archdiocese in 1981; after a series of meetings, joint encyclical issued, 1989.

22. Patriarch Elias IV of Antioch issues call for church unity in pastoral visit to America (Barringer 13).

23. Preliminary report on Orthodox Diaspora and unity issued at the Ecumenical Patriarchate Center in Switzerland in 1990 by Preparatory Commission for the Great and Holy Council.

24. Ecumenical Patriarch Demetrius speaks to OCA's Metropolitan Theodosius in Washington, D.C. during 1990 visit to America on the scandal of disunity in America.

25. Ecumenical Patriarchate and OCA issue joint statement on conclusion of talks following visit of OCA delegation led by Archbishop Peter of New York to the See of Constantinople, 1991 (Orthodox Church News, June 12, 1991).

26. First publication of Orthodox Unity by Fr. Vasile Hategan, 1991.

27. Ecumenical Patriarch Bartholomew hosts OCA delegation led by Metropolitan Theodosius at the Phanar for talks on unity, 1993 (The Orthodox Church February, 1993, 1 & 3).

NOTES TO APPENDIX III

1. For information in what is being hailed as the first "ecumenical" council in over a thousand years (the last one for the Orthodox Church was held in 787 A.D.), see Harakas, Something is Stirring in World Orthodoxy, op. cit., and Towards the Great Council (Chambesy, Switzerland: Orthodox Center of the Ecumenical Patriarchate, 1972). passim.

2. For the ramifications and discussions on this issue see Bogolepov, Trempelas, and Schmemann, "The Idea of Primacy in Orthodox Ecclesiology," pp. 49-75; also Andrew T. Kopan, "The Autocephaly of the Russian Metropolia," Diakonia, Vol. VI, No. 2 (1971), pp. 186-189.

APPENDIX IV

STANDING CONFERENCE OF CANONICAL ORTHODOX BISHOPS IN THE AMERICAS

Archbishop Iakovos
Chairman

Metropolitan Joseph
Secretary

Bishop Nicholas
Treasurer

Metropolitan Philip
Vice Chairman

Very Rev. Paul Schneirla
Recording Secretary

Rev. Milton B. Efthimiou
Consultant

GREEK ORTHODOX ARCHDIOCESE OF NORTH AND SOUTH AMERICA
Most Rev. Archbishop Iakovos
10 East 79th Street
New York, NY 10021
(212) 570-3500

ORTHODOX CHURCH IN AMERICA
Most Rev. Metropolitan Theodosius
Route 25A - P. O. Box 675
Syosset, NY 111791
(516) 922-0550

ALBANIAN ORTHODOX DIOCESE OF AMERICA
Rev. Ilia Katre, Vicar General
2100 S. Stockton Avenue
Las Vegas, NV 89104
(702) 382-2750

ROMANIAN ORTHODOX MISSIONARY ARCHDIOCESE IN AMERICA AND CANADA
Most Rev. Archbishop Victorin
19959 Riopelle Avenue
Detroit, MI 48203
(313) 893-8390

AMERICAN CARPATHO-RUSSIAN ORTHODOX GREEK CATHOLIC DIOCESE IN THE U.S.A.
Right Rev. Bishop Nicholas of Amissos
312 Garfield Street
Johnstown, PA 15906
(814) 539-9143

ANTIOCHAN ORTHODOX CHRISTIAN ARCHDIOCESE OF NORTH AMERICA
Most Rev. Metropolitan Philip
358 Mountain Road
Englewood, NJ 97631
(201) 871-1355

SERBIAN ORTHODOX CHURCH IN THE UNITED STATES AND CANADA
Most Rev. Metropolitan Christopher
St. Sava Monastery
Route 176
Libertyville, IL 60048
(708) 362-1760

UKRAINIAN ORTHODOX CHURCH IN AMERICA AND CANADA
· Right Rev. Bishop Vsevolod of Scopelos
90-34 139th Street
Jamaica, NY 11435
(718) 297-2407

APPENDIX V

Inter-Orthodox Preparatory Commission
Chambesy, November 10-17, 1990
ORTHODOX DIASPORA
Adopted Text

Introduction

The Inter-Orthodox Preparatory Commission met at the Orthodox Center of the Ecumenical Patriarchate in Chambesy from November 10 through 17 under the Chairmanship of His Eminence Metropolitan Bartholomew of Chalcedon and with the representatives and their advisers of all the Orthodox Churches participating in the project of determining an Orthodox consensus on the topic of the "Orthodox Diaspora."

After the opening address of the Chairman and the reading of the report of the Secretary, His Eminence Metropolitan Damascene of Switzerland, regarding the preparation for the Great and Holy Council, the Commission discussed in detail the whole question of the "Orthodox Diaspora" based on the contributions of the Holy Orthodox Churches, and arrived at the decision to submit its proposal on the question to the coming Fourth Pre-Conciliar Pan-Orthodox Conference.

1. a) The Commission stated that every Orthodox Church is unanimous that the problem of the Orthodox Diaspora be resolved as quickly as possible and that it be organized in a way that is in accordance with Orthodox ecclesiological tradition and the canonical praxis of the Orthodox Church.

b) The Commission also stated that during the current phase it is not possible to follow exactly the Church's strict canonical order in this matter. For this reason, the Commission arrived at the conclusion to propose the creation of a transitional structure that would prepare the groundwork for a strictly canonical solution to the problem that will be based on principles and directives defined below. This preparatory phase should not go beyond the convocation date of the Great Council of the Orthodox Church, so that the Great Council might confirm the canonical solution to the problem.

2. a) As the canonical solution to the question is being prepared, the Commission proposes that "Episcopal Assemblies" be created in each of the regions defined below bringing together all the canonically recognized bishops of that region, who will continue in their relationship with their current jurisdictions during the transitional phase.

b) The Assemblies will be comprised of all bishops of each region, who are in canonical communion with all the Holy Orthodox Churches. They will have as their president the primate of the jurisdiction of the Church of Constantinople, and in his absence, the president will be according to order of the diptychs. The Assemblies will have an executive committee formed from among the presiding hierarchs of the various jurisdictions that exist in the region.

c) The work and responsibility of these Episcopal Assemblies will bear witness to the unity of Orthodoxy. They will begin to develop a common ministry for all Orthodox living in the region; to project inter-Orthodox cooperation in the relationship with other confessions, as well as in the society at large; to cultivate theological and religious education; etc. Decisions on matters will be made by majority vote (of the Assembly members).

POSTSCRIPT: PROGRESS AND REGRESSION

HISTORICAL REFLECTIONS[*]
on the Constitutions
of the Greek Orthodox Archdiocese
of North and South America, 1922-1982

by Dr. James Steve Counelis[**]

INTRODUCTION:

The sixtieth anniversary of the organizational establishment of the American Archdiocese is an event to celebrate joyfully. And given the fact that the constitutional structure of this church was changed in 1977, it is an apt opportunity to reflect historically on the constitutional structure of this church. Also, it is an appropriate opportunity to reflect upon practical Orthodox ecclesiology in the American legal milieu. For purposes of this discussion, the church structures in Canada and Latin America will be excluded, each requiring a separate study.

Within the American political doctrine of the separation of church and state, the formation and operation of churches is a private matter for people to group themselves under the legal structure of a non-profit corporate body. Under this American legal structure, the Greek Archdiocese of North and

---

* Source: Greek Orthodox Archdiocese, <u>Album of the 26th Biennial Clergy-Laity Congress</u>, July 4-8, 1982, San Francisco. Reprinted with the permission of the author.

** Dr. James Steve Counelis is Professor of Education in the School of Education of the University of San Francisco, San Francisco, California 94117. He is also *Archon Chartoularius* of the Ecumenical Patriarchate of Constantinople and New Rome.

South America was incorporated under New York statute in 1921.[1] This corporate charter and the uniform parish by-laws made thereunder constitute one part of the legal structure of the Greek Archdiocese of North and South America. A second element in the archdiocesan constitutional structure is, collectively, the several archdiocesan constitutions granted by the Ecumenical Throne. These constitutions are of 1922,[2] 1927,[3] 1931,[4] and 1977,[5] the last being the current document under which this Archdiocese operates. The third of these constitutional elements in the structure of the American Archdiocese are the over 450 independent, separate parish church corporations, which govern directly all parochial resources and provide direct parochial services to the members of the parishes.[6] But before this structure of documents can be reviewed with profit, the nature and principles of American constitutionalism and Orthodox Christian ecclesiology require delineation.

AMERICAN CONSTITUTIONALISM:

Professor of History Andrew C. McLaughlin of the University of Chicago gave the 1932 Anson G. Phelps Lectures at New York University. This lecture series was titled, "The Foundations of American Constitutionalism." In these justly famous lectures, McLaughlin characterized American constitutionalism by five institutionalized ideas: (1) the social compact; (2) representation; (3) the constitutional convention; (4) the reign of law; (5) federalism.[7] From these notions have risen the democratic expectations of American Orthodox Christians for an ecclesial structure that comports with the American constitutional experience.

The American Orthodox Christian buttresses these democratic notions theologically when he construes the church as the Eucharistic Community of right believers[8] and as a royal priesthood or holy nation, [9] wherein all persons are equal before the footstool of God.[10] For the American Orthodox Christian, the Apostolic Counsel of Jerusalem, documented in the Book of Acts, is the model of the collegium of saints on earth who gather to elect their deacons and other clergy, who gather to make useful rules for church governance, and who gather to decide in the presence of the Holy Spirit the

292

teachings or dogmata of the Church.[11]   The ecclesiological concerns of laymen in the United States are not unique, for the Cotsonis documents the same concerns among laymen of the Church of Greece.[12]   In a significant way the Puritan Divines of New England and American Orthodox Christians meet in the twentieth century.

ORTHODOX CHRISTIAN ECCLESIOLOGY:

Orthodox Christian ecclesiology is discussed in one of two contexts. The one context is in Eucharistic theology; the other is in cannon law. In the first context, the Church is construed theologically as the praying Eucharistic community, wherein the whole spiritual edifice of the Church is constructed and Orthodox Christian anthropology finds its finest expression.[13]   The context of canon law construes the Church as a legal body within the cultural framework of Roman law as it evolved in the Christian Byzantine East. From within this framework, the canon law is the one half of the Byzantine code that has survived to this day.[14]   Unfortunately, Eucharistic theology and its theology of man has not been instructive in the formation and implementation of the canon law.

The 1921 articles of incorporation contain the following language on the purposes of the Greek Archdiocese of North and South America:

> *To edify the religious and moral life of the Greek Orthodox Christians in North and South America on the basis of the Holy Scriptures, the rules and canons of the Holy Apostles and the seven Oecumenical Counsels of the ancient undivided church as they are or shall be actually interpreted by the Great Church of Christ in Constantinople and to exercise governing authority over and to maintain advisory relations with Greek Orthodox Churches throughout North and South America and to maintain spiritual and advisory relations with synods and other governing authorities of the said church located elsewhere.*[15]

The reference to Holy Writ, canons of the church councils and the Ecumenical Throne's jurisdictional competence to interpret these sources placed an hierarchial and undemocratic system of church governance within the purview and control of American law. Byzantine monarchy and its caesaropapistic pretensions are part of the model of Orthodox Christian church governance. The model of the Orthodox bishop in canon law is that of the emperor-bishop — a caesaropapistic notion that has been reversed for churchmen by modern historical experience into "ethnarch" or "head of nation." Canon law defines dioceses as fiefs and benefices. Canon law regulates clerical and lay statuses within the church, especially episcopal status and relations among bishops, synods, and churches. Canon law defines and regulates a bishop's religious, administrative, legislative, and judicial functions. Canon law defines the clergy as a guild; and a synod of bishops as government. And canon law defines the substance of theological creed, *viz.*, the issues which define "right believers" or "orthodox" from "other believers" or "heterodox," whatever their type.

> *But you are a chosen people, a royal priesthood, a consecrated nation, a people set apart to sing the praises of God who calls you out of the darkness into his wonderful light.*
> —I Peter 2:9

Without the practical restraint of the Emperor and Roman law or the restraint of current civil governments of nation-states, canon law defines the church hierarchically in absolute terms with the bishop as absolute monarch.

In her history, the Orthodox Church has had to be flexible and to adapt to a wide range of political; social and economic systems. In the United States, America's democratic ethos does not tolerate extreme arbitrary behavior of anyone, clergy or no. Indeed, American democratic expectations are that there is accountability for everyone's behavior in this world, regardless of status. In particular, there is accountability for everyone's behavior in this world, regardless of status. In particular, there is a restraining effect upon gross absolutism because American civil law guarantees to every church member his or her say and vote. And in the American version of the Greek Orthodox Church, lay participation in the control over real estate and fiscal resources has an added restraining effect upon arbitrary clerical behavior of whatever type. There is the further fact that several Orthodox bishops have been brought into civil courts, the effect being to reduce arbitrary episcopal behavior over time.[16]

There is a creative tension in the American Archdiocese between the American democratic ethos and Byzantine ecclesial autocracy. Out of this creative tension, this writer believes that a new mode of episcopal service is evolving within American Orthodox Christian church life. It is a model of episcopal service that is built upon the theological anthropology of the Church. The traditional Orthodox episcopal model of emperor-bishop is being replaced by the ideal of Christ as rabbi and *kathegetes*. This mode of episcopal service is more American and Orthodox than Greek Orthodox as evidenced by the church's historical practice in modern times.[17]

CONTINUING CONSTITUTIONAL CHARACTERISTICS:

A document-by-document comparison of the four constitutions of this American Archdiocese reveals five continuing constitutional characteristics, each of which is found in the current 1977 church constitution.

The first structural characteristic of the American Archdiocese is the fact that it is an international rather than a national church. In name and operations, the Greek Orthodox Archdiocese of North and South America comprehends Canadian, Latin American and United States parishes and diocesan structures.[18] The practical degree to which the Chancellory's administration has been effective over the years in serving multinational parochial needs requires study. But the presence of parishes throughout the western hemisphere requires at least parochial clergy for these established communities.

The establishment of an hierarchical ecclesial structure with an archbishop for the whole archdiocese, bishops or dioceses, and priests for parish churches is the second continuing constitutional characteristic.[19] Also, this hierarchical principle extends above the American Archdiocese to that of the Ecumenical Patriarchate. Each of the four constitutions explicitly states the superior jurisdiction of the Great Church of Christ over the American Church.[20]

The third continuing constitutional characteristic is the autonomous status of the American Archdiocese. The appointment of all bishops, the approval of all churchwide legislation, and the direct control over all bishops, the approval of all churchwide legislation, and the director control over all theological, inter-religious and inter-church relations are all current prerogatives of the Ecumenical Throne.[21] For the most part, the practical matters of internal governance and policy are not subject to detailed scrutiny and control by the Ecumenical Patriarchate.

CHART NO. 1.

ECUMENICAL PATRIARCHS
SINCE 1923*

Gregory VII 1923
Constantine 1924-25
Basil III 1925-1929
Photius II 1929-1936
Benjamin I 1936-1946
Maximus V 1046-1948
Athenagoras I 1948-1972
Demetrius 1972-1991
Bartholomew . . . . ·. . . 1991-present

* Basil K. Stephanides, *Ekklesiastiki Istoria: Ap Archis Mechri Simeron [Church History: From the Beginning until Today]* (Greek text: Athens: Starr Publishers — A.E. Papademetriou 1948), p. 739.

Lay representation in some form at all levels of church governance is the fourth characteristic that continues across all four constitutions. Church congresses, diocesan assemblies, councils of all varieties and levels, and parish

296

trustees are the typical organs for lay participation along with the lower clergy.[22] With the exceptions of parish church boards of trustees, the parish clergy participate as equals.

The last characteristic is the mention and support of specific archdiocesan institutions for education and philanthropy. In particular, a theological school or seminary is mentioned in all four constitutional documents.[23]

All five of these continuing constitutional characteristics of the American Archdiocese embodied in the 1977 constitution also, are important to recognize. They represent the historical common denominator of requisite ecclesial institutions that fit a hybrid American Orthodox Church at this time. But a document-by-document review of these four archdiocesan constitutions reveals some other facts of importance.

PROGRESSIVE CONSTITUTIONAL DEVELOPMENTS:

Three important constitutional developments over the 1922-1982 period can be construed to be progressive. The first of these is the increased scope of Orthodox Christians under the jurisdiction of the American Archdiocese. In the 1922 and 1927 constitutions, only Greek-speaking Orthodox were considered to be within archdiocesan purview.[24] The 1931 constitution broadens the archdiocesan jurisdiction to other Orthodox Christians who are not Greek-speaking.[25] The 1977 constitution reads: "The Archdiocese of North and South America serves all Orthodox living in the western hemisphere.[26] Such an umbrella statement is most progressive when contrasted to the 1922 and 1927 constitutions.

All baptized in Christ, you have all clothed ourselves in Christ;
and there are no more distinctions between Jew and Greek,
slave and free, male and female, but all of you are one in
Christ Jesus.

— Galatians 3:27-28

When all four constitutions are examined side-by-side, the second progressive development is the rising level of generality of goals. The 1922 constitution contained only one goal, *viz.* the cultivation and improvement of the religious and ethical life of Greek-speaking Orthodox.[27] In 1927, the teaching and maintenance of the Orthodox Christian faith and the teaching of the "prototype language of the Gospel," *viz.,* Greek, were added.[28] However, the 1977 constitution states the archdiocese's purposes in the following:

> *The purpose of the Archdiocese is to administer the life of the church in the Americas according to the Eastern Orthodox faith and tradition, sanctifying the faithful through the divine liturgy and the holy sacraments and edifying the religious and ethical life of the faithful in accordance with the holy scriptures, the decrees and canons of the holy apostles and the seven ecumenical councils of the Ancient Undivided Church, as interpreted by the practice of the Great Church of Christ in Constantinople. As to its ecumenical activities, both inter-christian and inter-religious, the Archdiocese shall follow the position and guidelines established by the Ecumenical Patriarchate.*[29]

Certainly, the raising of the purposes of the American Church to a higher level of generality is progressive, to say nothing of including ecumenical activities within archdiocesan concerns.

The third progressive constitutional development is the return to a synodical structure with a decentralized form of canonical dioceses and bishops. The constitutions of 1922 and 1927 provided synods;[30] but the constitution of 1931 provided for a single canonical archbishop, quite monarchical in power and type.[31] With the 1977 constitution, the movement toward decentralization was accomplished.[32] This canonical pattern provided an overall solution to the problem of greater lay and lower clergy participation in the governance of a hierarchical church. It is in this sense of greater participation in the decision-making of an hierarchical church that the synodical form of church governance can be construed to be progressive.

298

CONSTITUTIONAL RETROGRESSIONS:

From the viewpoint of American Orthodox Christians, a document-by-document review of the four constitutions reveals that two retrogressions have occurred. These retrogressions are: (1) the participation and approval of the archdiocesan constitution by laymen and lower clergy; (2) the method of selecting bishops.

The constitution of 1922 was developed and approved by the 2nd Clergy-Laity Congress in 1922.[33] This constitution was intended to be temporary, a document to be revised in two years. The revision did not occur until 1927,[34] And it was approved at a general meeting in the then Cathedral of St. Basil in Chicago. As to the monarchical constitution of 1931, it is a well known fact that it was imposed by the Ecumenical Patriarchate and the Greek Government.[35] And as for the 1977 constitution, it was never presented at a referendum at any Clergy-Laity Congress, though a small committee of bishops, lower clergy and laymen participated in its construction. It appears that the Ecumenical Patriarchate was more Christian and more trusting in the past than in the present.

The method of selecting bishops has also retrogressed since the 1922 and 1927 constitutions. In these two earlier constitutions, the Clergy-Laity Congress had the opportunity to submit the names of three clergymen for transmission to the American Synod of Bishops. They, in turn, would nominate one of the three, sending that candidate's name on to Constantinople. The Synod of the Ecumenical Patriarchate would accept the decision of the American Synod and would elect that candidate to episcopal office.[36] No such process is available in the 1977 constitution; and certainly nothing is said in the 1931 constitution. In the 1977 constitution there is a vaguely worded reference to the American Synod of Bishops consulting with the Archdiocesan Council on which laymen and lower clergy are present. However, the Ecumenical Patriarchate reserves the right to name bishops to American dioceses.[37] Obviously, the ancient tradition of the local diocese selecting its own bishop and proclaiming him "Axios," is dead. There is no doubt that the 1922 and 1927 constitutions were superior to the 1977 constitution in both the constitutional procedures and the method of selecting bishops.

AMERICAN CONSTITUTIONALISM AND THE ARCHDIOCESAN CONSTITUTION OF 1977:

For the American Archdiocese, it is in the parish church that the fullest meaning and most direct application of American constitutional principles are found. Certainly, the acts of a group of religious faithful coming together to form a parish church and incorporate it illustrates the social compact characteristic of McLaughlin's understanding of American constitutionalism. Certainly, the election of boards of trustees and the general assembly meetings of the church corporation constitute the institutionalization of representation in the best sense of the word and practice. And the creation of on-going corporate by-laws under state law through specific procedures for the church corporation to follow illustrates the basic ideas of constitutional convention and the reign of law. However, there is little doubt that the concept of federalism is not an applicable principle for a single parish church, lest two or more parish churches come together under some confederal or federal arrangement. McLaughlin's principles project our understanding of the Orthodox parish church of this Archdiocese to be by nature an American constitutional structure.

At the level of the Archdiocese, however, McLaughlin's principles of American constitutionalism are not fully present. The original 1921 incorporation of the Archdiocese resulted from a meeting; and the constitutions of 1922 and 1927 were ratified by congresses. These actions of laymen and clergy reflected the principle of social compact and partially the notion of the constitutional convention. But the 1931 and 1977 constitutions were installed in specific and bald denial of American constitutional notions — indeed, contrary to American Orthodox Christians' democratic expectations. Though it is true that the enactment of uniform parish by-laws is still a function of the Clergy-Laity Congress (even though they are approved by Constantinople), this is so because the reign of law through New York corporate statutes can not be shut down totally be ecclesial behavior that is Byzantine and autocratic. It

300

appears that American civil law has a higher regard for the dignity and integrity of religious people than does an official church whose theological anthropology espouses the same principles.

Representation at the Clergy-Laity Congresses and Diocesan Assemblies is probably the one constitutional characteristic that still obtains. But this too, is the result of the reign of law where American corporate law guarantees each church member a say and a representative vote.

The principle of federalism is seen operating in the pragmatic relations of the several Orthodox parish corporations to the American Archdiocese. Through the assignment of clergy and the application of the Uniform Parish By-Laws, a type of confederal structure obtains, though this structure is being eroded over time by a gradual amending process of these by-laws.

> *He loves us and has washed away our sins with his blood, and*
> *made us a line of kings, priests to serve his God and Father.*
> — Revelations 1:6

The degree to which the Greek Orthodox Archdiocese of North and South America conforms to American principles of constitutionalism rests upon the determined vigilance of American Orthodox Christians to see to the application of the reign of law in all ecclesial affairs. And more precisely, the power of the Congresses and Assemblies of the Church to frame and pass resolutions is theologically important. The Church in assembly and prayer theologizes, proclaiming the "Good News" through current concerns and issues of society and polity, through the application of theology to ecclesial order and affairs, through the defense of the Church against her internal and external enemies, and through the advocacy and practice of the theological pedagogy for *agape*. Indeed, every Congress and Assembly of the American Church should conclude its sessions with the apostolic formula. "it is good to the Holy Spirit and to Us."

CONCLUSIONS:

Through the sixty years of the constitutional elaboration of the American Orthodox Church, the American Archdiocese has a straight development. There is no doubt that the American Archdiocese represents one of adaptive forms of the Orthodox Church through her nineteen centuries of history. And it should not come as a surprise that the American Orthodox ecclesial structure will take longer than sixty years fully to be indigenized. This writer believes that the development of on operative democratic church within the title of the Greek Archdiocese of North and South America is inevitable, though he may not live to see it. Further, this democratization will occur only when the American Church takes seriously the theological anthropology of the Church and sees that the anthropology becomes the structural basis of a Christ-like church — a Christ-like ecclesiology in living practice. The true ecclesial independence of the American Orthodox Church rests in the achievement of a Christ-like ecclesiology, for creativity, wisdom and piety will be her gifts. The Church is one priesthood of believers, clergy and lay, with one Head-the Christ.[38]

At the 1892-1893 Columbian Exposition, the World Parliament of Religions met in Chicago simultaneously. The Church of Greece was represented by the Most Reverend Dionysios Latas, Archbishop of Zante (1835-1894).[39] To the knowledge of this writer he was the first Greek orthodox prelate to visit the United States. At this international meeting, Archbishop Dionysios made a brief presentation on the Church. He closed that presentation with this wonderful historic prayer:

> *Almighty King, High Omnipotent God, look upon humankind; enlighten us that we may know Thy will, Thy ways, Thy Holy Truths; bless Thy Holy Truths; bless Thy Holy Church. Bless this country. magnify the renown people of the United States of America, which in its greatness and happiness invited us to*

this place from the remotest parts of the earth, and gave us a place of honor in this Columbian Year to witness with them the evidences of their great progress, and the wonderful achievement of the human mind.[40]

Prophetic prayer! Amen.

+ + + + + + + + +

FOOTNOTES

1. Certificate of Incorporation of [the] Greek Archdiocese of North and South America, 17 September 1921, (Certified True Copy, County Clerk and Clerk of the Superior Court, New York County, New York File No. 7650. This text is also in Basil T. Zoustis, *The Greeks In America and Their Work* (Greek text: New York: D.C. Divry, 1954, 1954) pp. 133-135.

2. Constitution of the Greek Archdioceses of North and South America, 11 August 1922. Certified True Copy, Greek Text, from *Patriarchikos Kodix: Synodikon Tomon ka: Sigillion, anef Chronologia,* Tome 979, pp. 1-11. The Archive of the Ecumenical Patriarchate of Constantinople and New Rome, Istanbul, Turkey.

3. Constitution of the Greek Archdiocese of North and South America, [12-14 October 1927], *Ibid.,* 97-111.

4. Constitution of the Greek Archdiocese of North and South America, 10 January 1931. Certified True Copy Greek text. The Archives of the Ecumenical Patriarchate of Constantinople and New Rome, Istanbul Turkey.

5. *Charter of the Greek Archdiocese of North and South America,* 29 November 1977 (Brookline, MA: Holy Cross Orthodox Press, 1978).

303

6. For a Complete listing of archdiocesan institutions and parishes, see: Demitri Gemelos and Reverend Kosmas Karavellas (eds.), *Year Book 1982* (New York, NY: Greek Orthodox Archdiocese of North and South America, 1982).

7. Andrew C. McLaughlin, *The Foundations of American Constitutionalism* (New York, NY: New York University Press, 1932).

8. John D. Zizoulas, "The Eucharistic Community and the Catholicity of the Church," in John Meyendorff and Joseph McLelland (eds.), *The New Man: An Orthodox and Reformed Diologue* (New Brunswick, NJ: Agora Books/Standard Press, 1973), pp. 107-131.

9. I Pet. 1:9-10.

10. Gal. 2:26, 28; Col. 3:11; Rev. 1:16.

11. Acts 1-23-26; 6:1-7; 15-1-31.

12. Jerome I. Cotsonis, *The Place of the Laity within the Ecclesial Organism according to the Canon Law of the Eastern Orthodox Church* (Greek text; Athens, 1956), pp. 15-17. See also, Athenagoras Kokkinakis, *Parents and Priests as Servants of Redemption* (New York, NY: Morehouse-Gorham Company, 1958), Chs. XXI-XXII.

13. Zizoulas, *op. cit.* See also: (1) Alexander Schmemann, *Introduction to Liturgical Theology*, translated by A. E. Moorehouse (London: The Faith Press, Ltd., 1966); (2) Alexander Schmemann, *For the Life of the World: Sacraments and Orthodoxy* ([Crestwood, NY]; St. Vladimir's Seminary Press, 1973)

14. For an overview of canon law sources, see: John Meyendorff, *Byzantine Theology: Historical Trends and Doctrinal Themes* (New York, NY; Fordham University Press, 1974), Ch. VI. For an English translation of the traditional *Pedalion of Agapius and Nicodemus*, see D. Cummings

(trans.), *The Rudder. . .* (Chicago, IL.: The Orthodox Christian Educational Society, 1957). For English translation of Byzantine civil and canon law, see: (1) Clyde Phart (trans. and ed.) *The Theodosian Code and Novels and the Sirmondian Constitutions* (Princeton, NJ: Princeton University Press, 1952); (2) Philip Schaff and Henry Wace (eds.) *A select Library of Nicene and Post-Nicene Fathers of the Christian Church. . .* (Cincinnati, Ohio: The Central Trust Company, 1932). Vols. XII-XVII.

15. 1921 Articles of Incorporation. *op. cit.* Pg. 5.

16. During the 1920's Venizelist-Royalist controversy over American church control, the American civil courts were used often to control arbitrary episcopal behavior regardless of political persuasion.   Also for local control issues, civil suits and injunctive relief had been sought to control clerical behavior.   To the knowledge of this writer, no systematic study of this matter has been made for any of the ethnic Orthodox Churches. For a sample, see, John Papas (ed. and publisher), *Greek Church in the Courts* (Printed booklet: Stanford, Conn: n.d., 1945?).   This does not mean, however, that court cases involving the Orthodox Church have not made their imprint upon American case law involving religious societies. In a rapid review of encyclopaedic articles, titled, "Religious Societies" in *Corpus Juris Secundum* (1952) and *American Jurisprudence* (1973) some 28 cases were readily identifiable by title in the footnotes of these articles.   Most of these cases involved the Russian Orthodox Church. The most significant case seems to be one ruled upon by the United States Supreme Court *viz.,* Kedroff v. St. Nicholas Cathedral of the Russian Orthodox Church, 344 U.S. 94, 97 L.Ed. 120, 73 S.Ct. 143. For the Greek Archdiocese under Archbishop Athenagoras, some legal problems are described in: George Papaioannou.   *From Mars Hill to Manhattan. . .* " (Minneapolis, MN: Light and Life Publishing Company, 1976)." pp. 98-121; and some of the legal documentation is found in Papas, *supra.*

17. James Steve Counelis, "Polis and Ecclesia: Toward an American Orthodox Church," *Diakonia*, Vol. VII, No. 4 (1972), — 310-325. Also, see: (1) Charles A. Frazee, *The Orthodox Church and Independent Greece, 1921-1852* (Cambridge at the University Press, 1969; (2) L.S. Stavrianos, *The Balkans since 1453* (New York, NY: Holt, Rinehart, and Winston, 1958; (3) Mario Rinvolucri, *Anatomy of a Church; Greek Orthodoxy Today* (New York, NY: Fordham University Press, 1966).

18. 1922 Const., art. 1, 4; 1927 Const. art. 1, 4; 1931 Const. art. 1; 1977 Const., art 1, 4.

19. 1922 Const., art. 4, 8, 9; 1927 Const., art. 1, 4; 1931 Const. art. 6; 1977 Const., art. 5, 7, 8, 9.

20. 1922 Const., art. 2, 3; 1927 Const., art. 2a, 3; 1931 Const., art. 3; 1977 Const., art. 2, 3.

21. 1977 Const., art. 2, 11, 13, 14.

22. 1922 Const., art. 12, 13; 1927 Const., art. 13, 13; 1977 Const., art. 12.

23. 1922 Const., art. 24; 1927 Const., art. 23; 1931 Const., art. 12, 13, 14; 1977 Const., art. 18, 19.

24. 1922 Const., art. 2; 1927 Const., art. 2.

25. 1931 Const., art. 2.

26. 1977 Const. art. 1.

27. 1922 Const., art. 1.

28. 1927 Const., art. 2.

29. 1977 Const., art. 2.

30. 1922 Const., art. 7; 1927 Const., art. 7.

31. 1931 Const., art. 6.

32. 1977 Const. art. 6

33. Zoustis, *op. cit.*, p. 160.

34. 1927 Const., art. 28.

35. The Most Reverend Damaskinos, Metropolitan of Corinth and Patriarchal Exarch, Encyclical of May 20, 1930 (?), Zoustis, *op. cit.*, pp. 195-201; The Most Reverend Damaskinos, Metropolitan of Corinth and Patriarchal Exarch, Encyclical of December 30, 1930. (Original text copy distributed to parishes in writer's Library.) Also Mr. Paul Manolis, having amassed Greek Government documentation for this period is preparing an historical study for publication.

36. 1922 Const., art. 16-19; 1927 Const., art. 18-20.

37. 1977 Const., art. 13-14.

38. I Pet. 2:9-10; Col. 1-18.

39. Basil Atesi. *Brief Episcopal History of the Church of Greece from 1833 until Today* (Greek text; Athens, A. T. Pountza, 1948), Vol. I, pp. 122-123.

40. The Most Reverend Dionysios Latas (Archbishop of Zante, "The Greek Church," [Address given on September 13, 1893], in John H. Barrows (ed.), *The World's Parliament of Religions . . . The Columbian Exposition of 1893* (Chicago, IL; The Parliament Publishing Company, 1893), Vol. I, pp. 114, 352-359. An illustration depicting Archbishop Dionysios appears on p. 357.

ORTHODOX
CHRISTIAN
LAITY

BIBLIOGRAPHY —— WORKS CITED

Agnnides, Thanassis. The Ecumenical Patriarchate of Constantinople in the Light of the Treaty of Lausanne. New York: Privately Printed, 1954).

Behr-Sigel, Elisabeth. The Ministry of Women in the Church., Redondo Beach, CA: Oakwood Publications, 1991.

Barringer, Robert, ed. Rome and Constantinople: Essays in the Dialogue of Love. Brookline, MA: Holy Cross Orthodox Press, 1984.

Bogolepov, Alexander A. Toward an American Orthodox Church: The Establishment of an Autocephalous Orthodox Church. New York: Morehouse-Barlow Company, 1963.

Callinikos, Constantine. History of the Orthodox Church. Los Angeles, CA: Prothymos Press, 1957.

Cole, F. G. Mother of All Churches: Holy Eastern Orthodox Church. London: Skeffington, 1908.

"Commission: Archdiocesan on Theological Agenda." Report to His Eminence Archbishop Iakovos. Greek Orthodox Theological Review. Vol. 34, No. 3. 1989.

Constantinides, Michael. The Orthodox Church. London: Williams and Norgate, 1931.

Cotsonis, Jerome I. The Place of the Laity Within the Ecclesial Organism According to the Canon Law of the Eastern Orthodox Church (Greek text; Athens, 1956.

Cummings, D. The Rudder (Pedalion) of the Holy Orthodox Christians or All the Sacred and Divine Canons. Chicago: The Orthodox Christian Educational Society, 1957.

Conclusions of the Interorthodox Consultation on the Place of The Woman in the Orthodox Church. . . (Rhodes, Greece, 30 Oct.-7 Nov., 1988), Light and Life Publishing Company, Minneapolis, MN, 1990.

Council of Jewish Federation Study; New York Times, June 7, 1991.

Efthimiou, Miltiades B., and George A. Christopoulos, (ed.) History of the Greek Orthodox Church in America New York: Greek Orthodox Archdiocese of North and South America, 1984.

Florovsky, George. Bible, Church, Tradition: An Eastern Orthodox View. Vol. I (in collected works). Belmont, Massachusetts: Norland Publishing Company, 1972.

—— Creation and Redemption. Vol III (in collected works). Belmont, Massachusetts: Nordland Publishing Company, 1976.

Frazee, Charles A. The Orthodox Church and Independent Greece 1821-1852 Cambridge: At the University Press, 1969.

Giannakakis, Basil S. International Status of the Ecumenical Patriarchate. Cambridge, MA: Privately Printed, 1959.

Gryson, Roger. The Ministry of Women in the Early Church. The Liturgical Press, Collegeville, MN, 1980.

Gvosdev, Ellen. The Female Diaconate: An Historical Perspective. Light and Life Publishing Company, Minneapolis, MN, 1991.

Hagioreites, Nikodemos. Synaxaristes II. Athens, 1868.

Harakas, Stanley S. Toward Transfigured Life. "The Theoria of Eastern Orthodox Ethics." Minneapolis, Minnesota: Light and Life Publishing Company, 1983.

—— Something is Stirring in World Orthodoxy. Light and Life Publishing Co. Minneapolis, MN, 1978.

Hopko, Thomas. Administration and Ministry, Crestwood, New York: St. Vladimir's Seminary Press.

—— All the Fullness of God. Crestwood, New York: St. Vladimir's Seminary Press, 1982.

—— et al. God and Charity Images of Eastern Orthodox Theology, Spirituality and Practice, Essay, "God and Man in the Orthodox Church," Brookline, Massachusetts: Holy Cross Orthodox Press, 1979.

ed., Women and the Priesthood. St. Vladimir's Press, Crestwood, NY, 1983.

Jurgens, W. A. The Faith of the Early Fathers. Collegeville, MN: The Liturgical Press, 1970.

—— The Priesthood. A Translation of the Peri Hierosynes of St. John Chrysostom. New York, 1950.

Kakkinakis, Athenagoras. Parents and Priests as Servants of Redemption. New York: Morehouse-Gorham Company, 1958.

Kopan, Andrew T. "A Greek-Layman Views Autocephaly." Diakonia, Vol. VI, No. 2 (1972), pp. 186-189.

Kosmin, Barry A. "Research Report: The National Survey of Religious Identification 1980, - 90." Graduate School and University Center of the City University of New York, March, 1991.

Langford, James and Richard Lloyd. A Dictionary of the Eastern Orthodox Church. London: Faith Press, 1923.

Lossky, Vladimir. The Mystical Theology of the Eastern Church. Crestwood, New York: St. Vladimir's Seminary Press, 1976.

Mantzarides, Georgios I. The Deification of Man, St. Gregory Palamas and the Orthodox Tradition. Crestwood, New York: St. Vladimir's Seminary Press, 1984.

Mastrantonis, George. A New-Style Catechism on the Eastern Orthodox Faith for Adults. St. Louis: The O LOGOS Mission, 1969.

Maximos, Bishop of Pittsburgh. Women Priests?. Holy Cross Orthodox Press, Brookline, MA, 1976.

McManus, Bishop William E. "The Rights of Laity In Governing the Church." America, November, 1992.

Merton, J. Gordon. The Encyclopedia of American Religions. 3rd ed., Detroit: Gale Research Inc., 1989.

Meyendorff, John. Catholicity and the Church. Crestwood, NY: St. Vladimir's Press, 1983.

—— Living Tradition Crestwood, New York: St. Vladimir's Seminary Press, 1984.

—— "Was There Ever a Third Rome? Research on the Byzantine Legacy in Russia," in John J. Yiannias, ed. The Byzantine Tradition After the Fall of Constantinople. Charlottesville, VA: University of Virginia Press, 1991, pp. 45-60.

—— The Vision of Unity. Crestwood, NY: St. Vladimir's Seminary Press, 1987.

Migne. Patrologia Graeca.

Neale, John Mason. A history of the Holy Eastern Orthodox Church. London: 1847, 1873.

Neofotistos, George. "A Reflection: Syndiakonia." The Way to Life, The Greek Orthodox Voice of the Southeast, Vol. 2, Easter, 1990.

Orthodox Women: Their Role and Participation in the Orthodox Church, Report on the Consultation of Orthodox Women. Agapia, Roumania, 1976, World Council of Churches, Geneva, 1977.

Papadakis, Aristeides. "St. Vladimir's Orthodox Seminary Commencement Address, 16 May 1992," St. Vladimir's Theological Quarterly Vol. XXXVI, No. 3 1992.

Papaioannou, George. From Mars Hill to Manhattan: The Greek Orthodox in America Under Athenagoras I. Minneapolis: Light and Life Publishing Company, 1976.

Parvey, Constance F., ed. Ordination of Women in Ecumenical Perspective. World Council of Churches, Geneva 1980.

Patrinacos, Nicon D. A Dictionary of Greek Orthodoxy. New York: Greek Orthodox Archdiocese of North and South America, 1984.

Patsavos, Lewis. "The Role of the Priest and the Apostolate of the Laity," Hellenic Chronicle. [Boston, Mass.], Fall, 1990. (Article two in a three part series, Lewis J. Patsavos quoting Stanley S. Harakas).

Reinken, Tom. Gallup Organization; personal communication, August 4, 1976.

Report of Commission: Archdiocesan Theological Agenda. Greek Orthodox Theological Review, Vol. 34, No. 3, 1989.

Report of Committee on Spiritual Renewal. Chicago, Illinois: 22nd Clergy-Laity Congress, 1974.

Runciman, Steven. The Great Church in Captivity: A Study of the Patriarchate of Constantinople from the Eve of the Turkish Conquest to the Greek War of Independence. Cambridge: At the University Press, 1968.

Russian Autocephaly and Orthodoxy in America. New York: The Orthodox Observer Press, 1972.

Schaff, Philip and Henry Wace. Decrees and Canons of the Seven Ecumenical Councils; Series Two, Vol. IIV of A Select Library of the Nicene and Post-Nicene Fathers. Grand Rapids, MI: William B. Eerdmans Publishing Co., 1956.

Schmemann, Alexander. The Eucharist: Sacrament of the Kingdom. Crestwood, New York: St. Vladimir's Seminary Press, 1988.

—— "The Idea of Primacy in Orthodox Ecclesiology," St. Vladimir's Seminary Quarterly, Vol. IV, Nos. 2-3 1960.

Sfekas, Stephen J. "The Restoration of Orthodox Traditions." Paper presented to the Follows Conference of the Society for Values in Higher Education, University of Tennessee. [Tennessee] August, 1986.

Shaw, Plato Ernest. American Contacts with the Eastern Church: 1820-1870. Chicago: The American Society of Church History, 1937.

Skordallos, Sabastian. "Orthodoxy/Orthopraxia, Syndiakonia in Practice," Keynote Address May 30, 1991, Clergy Laity Conference, Atlanta Diocese, Birmingham, Alabama.

Stephanou, Eusebius. Letter to OCL Task Force Committee on Spiritual Renewal, November, 1991.

Stylianopoulos, Theodore. Christ in Our Midst, Spiritual Renewal in the Orthodox Church. Brookline, Massachusetts: Greek Orthodox Archdiocese, Department of Religious Education, 1981.

—— Christ in Our Midst, Spiritual Renewal in the Orthodox Church. Greek Orthodox Archdiocese, Department of Religious Education, 1981.

Surrency, Serafim. The Quest for Orthodox Unity in America. New York: SS. Boris and Gleb Press, 1973.

Tavard, George H. Woman in Christian Tradition. University of Notre Dame Press, Notre Dame, IN, 1973.

The Holy Bible. Revised Standard Version containing the Old and New Testaments. Grand Rapids, Michigan, Zondervan Publishing House.

Theodorou, E. "He 'cheirotonia' e 'cheirothsia' ton diakonisson," Theologia 1954, pp. 430-469; 26 1955, pp. 275-76.

Topping, Eva C. Holy Mothers of Orthodoxy; Women and the Church. Light and Life Publishing Company, Minneapolis, MN, 1987.

—— Orthodox Eve and Her Church. The Patriarch Athenagoras Orthodox Institute, Occasional Papers, No.2, Berkeley CA, 1991.

—— Saints and Sisterhood: The Lives of 48 Holy Women. Light and Life Publishing Company, Minneapolis, MN, 1990.

—— "Patriarchal Prejudice and Pride in Greek Christianity: Some Notes on Origins." Journal of Modern Greek Studies 1 1982.

Trempelas, Panagiotis. Religious and Ethical Encyclopedia (Thriskeftiki kai Ithiki Enkyklopaedia), Volume 7, article on the Clergy (Kleros) and the section "The Selection of the Shepherds."

Tsongas, Paul. Heading Home. N.Y.: Knopf, 1984.

Ugolnik, Anthony. "The Image of God: Spirituality for the Busy Man." Lenten Retreat. School of Orthodox Studies, St. Mark Greek Orthodox Church. [Boca Raton, Florida] March 9, 1991.

Ware, Timothy (Kallistos). The Orthodox Church. Baltimore, MD: Penguin Books, 1963.

—— The Orthodox Way. Crestwood, NY: St. Vladimir's Orthodox Theological Seminary, 1979.

Wills, Gary. Under God N.Y.: Simon and Schuster, 1990.

An extensive Bibliography, i.e., Books and Articles relating to Orthodoxy in America is available for further study on the topic. If you are interested, please request a copy from:

Orthodox Christian Liaty Headquarters
30 North LaSalle Street, Suite 4020
Chicago, Illinois 60602-2507

Please send $3.00 to cover the cost of postage and handling.

INDEX

democratic 57, 122, 140, 141, 151, 168, 170, 174, 292, 294, 295, 300, 302
demographics 18, 210
desert fathers 67
desert mothers 67
diaconate 5, 8, 11, 71, 86, 87, 112, 113, 309
diakonia 66, 67, 69, 70, 72, 73, 76, 87, 97, 103, 230, 283, 295, 310
diaspora 15-17, 24, 194, 202, 203, 209, 213, 219, 228, 233-235, 240, 250, 251, 252-254, 263, 281, 283, 284, 288
diocesan assembly 167
diocesan council 168, 169
Diocesan Level 11
diocese 10-12, 16, 50, 137, 142, 144, 158-163, 167-170, 172, 174, 201, 205, 210, 227, 229, 245, 248, 252, 266, 270, 273, 275-279, 286, 287, 299, 314
discipleship 67-69, 72, 80, 185
dispensation 118
divine image 65, 73, 77-80
Divine Liturgy 8, 35, 56, 83, 86, 91, 103, 107, 109, 125, 129, 215, 217, 298
divorce 8, 9, 22, 92, 104, 113, 118-120
dogma 97, 159
donations 110
drifting away 22
early migration 19
Eastern Orthodoxy 25, 224
ecclesia 230, 238, 295
Ecclesiology 141, 150, 186, 187, 218, 241, 251, 254, 283, 291-293, 302, 313
Ecumenical Council 138, 195, 197-201, 204, 205, 219, 226, 233, 234

Ecumenical Movement 100, 206, 208, 209
Ecumenical Patriarchate 14-16, 141, 142, 145, 152-154, 195, 196, 202, 207, 208, 220-223, 228, 229, 231-240, 246, 247, 264, 266, 272, 273, 276, 277-279, 281-284, 288, 291, 292, 295, 296, 298, 299, 308, 309
Ecumenical Synod 137, 138, 198
Eden 76, 116
Efthimiou, Miltiades B. 208, 286, 309
eighth day 126
ekklesia 66, 67
election 9, 49, 134-140, 143-147, 149-155, 163, 164, 168, 175, 197, 238, 300
emotional development 85
enanthropeo 79
English 1, 2, 5-7, 14, 21, 25-27, 35, 47, 61, 91, 100, 102, 107, 108, 110, 166, 177, 208, 216, 217, 240, 248, 293
English-language liturgy 27
Episcopate 136, 138, 147, 153, 154, 201, 204, 206, 229, 253, 275, 280
ethnic factor 224
ethnically-correct 57
ethnicity 20, 21, 24, 28-30, 47, 56, 196, 197, 211, 212, 225, 249
ethno-religious 148
ethnos 211
Eucharist 25, 34, 35, 38, 41, 51, 115, 122, 204, 215, 235, 313
Eucharistic community 36, 40, 292, 293
Eustathius 136
Evangelical Orthodox 218, 272, 283
evangelism 6, 91, 93, 97, 98, 102
evangelizing 6, 93, 99
Eve 74, 76, 80, 114, 115, 313, 314

external conditions 54
Fabian 136
falsify church history 81
family kinship 22
fellowship 7, 56, 91, 93, 102-104, 106,
    111, 112, 119, 121, 123
female nature 76
feminists 64
fertility rates 20
festivals 7, 106
final agenda 12, 173
financial irregularities 159
financial management 13, 175, 176
First Ecumenical Synod 137, 138
first mother 74
Florovsky, George 36, 42, 52, 53, 309
fragmentation 114
Frazee, Charles A. 207, 295, 309
free will 123
Gallup poll 21
gap 65
gender 66-69, 71, 72, 78-80, 114, 125,
    130
General Assembly 198, 300
Georgakas 28
Germanos 136
Giannakakis, Basil S. 232, 309
global village 63
Godparent 163
golden age 110, 165
good news 69, 91, 93, 100, 301
GOYA 25, 110, 228
Great Schism 195, 196, 206, 220, 226,
    233
great wave 19
Greek background 22, 28
Greek identity 3, 27, 29, 30
Greek Revolution 196
Greek-Americana 3, 28
Greekness 15, 232, 237

Gregory 38, 45, 75, 78, 79, 86, 136,
    138, 272, 274, 296, 311
Gregory of Nazianzos 78, 79, 136
Gregory of Nyssa 75, 79
Gregory Palamas 38, 45, 311
Gryson, Roger 309
Gvosdev, Ellen 71, 309
hagia 80, 86
Hagia Sophia 86
Hagioreites, Nikodemos 71, 309
hamartia 76
Harakas, Stanley S. 41, 43, 146, 148,
    219, 282, 310, 312
hardness of heart 120
heart of flesh 120
heart of stone 120
heavenly illumination 87
Hebrew 28
Hellenic 6, 24, 29, 98, 231, 312
heterodox 9, 92, 96, 99, 105, 121, 281,
    294
heterodox Christians 99, 121
heterosexual 123
hierarchy ii, 3, 11, 34-36, 42, 43, 45,
    46, 50, 51, 55, 57-59, 65, 69, 74,
    80, 91, 133-135, 138, 139, 143,
    149, 157, 182, 187, 198, 202, 242
hierosyne 86
high school 2, 27, 28
Hippolytos 137
historical experience 64, 294
Historical Reflections 238
holiness 57, 79, 80, 99, 109, 207
Holy Canons 137, 207
Holy Communion 45, 119, 120, 126,
    128
Holy Cross School 30, 143, 229
holy fathers 83, 186, 200
holy mothers 66, 80, 83, 87, 314
holy oil 34

ORTHODOX
CHRISTIAN
LAITY

CLIP AND MAIL

Yes! I am concerned about my Church and I suscribe to the mission and goals of OCL. Please enroll me as
a member ☐ Individual Membership ☐ Family Membership ☐ 1993 Renewal

Founding Member: $500 to $1,000 ☐   Supporting Member: $50 to $100 ☐
Charter Member: $250 to $500 ☐   Contributing Member: $25 ☐
Sustaining Member: $100 to $250 ☐   OCL FORUM AND OCL NEWSLETTER $25 ☐
                                      SUBSCRIBER (non-member) $25 ☐

Name: _____

Address: _____ AC/Telephone _____

City, State,Zip: _____ Church Affiliation _____

Parish Affiliation _____

Mail To: ORTHODOX CHRISTIAN LAITY,
30 North LaSalle Street, Suite 4020, Chicago, IL 60602-2507
Contributions are tax deductible as allowed by law

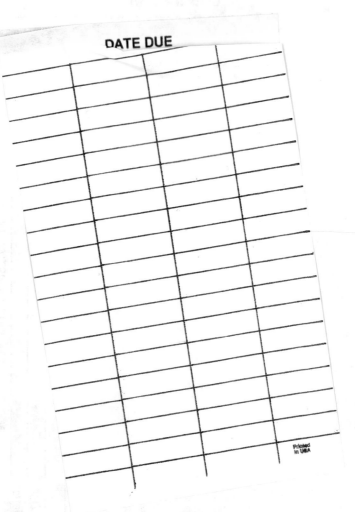

DATE DUE

Printed
in USA